A PROGRAMMER'S COMPANION
TO ALGORITHM ANALYSIS

A PROGRAMMER'S COMPANION TO ALGORITHM ANALYSIS

Ernst L. Leiss

University of Houston,
Texas, U.S.A.

CRC Press
Taylor & Francis Group
Boca Raton London New York

CRC Press is an imprint of the
Taylor & Francis Group, an **informa** business

A CHAPMAN & HALL BOOK

CRC Press
Taylor & Francis Group
6000 Broken Sound Parkway NW, Suite 300
Boca Raton, FL 33487-2742

First issued in hardback 2017

© 2007 by Taylor & Francis Group, LLC
CRC Press is an imprint of Taylor & Francis Group, an Informa business

No claim to original U.S. Government works

ISBN 13: 978-1-138-40225-6 (hbk)
ISBN 13: 978-1-58488-673-0 (pbk)

Library of Congress Cataloging-in-Publication Data

Leiss, Ernst L., 1952-
   A programmer's companion to algorithm analysis / Ernst L. Leiss.
      p. cm.
   Includes bibliographical references and index.
   ISBN 1-58488-673-0 (acid-free paper)
   1. Programming (Mathematics) 2. Algorithms--Data processing. I. Title.

QA402.5.L398 2006
005.1--dc22   2006044552

Visit the Taylor & Francis Web site at
http://www.taylorandfrancis.com

and the CRC Press Web site at
http://www.crcpress.com

Preface

The primary emphasis of this book is the transition from an algorithm to a program. Given a problem to solve, the typical first step is the design of an algorithm; this algorithm is then translated into software. We will look carefully at the interface between the design and analysis of algorithms on the one hand and the resulting program solving the problem on the other. This approach is motivated by the fact that algorithms for standard problems are readily available in textbooks and literature and are frequently used as building blocks for more complex designs. Thus, the correctness of the algorithm is much less a concern than its adaptation to a working program.

Many textbooks, several excellent, are dedicated to algorithms, their design, their analysis, the techniques involved in creating them, and how to determine their time and space complexities. They provide the building blocks of the overall design. These books are usually considered part of the theoretical side of computing. There are also numerous books dedicated to designing software, from those concentrating on programming in the small (designing and debugging individual programs) to programming in the large (looking at large systems in their totality). These books are usually viewed as belonging to software engineering. However, there are no books that look systematically at the gap separating the theory of algorithms and software engineering, even though many things can go wrong in taking several algorithms and producing a software product derived from them.

This book is intended to fill this gap. It is not intended to teach algorithms from scratch; indeed, I assume the reader has already been exposed to the ordinary machinery of algorithm design, including the standard algorithms for sorting and searching and techniques for analyzing the correctness and complexity of algorithms (although the most important ones will be reviewed). Nor is this book meant to teach software design; I assume that the reader has already gained experience in designing reasonably complex software systems. Ideally, the readers' interest in this book's topic was prompted by the uncomfortable realization that the path from algorithm to software was much more arduous than anticipated, and, indeed, results obtained on the theory side of the development process, be they results derived by readers or acquired from textbooks, did not translate satisfactorily to corresponding results, that is, performance, for the developed software. Even if the reader has never encountered a situation where the performance predicted by the complexity analysis of a specific algorithm did not correspond to the performance observed by running the resulting software, I argue that such occurrences are increasingly more likely, given the overall development of our emerging hardware platforms and software environments.

In many cases, the problems I will address are rooted in the different way memory is viewed. For the designer of an algorithm, memory is inexhaustible, has uniform access properties, and generally behaves *nicely* (I will be more specific later about the meaning of *niceness*). Programmers, however, have to deal with memory hierarchies, limits on the availability of each class of memory, and the distinct nonuniformity of access characteristics, all of which imply a definite absence of niceness. Additionally, algorithm designers assume to have complete control over their memory, while software designers must deal with several agents that are placed between them and the actual memory — to mention the most important ones, compilers and operating systems, each of which has its own idiosyncrasies. All of these conspire against the software designer who has the naïve and often seriously disappointed expectation that properties of algorithms easily translate into properties of programs.

The book is intended for software developers with some exposure to the design and analysis of algorithms and data structures. The emphasis is clearly on practical issues, but the book is naturally dependent on some knowledge of standard algorithms — hence the notion that it is a companion book. It can be used either in conjunction with a standard algorithm text, in which case it would most likely be within the context of a course setting, or it can be used for independent study, presumably by practitioners of the software development process who have suffered disappointments in applying the theory of algorithms to the production of efficient software.

Contents

**Part 2   The Software Side: Disappointments and
           How to Avoid Them**

Foreword

The foremost goal for (most) computer scientists is the creation of efficient and effective programs. This premise dictates a disciplined approach to software development. Typically, the process involves the use of one or more suitable algorithms; these may be standard algorithms taken from textbooks or literature, or they may be custom algorithms that are developed during the process. A well-developed body of theory is related to the question of what constitutes a good algorithm. Apart from the obvious requirement that it must be correct, the most important quality of an algorithm is its efficiency. Computational complexity provides the tools for determining the efficiency of an algorithm; in many cases, it is relatively easy to capture the efficiency of an algorithm in this way. However, for the software developer the ultimate goal is efficient software, not efficient algorithms. Here is where things get a bit tricky — it is often not well understood how to go from a good algorithm to good software. It is this transition that we will focus on.

This book consists of two complementary parts. In the first part we describe the idealized universe that algorithm designers inhabit; in the second part we outline how this ideal can be adapted to the real world in which programmers must dwell. While the algorithm designer's world is idealized, it nevertheless is not without its own distinct problems, some having significance for programmers and others having little practical relevance. We describe them so that it becomes clear which are important in practice and which are not. For the most part, the way in which the algorithm designer's world is idealized becomes clear only once it is contrasted with the programmer's.

In Chapter 1 we sketch a taxonomy of algorithmic complexity. While *complexity* is generally used as a measure of the performance of a program, it is important to understand that there are several different aspects of complexity, all of which are related to performance but reflect it from very different points of view. In Chapter 2 we describe precisely in what way the algorithm designer's universe is idealized; specifically, we explore the assumptions that fundamentally underlie the various concepts of algorithmic complexity. This is crucially important since it will allow us to understand how disappointments may arise when we translate an algorithm into a program.

This is the concern of the second part of this book. In Chapter 4 we explore a variety of ways in which things can go wrong. While there are many causes of software behaving in unexpected ways, we are concerned only with those where a significant conceptual gap may occur between what the algorithm analysis indicates and what the eventual observations of the resulting program demonstrate. Specifically, in this chapter we look at ways in which slight variations in the (implied) semantics of algorithms and software may cause the software to be incorrect, perform much worse than predicted by algorithmic analysis, or perform unpredictably. We also touch upon occasions where a small change in the goal, a seemingly innocuous generalization, results in (quite literally) impossible software. In order for this discussion to develop in some useful context, Part 1 ends (in Chapter 3) with a discussion of analysis techniques and sample algorithms together with their worked-out analyses. In Chapter 5 we discuss extensively the rather significant implications of the memory hierarchies that typically are encountered in modern programming environments, whether they are under the direct control of the programmer (e.g., out-of-core programming) or not (e.g., virtual memory management). Chapter 6 focuses on issues that typically are never under the direct control of the programmer; these are related to actions performed by the compiling system and the operating system, ostensibly in support of the programmer's intentions. That this help comes at a sometimes steep price (in the efficiency of the resulting programs) must be clearly understood. Many of the disappointments are rooted in memory issues; others arise because of compiler- or language-related issues.

The next three chapters of Part 2 are devoted to somewhat less central issues, which may or may not be of concern in specific situations. Chapter 7 examines implicit assumptions made by algorithm designers and their implications for software; in particular, the case is made that exceptions must be addressed in programs and that explicit tests for assumptions must be incorporated in the code. Chapter 8 considers the implications of the way numbers are represented in modern computers; while this is mainly of interest when dealing with numerical algorithms (where one typically devotes a good deal of attention to error analysis and related topics), occasionally questions related to the validity of mathematical identities and similar topics arise in distinctly nonnumerical areas. Chapter 9 addresses the issue of constant factors that are generally hidden in the asymptotic complexity derivation of algorithms but that matter for practical software performance. Here, we pay particular attention to the notion of crossover points. Finally, in Chapter 10 we look at the meaning of undecidability for software development; specifically, we pose the question of what to do when the algorithm text tells us that the question we would like to solve is undecidable. Also examined in this chapter are problems arising from excessively high computational complexities of solution methods.

Four appendices round out the material. Appendix I briefly outlines which basic algorithms should be familiar to all programmers. Appendix II presents a short overview of some systems that are implicated in the disappointments addressed in Part 2. In particular, these are the memory hierarchy, virtual memory management, optimizing compilers, and garbage collection. Since each of them can have dramatic effects on the performance of software, it is sensible for the programmer to have at least a rudimentary appreciation of them. Appendix III gives a quick review of NP-completeness, a concept that for many programmers appears rather nebulous. This appendix also looks at higher-complexity classes and indicates what their practical significance is. Finally, Appendix IV sketches undecidability, both the halting problem for Turing machines and the Post's Correspondence Problem. Since undecidability has rather undesirable consequences for software development, programmers may want to have a short synopsis of the two fundamental problems in undecidability.

Throughout, we attempt to be precise when talking about algorithms; however, our emphasis is clearly on the practical aspects of taking an algorithm, together with its complexity analysis, and translating it into software that is expected to perform as close as possible to the performance predicted by the algorithm's complexity. Thus, for us the ultimate goal of designing algorithms is the production of efficient software; if, for whatever reason, the resulting software is not efficient (or, even worse, not correct), the initial design of the algorithm, no matter how elegant or brilliant, was decidedly an exercise in futility.

A Note on the Footnotes

The footnotes are designed to permit reading this book at two levels. The straight text is intended to dispense with some of the technicalities that are not directly relevant to the narrative and are therefore relegated to the footnotes. Thus, we may occasionally trade precision for ease of understanding in the text; readers interested in the details or in complete precision are encouraged to consult the footnotes, which are used to qualify some of the statements, provide proofs or justifications for our assertions, or expand on some of the more esoteric aspects of the discussion.

Bibliographical Notes

The two (occasionally antagonistic) sides depicted in this book are analysis of algorithms and software engineering. While numerous other fields of computer science and software production turn out to be relevant to our discussion and will be mentioned when they arise, we want to make at least some reference to representative works of these two sides. On the algorithm front, Knuth's *The Art of Computer Programming* is the classical work on algorithm design and analysis; in spite of the title's emphasis on programming, most practical aspects of modern computing environments, and especially the interplay of their different components, hardly figure in the coverage. Another influential work is Aho, Hopcroft, and Ullman's *The*

Design and Analysis of Computer Algorithms. More references are given at the end of Chapter 1.

While books on algorithms have hewn to a fairly uniform worldview over the decades, the software side is considerably more peripatetic; it has traditionally been significantly more trendy, prone to fads and fashions, perhaps reflecting the absence of a universally accepted body of theory that forms the backbone of the discipline (something clearly present for algorithms). The list below reflects some of this.

Early influential works on software development are Dijkstra, Dahl, et al.: *Structured Programming*; Aron: *The Program Development Process*; and Brooks: *The Mythical Man Month.* A historical perspective of some aspects of software engineering is provided by Brooks: *No Silver Bullet: Essence and Accidents of Software Engineering* and by Larman and Basili: *Iterative and Incremental Development: A Brief History.* The persistence of failure in developing software is discussed in Jones: *Software Project Management Practices: Failure Versus Success*; this is clearly a concern that has no counterpart in algorithm design. Software testing is covered in Bezier: *Software Testing Techniques*; Kit: *Software Testing in the Real World: Improving the Process*; and Beck: *Test Driven Development: By Example.* Various techniques for and approaches to producing code are discussed in numerous works; we give, essentially in chronological order, the following list, which provides a bit of the flavors that have animated the field over the years: Liskov and Guttag: *Abstraction and Specification in Program Development*; Booch: *Object-Oriented Analysis and Design with Applications*; Arthur: *Software Evolution*; Rumbaugh, Blaha, et al.: *Object-Oriented Modeling and Design*; Neilsen, *Usability Engineering*; Gamma, Helm, et al.: *Design Patterns: Elements of Reusable Object-Oriented Software*; Yourdon: *When Good-Enough Software Is Best*; Hunt and Thomas: *The Pragmatic Programmer: From Journeyman to Master*; Jacobson, Booch, and Rumbaugh: *The Unified Software Development Process*; Krutchen: *The Rational Unified Process: An Introduction*; Beck and Fowler: *Planning Extreme Programming*; and Larman: *Agile and Iterative Development: A Manager's Guide.*

Quite a number of years ago, Jon Bentley wrote a series of interesting columns on a variety of topics, all related to practical aspects of programming and the difficulties programmers encounter; these were collected in two volumes that appeared under the titles *Programming Pearls* and *More Programming Pearls: Confessions of a Coder.* These two collections are probably closest, in goals and objectives as well as in emphasis, to this book.

Part 1

The Algorithm Side: Regularity, Predictability, and Asymptotics

This part presents the view of the designer of algorithms. It first outlines the various categories of complexity. Then it describes in considerable detail the assumptions that are fundamental in the process of determining the algorithmic complexity of algorithms. The goal is to establish the conceptual as well as the mathematical framework required for the discussion of the practical aspects involved in taking an algorithm, presumably a good or perhaps even the best (defined in some fashion), and translating it into a good piece of software.[1]

The general approach in Chapter 1 will be to assume that an algorithm is given. In order to obtain a measure of its goodness, we want to determine its complexity. However, before we can do this, it is necessary to define what we mean by *goodness* since in different situations, different measures of quality might be applicable. Thus, we first discuss a taxonomy of complexity analysis. We concentrate mainly on the standard categories, namely time and space, as well as average-case and worst-case computational complexities. Also in this group of standard classifications falls the distinction

---

[1] It is revealing that optimal algorithms are often a (very legitimate) goal of algorithm design, but nobody would ever refer to optimal software.

between word and bit complexity, as does the differentiation between on-line and off-line algorithms. Less standard perhaps is the review of parallel complexity measures; here our focus is on the EREW model. (While other models have been studied, they are irrelevant from a practical point of view.) Also, in preparation of what is more extensively covered in Part 2, we introduce the notion of I/O complexity. Finally, we return to the fundamental question of the complexity analysis of algorithms, namely what is a good algorithm, and establish the importance of lower bounds in any effort directed at answering this question.

In Chapter 2 we examine the methodological background that enables the process of determining the computational complexity of an algorithm. In particular, we review the fundamental notion of statement counts and dis-cuss in some detail the implications of the assumption that statement counts reflect execution time. This involves a detailed examination of the memory model assumed in algorithmic analysis. We also belabor a seemingly obvious point, namely that mathematical identities hold at this level. (Why we do this will become clear in Part 2, where we establish why they do not neces-sarily hold in programs.) We also discuss the asymptotic nature of complex-ity analysis, which is essentially a consequence of the assumptions underlying the statement count paradigm.

Chapter 3 is dedicated to amplifying these points by working out the complexity analysis of several standard algorithms. We first describe several general techniques for determining the time complexity of algorithms; then we show how these are applied to the algorithms covered in this chapter. We concentrate on the essential aspects of each algorithm and indicate how they affect the complexity analysis.

Most of the points we make in these three chapters (and all of the ones we make in Chapter 2) will be extensively revisited in Part 2 because many of the assumptions that underlie the process of complexity analysis of algo-rithms are violated in some fashion by the programming and execution environment that is utilized when designing and running software. As such, it is the discrepancies between the model assumed in algorithm design, and in particular in the analysis of algorithms, and the model used for software development that are the root of the disappointments to be discussed in Part 2, which frequently sneak up on programmers. This is why we spend con-siderable time and effort explaining these aspects of algorithmic complexity.

1

A Taxonomy of Algorithmic Complexity

About This Chapter

This chapter presents various widely used measures of the performance of algorithms. Specifically, we review time and space complexity; average, worst, and best complexity; amortized analysis; bit versus word complexity; various incarnations of parallel complexity; and the implications for the complexity of whether the given algorithm is on-line or off-line. We also introduce the input/output (I/O) complexity of an algorithm, even though this is a topic of much more interest in Part 2. We conclude the chapter with an examination of the significance of lower bounds for good algorithms.

1.1   Introduction

Suppose someone presents us with an algorithm and asks whether it is good. How are we to answer this question? Upon reflection, it should be obvious that we must first agree upon some criterion by which we judge the quality of the algorithm. Different contexts of this question may imply different criteria.

At the most basic level, the algorithm should be correct. Absent this quality, all other qualities are irrelevant. While it is by no means easy to ascertain the correctness of an algorithm,[1] we will assume here that it is given. Thus, our focus throughout this book is on performance aspects of the given (correct) algorithm. This approach is reasonable since in practice we are most likely to use algorithms from the literature as building blocks of the ultimate solution we are designing. Therefore, it is sensible to assume that these algorithms are correct. What we must, however, derive ourselves is the

---

[1] There are different aspects of correctness, the most important one relating to the question of whether the algorithm does in fact solve the problem that is to be solved. While techniques exist for demonstrating formally that an algorithm is correct, this approach is fundamentally predicated upon a formal definition of what the algorithm is supposed to do. The difficulty here is that problems in the real world are rarely defined formally.

complexity of these algorithms. While the literature may contain a complexity analysis of an algorithm, it is our contention that complexity analysis offers many more potential pitfalls when transitioning to software than correctness. As a result, it is imperative that the software designer have a good grasp of the principles and assumptions involved in algorithm analysis.

An important aspect of the performance of an algorithm is its dependence on (some measure of) the input. If we have a program and want to determine some aspect of its behavior, we can run it with a specific input set and *observe* its behavior on that input set. This avenue is closed to us when it comes to algorithms — there is no execution and therefore no observation. Instead, we desire a much more universal description of the behavior of interest, namely a description that holds for any input set. This is achieved by abstracting the input set and using that abstraction as a parameter; usually, the size of the input set plays this role. Consequently, the description of the behavior of the algorithm has now become a function of this parameter. In this way, we hope to obtain a universal description of the behavior because we get an answer for any input set. Of course, in this process of abstracting we have most likely lost information that would allow us to give more precise answers. Thus, there is a tension between the information loss that occurs when we attempt to provide a global picture of performance through abstraction and the loss of precision in the eventual answer.

For example, suppose we are interested in the number of instructions necessary to sort a given input set using algorithm A. If we are sorting a set S of 100 numbers, it stands to reason that we should be able to determine accurately how many instructions will have to be executed. However, the question of how many instructions are necessary to sort any set with 100 elements is likely to be much less precise; we might be able to say that we must use at least this many and at most that many instructions. In other words, we could give a range of values, with the property that no matter how the set of 100 elements looks, the actual number of instructions would always be within the given range. Of course, now we could carry out this exercise for sets with 101 elements, 102, 103, and so on, thereby using the size n of the set as a parameter with the property that for each value of n, there is a range $F(n)$ of values so that any set with n numbers is sorted by A using a number of instructions that falls in the range $F(n)$.

Note, however, that knowing the range of the statement counts for an algorithm may still not be particularly illuminating since it reveals little about the likelihood of a value in the range to occur. Clearly, the two extremes, the smallest value and the largest value in the range $F(n)$ for a specific value of n have significance (they correspond to the best- and the worst-case complexity), but as we will discuss in more detail below, how often a particular value in the range may occur is related to the average complexity, which is a significantly more complex topic.

While the approach to determining explicitly the range $F(n)$ for every value of n is of course prohibitively tedious, it is nevertheless the conceptual basis for determining the computational complexity of a given algorithm. Most importantly, the determination of the number of statements for solving a problem is also abstracted, so that it typically is carried out by examining the syntactic components, that is, the statements, of the given algorithm.

Counting statements is probably the most important aspect of the behavior of an algorithm because it captures the notion of execution time quite accurately, but there are other aspects. In the following sections, we examine these qualities of algorithms.

1.2 The Time and Space Complexities of an Algorithm

The most burning question about a (correct) program is probably, "How long does it take to execute?" The analogous question for an algorithm is, "What is its time complexity?" Essentially, we are asking the same question ("How long does it take?"), but within different contexts. Programs can be executed, so we can simply run the program, admittedly with a specific data set, and measure the time required; algorithms cannot be run and therefore we have to resort to a different approach. This approach is the statement count. Before we describe it and show how statement counts reflect time, we must mention that time is not the only aspect that may be of interest; space is also of concern in some instances, although given the ever-increasing memory sizes of today's computers, space considerations are of decreasing import. Still, we may want to know how much memory is required by a given algorithm to solve a problem.

Given algorithm A (assumed to be correct) and a measure n of the input set (usually the size of all the input sets involved), the *time complexity* of algorithm A is defined to be the number $f(n)$ of atomic instructions or operations that must be executed when applying A to any input set of measure n. (More specifically, this is the worst-case time complexity; see the discussion below in Section 1.3.) The *space complexity* of algorithm A is the amount of space, again as a function of the measure of the input set, that A requires to carry out its computations, over and above the space that is needed to store the given input (and possibly the output, namely if it is presented in memory space different from that allocated for the input).

To illustrate this, consider a vector V of n elements (of type integer; V is of type [1:n] and $n \geq 1$) and assume that the algorithm solves the problem of finding the maximum of these n numbers using the following approach:

Algorithm Max to find the largest integer in the vector $V[1:n]$:

1. Initialize TempMax to $V[1]$.
2. Compare TempMax with all other elements of V and update Temp-Max if TempMax is smaller.

Let us count the number of atomic operations[2] that occur when applying the algorithm Max to a vector with n integers. Statement 1 is one simple assignment. Statement 2 involves $n - 1$ integers, and each is compared to TempMax; furthermore, if the current value of TempMax is smaller than the vector element examined, that integer must be assigned to TempMax. It is important to note that no specific order is implied in this formulation; as long as all elements of **V** are examined, the algorithm works. At this point, our statement count stands at n, the 1 assignment from statement 1 and the $n - 1$ comparisons in statement 2 that must always be carried out. The updating operation is a bit trickier, since it only arises if TempMax is smaller. Without knowing the specific integers, we cannot say how many times we have to update, but we can give a range; if we are lucky (if V[1] happens to be the largest element), no updates of TempMax are required. If we are unlucky, we must make an update after every comparison. This clearly is the range from best to worst case. Consequently, we will carry out between 0 and $n - 1$ updates, each of which consists of one assignment. Adding all this up, it follows that the number of operations necessary to solve the problem ranges from n to $2n - 1$. It is important to note that this process does not require any execution; our answer is independent of the size of n. More bluntly, if $n = 10^{10}$ (10 billion), our analysis tells us that we need between 10 and 20 billion operations; this analysis can be carried out much faster than it would take to run a program derived from this algorithm.

We note as an aside that the algorithm corresponds in a fairly natural way to the following pseudo code[3]:

```
TempMax := V[1];
for i:=2 to n do
  { if TempMax < V[i] then TempMax := V[i] };
Max := TempMax
```

However, in contrast to the algorithm, the language requirements impose on us a much greater specificity. While the algorithm simply referred to examining all elements of **V** other than **V**[1], the program stipulates a (quite unnecessarily) specific order. While any order would do, the fact that the language constructs typically require us to specify one has implications that we will comment on in Part 2 in more detail.

We conclude that the algorithm Max for finding the maximum of n integers has a time complexity of between n and $2n - 1$. To determine the space complexity, we must look at the instructions again and figure out how much additional space is needed for them. Clearly, TempMax requires space (one

---

[2] We will explain in Chapter 2 in much more detail what we mean by *atomic operations*. Here, it suffices to assume that these operations are arithmetic operations, comparisons, and assignments involving basic types such as integers.

[3] We use a notation that should be fairly self-explanatory. It is a compromise between C notation and Pascal notation; however, for the time being we sidestep more complex issues such as the method used in passing parameters.

unit[4] of it), and from the algorithm, it appears that this is all that is needed. This is, however, a bit misleading, because we will have to carry out an enumeration of all elements of **V**, and this will cost us at least one more memory unit (for example for an index variable, such as the variable i in our program). Thus, the space complexity of algorithm Max is 2, independent of the size of the input set (the number of elements in vector **V**). We assume that n, and therefore the space to hold it, was given.

It is important to note that the time complexity of any algorithm should never be smaller than its space complexity. Recall that the space complexity determines the additional memory needed; thus, it stands to reason that this is memory space that should be used in some way (otherwise, what is the point in allocating it?). Since doing anything with a memory unit will require at least one operation, that is, one time unit, the time complexity should never be inferior to the space complexity.[5]

It appears that we are losing quite a bit of precision during the process of calculating the operation or statement count, even in this very trivial example. However, it is important to understand that the notion of complexity is predominantly concerned with the *long-term behavior* of an algorithm. By this, we mean that we want to know the growth in execution time as n grows. This is also called the *asymptotic behavior* of the complexity of the algorithm. Furthermore, in order to permit easy comparison of different algorithms according to their complexities (time or space), it is advantageous to lose precision, since the loss of precision allows us to come up with a relatively small number of categories into which we may classify our algorithms. While these two issues, asymptotic behavior and comparing different algorithms, seem to be different, they turn out to be closely related.

To develop this point properly requires a bit of mathematical notation. Assume we have obtained the (time or space) complexities $f_1(n)$ and $f_2(n)$ of two different algorithms, A_1 and A_2 (presumably both solving the same problem correctly, with n being the same measure of the input set). We say that the function $f_1(n)$ is *on the order of* the function $f_2(n)$, and write

$$f_1(n) = O(f_2(n)),$$

or briefly $f_1 = O(f_2)$ if n is understood, if and only if there exists an integer $n_0 \geq 1$ and a constant $c > 0$ such that

$$f_1(n) \leq c \cdot f_2(n) \text{ for all } n \geq n_0.$$

---

[4] We assume here that one number requires one unit of memory. We discuss the question of what one unit really is in much greater detail in Chapter 2 (see also the discussion of bit and word complexity in Section 1.4).
[5] Later we will see an example where, owing to incorrect passing of parameters, this assertion is violated.

Intuitively, $f_1 = O(f_2)$ means that f_1 does not grow faster asymptotically than f_2; it is asymptotic growth because we are only interested in the behavior from n_0 onward. Finally, the constant c simply reflects the loss of precision we have referred to earlier. As long as f_1 stays "close to" f_2 (namely within that constant c), this is fine.

Example: Let $f(n) = 5 \cdot n \cdot \log_2(n)$ and $g(n) = n^2/100 - 32n$. We claim that $f = O(g)$. To show this, we have to find n_0 and c such that $f(n) \le c \cdot g(n)$ for all $n \ge n_0$. There are many (in fact, infinitely many) such pairs (n_0, c). For example, $n_0 = 10{,}000$, $c = 1$, or $n_0 = 100{,}000$, $c = 1$, or $n_0 = 3{,}260$, $c = 100$.

In each case, one can verify that $f(n) \le c \cdot g(n)$ for all $n \ge n_0$. More interesting may be the fact that $g \ne O(f)$; in other words, one can verify that there do not exist n_0 and c such that $g(n) \le c \cdot f(n)$ for all $n \ge n_0$.

It is possible that both $f_1 = O(f_2)$ and $f_2 = O(f_1)$ hold; in this case we say that f_1 and f_2 are equivalent and write $f_1 \equiv f_2$.

Let us now return to our two algorithms A_1 and A_2 with their time complexities $f_1(n)$ and $f_2(n)$; we want to know which algorithm is faster. In general, this is a bit tricky, but if we are willing to settle for asymptotic behavior, the answer is simple: if $f_1 = O(f_2)$, then A_1 is no worse than A_2, and if $f_1 \equiv f_2$, then A_1 and A_2 behave identically.[6]

Note that the notion of asymptotic behavior hides a constant factor; clearly if $f(n) = n^2$ and $g(n) = 5 \cdot n^2$, then $f \equiv g$, so the two algorithms behave identically, but obviously the algorithm with time complexity f is five times faster than that with time complexity g.

However, the hidden constant factors are just what we need to establish a classification of complexities that has proven very useful in characterizing algorithms. Consider the following eight categories:

$$\varphi_1 = 1, \ \varphi_2 = \log_2(n), \ \varphi_3 = \sqrt[2]{n}, \ \varphi_4 = n, \ \varphi_5 = n \cdot \log_2(n), \ \varphi_6 = n^2, \ \varphi_7 = n^3, \ \varphi_8 = 2^n.$$

(While one could define arbitrarily many categories between any two of these, those listed are of the greatest practical importance.) Characterizing a given function $f(n)$ consists of finding the most appropriate category φ_i for the function f. This means determining φ_i so that $f = O(\varphi_i)$ but $f \ne O(\varphi_{i-1})$.[7] For example, a complexity $n^2/\log_2(n)$ would be classified as n^2, as would be $(n^2 - 3n + 10) \cdot (n^4 - n^3)/(n^4 + n^2 + n + 5)$; in both cases, the function is $O(n^2)$, but not $O(n \cdot \log_2(n))$.

We say that a complexity of φ_1 is *constant*, of φ_2 is *logarithmic* (note that the base is irrelevant because $\log_a(x)$ and $\log_b(x)$ for two different bases a and b

---

[6] One can develop a calculus based on these notions. For example, if $f_1 \equiv g_1$ and $f_2 \equiv g_2$, then $f_1 + f_2 \equiv g_1 + g_2$, $f_1 - f_2 \equiv g_1 - g_2$ (under some conditions), and $f_1 * f_2 \equiv g_1 * g_2$. Moreover, if f_2 and g_2 are different from 0 for all argument values, then $f_1/f_2 \equiv g_1/g_2$. A similar calculus holds for functions f and g such that $f = O(g)$: $f_i = O(g_i)$ for $i = 1,2$ implies $f_1 \circ f_2 = O(g_1 \circ g_2)$ for $\circ$ any of the four basic arithmetic operations (with the obvious restriction about division by zero).

[7] Note that if $f = O(\varphi_i)$, then $f = O(\varphi_{i+j})$ for all $j > 0$; thus, it is important to find the best category for a function.

are related by a constant factor, which of course is hidden when we talk about the asymptotic behavior of complexity[8]), of φ_4 is *linear*, of φ_6 is *quadratic*, of φ_7 is *cubic*, and of φ_8 is *exponential*.[9] It should be clear that of all functions in a category, the function that represents it should be the simplest one. Thus, from now on, we will place a given complexity into one of these eight categories, even though the actual complexity may be more complicated.

So far in our discussion of asymptotic behavior, we have carefully avoided addressing the question of the range of the operation counts. However, revisiting our algorithm Max, it should be now clear that the time complexity, which we originally derived as a range from n to $2n - 1$, is simply linear. This is because the constant factor involved (which is 1 for the smallest value in the range and 2 for the largest) is hidden in the asymptotic function that we obtain as final answer.

In general, the range may not be as conveniently described as for our algorithm Max. Specifically, it is quite possible that the largest value in the range is not a constant factor of the smallest value, for all n. This then leads to the question of best-case, average-case, and worst-case complexity, which we take up in the next section.

Today, the quality of most algorithms is measured by their speed. For this reason, the computational complexity of an algorithm usually refers to its time complexity. Space complexity has become much less important; as we will see, typically, it attracts attention only when something goes wrong.

1.3 The Worst-, Average-, and Best-Case Complexities of an Algorithm

Recall that we talked about the range of the number of operations that corresponds to a specific value of (the measure of the input set) n. The *worst-case complexity* of an algorithm is thus the largest value of this range, which is of course a function of n. Thus, for our algorithm Max, the worst-case complexity is $2n - 1$, which is linear in n. Similarly, the *best-case complexity* is the smallest value of the range for each value of n. For the algorithm Max, this was n (also linear in n).

Before we turn our attention to the average complexity (which is quite a bit more complicated to define than best- or worst-case complexity), it is useful to relate these concepts to practical concerns. Worst-case complexity is easiest to motivate: it simply gives us an upper bound (in the number of statements to be executed) on how long it can possibly take to complete a task. This is of course a very common concern; in many cases, we would

---

[8] Specifically, $\log_a(x) = c \cdot \log_b(x)$ for $c = \log_a(b)$ for all $a, b > 1$.

[9] In contrast to logarithms, exponentials are not within a constant of each other: specifically, for $a > b > 1$, $a^n \neq O(b^n)$. However, from a practical point of view, exponential complexities are usually so bad that it is not really necessary to differentiate them much further.

like to be able to assert that under no circumstances will it take longer than this amount of time to complete a certain task. Typical examples are real-time applications such as algorithms used in air-traffic control or power-plant operations. Even in less dramatic situations, programmers want to be able to guarantee at what time completion of a task is assured. Thus, even if everything conspires against earlier completion, the worst-case time complexity provides a measure that will not fail. Similarly, allocating an amount of memory equal to (or no less than) the worst-case space complexity assures that the task will never run out of memory, no matter what happens.

Average complexity reflects the (optimistic) expectation that things will usually not turn out for the worst. Thus, if one has to perform a specific task many times (for different input sets), it probably makes more sense to be interested in the average behavior, for example the average time it takes to complete the task, than the worst-case complexity. While this is a very sensible approach (more so for time than for space), defining what one might view as average turns out to be rather complicated, as we will see below.

The best-case complexity is in practice less important, unless you are an inveterate gambler who expects to be always lucky. Nevertheless, there are instances where it is useful. One such situation is in cryptography. Suppose we know about a certain encryption scheme, that there exists an algorithm for breaking this scheme whose worst-case time complexity and average time complexity are both exponential in the length of the message to be decrypted. We might conclude from this information that this encryption scheme is very safe — and we might be very wrong. Here is how this could happen. Assume that for 50% of all encryptions (that usually would mean for 50% of all encryption keys), decryption (without knowledge of the key, that is, breaking the code) takes time 2^n, where n is the length of the message to be decrypted. Also assume that for the other 50%, breaking the code takes time n. If we compute the average time complexity of breaking the code as the average of n and 2^n (since both cases are equally likely), we obviously obtain again approximately 2^n (we have $(n + 2^n)/2 > 2^{n-1}$, and clearly $2^{n-1} = O(2^n)$). So, both the worst-case and average time complexities are 2^n, but in half of all cases the encryption scheme can be broken with minimal effort. Therefore, the overall encryption scheme is absolutely worthless. However, this becomes clear only when one looks at the best-case time complexity of the algorithm.

Worst- and best-case complexities are very specific and do not depend on any particular assumptions; in contrast, average complexity depends crucially on a precise notion of what constitutes the average case of a particular problem. To gain some appreciation of this, consider the task of locating an element x in a linear list containing n elements. Let us determine how many probes are necessary to find the location of x in that linear list. Note that the number of operations per probe is a (very small) constant; essentially, we must do a comparison. Then we must follow a link in the list, unless the comparison was the last one (determining this requires an additional simple test). Thus, the number of probes is the number of operations up to a constant factor — providing additional justification for our systematic hiding of constant factors when determining the asymptotic complexity of algorithms. It should be clear what are the best and worst cases in our situation. The best case occurs if the first element of the linear list contains x, resulting in one probe, while for the worst case we have two possibilities: either it is the last element of the linear list that contains x or x is not in the list at all. In both of these worst cases, we need n probes since x must be compared with each of the n elements in the linear list. Thus, the best-case time complexity is $O(1)$ and the worst case complexity is $O(n)$, but what is the average time complexity?

The answer to this question depends heavily on the probability distribution of the elements. Specifically, we must know what is the likelihood for x to be in the element of the linear list with number i, for $i = 1, ..., n$. Also, we must know what is the probability of x not being in the linear list. Without all this information, it is impossible to determine the average time complexity of our algorithm, although it is true that, no matter what our assumptions are, the average complexity will always lie between the best- and worst-case complexity. Since in this case the best-case and worst-case time complexities are quite different (there is no constant factor relating the two measures, in contrast to the situation for Max), one should not be surprised that different distributions may result in different answers. Let us work out two scenarios.

1.3.1 Scenario 1

The probability p_{not} of x not being in the list is 0.50; that is, the likelihood that x is in the linear list is equal to it not being there. The likelihood p_i of x to occur in position i is $0.5/n$; that is, each position is equally likely to contain x. Using this information, the average number of probes is determined as follows:

To encounter x in position i requires i probes; this occurs with probability $p_i = 0.5/n$. With probability 0.5, we need n probes to account for the case that x is not in the linear list. Thus, on average we have

$$1 \cdot p_1 + 2 \cdot p_2 + 3 \cdot p_3 + ... + (n - 1) \cdot p_{n-1} + n \cdot p_n + n \cdot 0.5 =$$
$$(1 + 2 + 3 + ... + n) \cdot 0.5/n + n \cdot 0.5 =$$
$$(n + 1)/4 + n/2 = (3n + 1)/4.^{10}$$

Thus, the average number of probes is $(3n + 1)/4$.

---

[10] In this computation, we used the mathematical formula $\Sigma_{i=1,...,n} i = n \cdot (n + 1)/2$. It can be proven by induction on n.

1.3.2   Scenario 2

Assume that x is guaranteed to be in the list; that is, $p_{not} = 0.00$, but now the probability of x being in position i is $1/2^i$ for $i = 1, ..., n - 1$ and $1/2^{n-1}$ for $i = n$. In other words, x is much more likely to be encountered at the beginning of the list than toward its end. Again, to encounter x in position i requires i probes, but now for the average number of probes we get

$$1 \cdot p_1 + 2 \cdot p_2 + 3 \cdot p_3 + ... + (n - 1) \cdot p_{n-1} + n \cdot p_n =$$

$$1 \cdot 1/2^1 + 2 \cdot 1/2^2 + 3 \cdot 1/2^3 + ... + (n - 1) \cdot 1/2^{n-1} + n \cdot 1/2^{n-1} =$$

$$= 2 - (n + 1) \cdot 1/2^{n-1} + n \cdot 1/2^{n-1} = 2 - 1/2^{n-1},[11]$$

and therefore the average time complexity in this scenario is always less than two probes. Note that this answer is independent of the number n of elements in the linear list.[12]

True, the situation in Scenario 2 is somewhat contrived since the probability decreases exponentially in the position number of a list element (for example, the probability of x occurring in position 10 is less than one tenth of 1%). Nevertheless, the two scenarios illustrate clearly the significance of the assumptions about the average case to the final answer. Thus, it is imperative to be aware of the definition of *average* before making any statements about the average complexity of an algorithm. Someone's average case can very possibly be someone else's completely atypical case.

1.4   Bit versus Word Complexity

Throughout our discussions, we have tacitly assumed that each of the numbers occurring in our input sets fits into one unit of memory. This is clearly a convenient assumption that greatly simplifies our analyses. However, it can be somewhat unrealistic, as the following example illustrates.

Recall our algorithm Max for determining the largest element in a vector **V** of n integers. We assumed that each memory unit held one integer. The time complexity (each of best, worst, average) of this algorithm is linear in

---

[11] In this computation, we used the mathematical formula $\Sigma_{i = 1, ..., n} i/2^i = 2 - (n + 2)/2^n$. It can be proven by induction on n.

[12] The last term, $n \cdot 1/2^{n-1}$, could be omitted since we know after $n - 1$ unsuccessful probes that x must be in the last position because $p_{not} = 0.00$. However, this last term is so small that its inclusion does not affect the final answer significantly.

n — assuming our operations apply to entire integers. This is the assumption we want to examine a bit closer in this section.

We have n integers in vector **V**. How realistic is it to assume that the memory units that accommodate the integers be independent of n? Assuming we wanted to have the n integers pairwise different, it is not difficult to see that we need a minimum of $\lceil \log_2(n) \rceil$ bits to represent each.[13] Clearly, this is not independent of n; in other words, if n grows, so does the number of bits required to represent the numbers. (One might object that this is true only if the numbers are to be pairwise different, but if one were to drop this assumption and restrict one's attention only to those integers that can be represented using, say 16 bits, then one effectively assumes that there are no more than 65,536 [i.e., 2^{16}] different integers — not a very realistic assumption.)

This example shows that we must be a bit more careful. On the one hand, assuming that all numbers fit into a given memory unit (typically a *word*, which may consist of a specific number, usually 4 or 8, of bytes, of 8 bits each) simplifies our analyses significantly; on the other hand, we are pretending that a fixed number of bits can accommodate an unlimited number of numbers. While we will not resolve this contradiction, we will make it clear which of the two (mutually contradictory) assumptions we use in a specific application. We will talk about *word complexity* if we assume that a (fixed-sized) word will accommodate our numbers, and we will talk about *bit complexity* if we take into consideration that the length of the words in terms of bits should grow with n, the number of these numbers. Given that bit complexity is much less often used, we will mean word complexity if we do not specify which of the two we are using.

It should be obvious that the bit complexity will never be smaller than the word complexity. In most cases it will be larger — in some cases substantially larger. For example, the word complexity of comparing two integers is $O(1)$. However, if the integers have m bits, the bit complexity of this operation is clearly $O(m)$ since in the positional representation (regardless of whether binary or decimal), we first compare the most significant digits of the two integers. If the two are different, the number with the larger digit is larger; if they are equal, we proceed to the next significant digit and repeat the process. Clearly, the worst case is where both sequences of digits are identical except for the least-significant one, since in this case m comparisons are necessary; the same bound holds for establishing that the two numbers are equal.

A somewhat more complicated example is provided by integer multiplication. The word complexity of multiplying two integers is obviously $O(1)$; however, if our integers have m bits, the bit complexity of multiplying them by the usual multiplication scheme is $O(m^2)$. To illustrate this, consider multiplying the two binary integers $x = 1001101$ and $y = 1100001$, each with

---

[13] If y is a real (floating-point) number, the ceiling $\lceil y \rceil$ of y is the smallest integer not smaller than y. Thus, $\lceil 1.001 \rceil = 2$, $\lceil 0.001 \rceil = 1$, $\lceil 1.0 \rceil = 1$, and $\lceil 0.5 \rceil = 1$.

7 significant bits. Since the second integer has three 1s, multiplication of x and y consists of shifting the first integer (x) by a number of positions and adding the resulting binary integers:

```
position  7654321    7654321
          1001101  *  1100001
position         3210987654321
                     1001101  x,  no shift,  from position 1 of y
                    1001101   x,  5 shifts,  from position 6 of y
                   1001101    x,  6 shifts,  from position 7 of y
                 1110100101101
```

It is clear that the only operations involved in this process are copying x, shifting x, and adding the three binary integers. In the general case of m-bit integers, copying and shifting take time $O(m)$, and adding two m-bit integers also takes time $O(m)$. Since there are at most m 1s in the second integer (y), the number of copying and shifting operations is also at most m. The grand total of the amount of work in terms of bit manipulations is therefore no larger than $m \cdot O(m) + O(m)$, which is $O(m^2)$. Thus, the bit complexity of this method of multiplying two m-bit binary integers is $O(m^2)$.

We note that this can be improved by using a divide-and-conquer strategy (for details, see Section 3.2.1). This involves rewriting the two integers, x and y, as (a,b) and (c,d) where a, b, c, and d are now of half the length of x and y (namely, $m/2$; this assumes that m is a power of two). We can then reconstitute the product $x \cdot y$ in terms of three products involving the a, b, c, and d integers, plus some additions and shift operations. The result of repeating this process yields a bit complexity of $O(m^{1.59})$, which is substantially better than $O(m^2)$ for larger m — but of course still much larger than the $O(1)$ word complexity.

Most analyses below are in terms of word complexity. Not only is this invariably easier, but it also reflects the fact that bit complexity has little to offer when one translates an algorithm into a program; clearly, in most instances a program will use fixed-length words to accommodate the numbers it manipulates. However, in certain applications bit complexity is quite relevant, for example in the design of registers for multiplication. Software developers, however, are less likely to be interested in bit complexity analyses; for them and their work, word complexity is a much more appropriate measure of the performance of an algorithm.[14]

---

[14] An exception is provided by cryptographic methods based on number-theoretic concepts (for example, the RSA public-key cryptography scheme) where arithmetic operations must be carried out on numbers with hundreds or thousands of bits.

1.5 Parallel Complexity

Parallelism is an aspect of software with which programmers are generally unfamiliar, but virtually all modern computing systems (for example, anything manufactured in the last decade or so) employ parallelism in their hardware. While producing parallel programs is probably not imminent for most application programmers, it is nevertheless useful to have some knowledge of the underlying software principles.

Parallel architectures are used because of their promise of increased performance. At the most primitive level, employing two or more devices that operate at the same time is expected to improve the overall performance of the system. A wide spectrum of different models of parallelism is available, from vector computing to shared-memory MIMD systems, to distributed memory MIMD systems.[15] Each requires specialized knowledge to allow programmers to exploit them efficiently. Common to most is the quest for speed-up, a measure of the improvement obtained by using several hardware devices in place of a single one.

Assume we are given a system with p processors, where $p > 1$. We use $T_s(n)$ to denote the time a given (parallel) algorithm AP requires to solve a given problem of size n using s processors, for $1 \leq s \leq p$. The speed-up that AP attains for a problem of size n on this parallel system is defined as follows:

$$\text{For } s < t, \; SP(s,t) = T_s(n)/T_t(n).$$

One is frequently interested in the effect that doubling the number of processors has on execution time; this corresponds to $SP(s,t)$, where $t = 2s$. It is also interesting to plot the curve one obtains by fixing $s = 1$ and increasing t by 1 until the maximum number p of processors in the system is reached.

In general, speed-up is dependent on the specific architecture and on the quality of the algorithm. Different architectures may permit differing speed-ups, independent of the quality of the algorithm. It may be impossible to take an algorithm that works very well on a particular parallel system and apply it effectively to a different parallel architecture.

Parallel algorithms frequently assume the shared memory paradigm; that is, they assume there are several processors but only one large memory space, which is shared by all processors. From a theoretical point of view, one can differentiate two types of access to a unit of memory: exclusive and concurrent. Exclusive access means that only one processor may access a specific memory unit at a time; concurrent access means that more than one processor can access the memory unit. Two types of access can be distinguished:

---

[15] Michael Flynn defined a very simple, yet effective classification of parallelism by concentrating on instruction streams (I) and data streams (D); the presence of a single stream (of type I or D) is then indicated by S, that of multiple streams by M. This gives rise to SISD, SIMD, and MIMD systems.

reading and writing. Therefore, we can image four types of combinations: EREW, ERCW, CREW, and CRCW, where E stands for exclusive, C for concurrent, R for read, and W for write. Of these four EREW is the standard mechanism implemented in all commercial systems (including all parallel shared-memory systems). ERCW, makes very little sense, since it is writing that is difficult to image being carried out in parallel. However, CREW is conceptually quite sensible; it simply means several processors can read a unit of memory at the same time.[16] However sensible concurrent reading may be, no commercially successful computing system has implemented it, so it is of no practical significance. Theoretically, one can, however, show that of the three models, EREW, CREW, and CRCW, certain problems can be solved more efficiently using CREW than EREW, and certain problems can be solved more efficiently using CRCW than CREW. In other words, CRCW is most powerful, and CREW is less powerful than CRCW but more powerful than EREW. However, these results are only of a theoretical nature and have no practical significance (at least as long as no commercial systems of CREW or CRCW types exist).

An alternative to the shared-memory approach assumes that each processor has its own (private) memory and that communication between processors relies on message passing. In this situation it is necessary to specify what messages are sent and at what time. While this creates significant problems for the programmer, it does not provide new programming paradigms that must be considered. Therefore, it does not give rise to new complexity considerations.

It should not come as a great surprise that programming parallel systems is significantly more difficult than programming sequential systems. When designing algorithms (or producing code), one must distinguish between covert and overt parallelism. In covert parallelism the designer ignores the parallel nature of the hardware and designs a standard sequential algorithm. It is only for overt parallelism that parallel algorithms must be devised. Here we are concentrating on sequential algorithms; they are not parallel, even though the hardware on which the software ultimately executes may contain a great deal of parallelism. Any exploitation of the available parallelisms in the hardware would be done by the compiling system, the operating system, or the run-time support system, all of which are typically outside of the designer's influence.

What is the promise of parallel hardware? Recall the notion of speed-up. If we have p processors instead of one, we might hope for a speed-up of p. After all, there is p times more hardware available. This ignores the ultimate crux in the difficulty of programming parallel systems: overhead, lack of balance, and synchronization.

Overhead refers to the coordination efforts that are necessary to have all processors cooperate to achieve a single goal. This typically involves the

---

[16] This occurs very frequently in practice, in different contexts. Consider a movie theater where many patrons see (that is, read) the same content at the same time. Clearly, writing is a completely different issue.

exchange of information between the processors that computed the information and the processors that require it for their own calculations.

Lack of balance refers to the fundamental problem that each processor should do essentially the same amount of work. This is difficult to achieve in practice. Most programming paradigms use a master–slave notion, whereby a single master process coordinates the work of many slave processes. Frequently (and in marked contrast to ordinary office work) the master process ends up having much more work than the slave processes. This lack of balance implies that the most overloaded process, which takes the longest, determines the overall execution time, since the entire problem is solved only when the last process is finished.

Synchronization refers to the fact that certain computations depend on the results of other computations, so the latter must be completed before the former may start. Ensuring that these dependences are satisfied is a necessary precondition for the correct functioning of the algorithm or software. Synchronization is the mechanism that achieves this. The downside is that it will make some processors wait for results. Forcing processors to wait results in a reduction of the efficiency that can be achieved by the parallel system.

The upshot of this (very brief) discussion is that the ideal speed-up, of p for p processors compared with one processor, is almost never attained. In many cases, significantly lower ratios (for MIMD systems perhaps 50% for smaller p, for example, p 32, and 20% or less for p on the order of thousands) are considered very respectable. An additional complication arises because a good parallel algorithm is not necessarily obtained by parallelizing a good sequential algorithm. In some cases parallelizing a *bad* sequential algorithm produces a much better parallel one.

1.6 I/O Complexity

I/O complexity is a nonstandard complexity measure of algorithms, but it is of great significance for our purposes. Some of the justification of and motivation for introducing this complexity measure will be provided in Part 2.

The I/O complexity of an algorithm is the amount of data transferred from one type of memory to another. We are primarily interested in transfers between disk and main memory; other types of transfer involve main memory and cache memory. In the case of cache memory the transfer is usually not under the control of the programmer. A similar situation occurs with disks when virtual memory management (VMM) is employed. In all these cases data are transferred in blocks (lines or pages). These are larger units of memory, providing space for a large number of numbers, typically on the order of hundreds or thousands. Not all programming environments provide VMM (for example, no Cray supercomputer has VMM); in the absence of

VMM, programmers must design *out-of-core* programs wherein the transfer of blocks between disk and main memory is directly controlled by them. In contrast, an *in-core* program assumes that the input data are initially transferred into main memory, all computations reference data in main memory, and at the very end of the computations, the results are transferred to disk. It should be clear that an in-core program assumes the uniformity of memory access that is almost always assumed in algorithms.

Let us look at one illustration of the concept of an out-of-core algorithm. Consider a two-dimensional (2D) finite difference method with a stencil of the form

$$
\begin{aligned}
s[i,j] = \quad & s[i-2,j] + \\
& s[i-1,j-1] + s[i-1,j] + s[i-1,j+1] + \\
s[i,j-2] + s[i,j-1] + \quad & s[i,j] + \quad s[i,j+1] + s[i,j+2] + \\
& s[i+1,j-1] + s[i+1,j] + s[i+1,j+1] + \\
& s[i+2,j],
\end{aligned}
$$

where we omitted the factors (weights) of each of the 13 terms. Suppose the matrix **M** to which we want to apply this stencil is of size $[1:n,1:n]$, for $n = 2^{18}$. Consequently, we must compute another matrix **M'**, whose $[i,j]$ element is exactly the stencil applied to the matrix **M** at the $[i,j]$ position. (For a somewhat different approach, see Exercise 11, page 35.) Now comes the problem: we have only space of size 2^{20} available for this operation. Because of the size of the two matrices (which is 2^{36}), we can only bring small portions of **M** and **M'** into main memory; the rest of the matrices must remain on disk. We may use VMM or we can use out-of-core programming, requiring us to design an algorithm that takes into consideration not only the computation, but also the movement of blocks between disk and main memory.

It is clear that we must have parts of **M** and **M'** in main memory. The question is which parts and how much of each matrix. Let us consider several possibilities:

1.6.1 Scenario 1

Assume that one block consists of an entire row of the matrices. This means each block is of size 2^{18}, so we have only room for four rows. One of these rows must be the ith row of **M'**; the other three rows can be from **M**. This presents a problem since the computation of the $[i,j]$ element of **M'** requires five rows of **M**, namely the rows with numbers $i-2$, $i-1$, i, $i+1$, and $i+2$. Here is where the I/O complexity becomes interesting. It measures the data transfers between disk and main memory, so in this case, it should provide us with the answer of how many blocks of size 2^{18} will have to be transferred. Let us first take the rather naïve approach formulated in the following code fragment:

```
for i:=1 to n do
  for j:=1 to n do
    M'[i, j] :=              M[i-2,j]+
             M[i-1,j-1]+M[i-1,j]+M[i-1,j+1]+
    M[i,j-2] + M[i,j-1]   +M[i,j]   +M[i,j+1]   +M[i,j+2]+
             M[i+1,j-1]+M[i+1,j]+M[i+1,j+1]+
                    M[i+2,j]
```

This turns out to have a truly horrific I/O complexity. To see why, let us analyze what occurs when $M'[i,j]$ is computed. Since there is space for just four blocks, each containing one matrix row, we will first install in main memory the rows $i - 2, i - 1, i$, and i + 1 of M and compute $M[i - 2,j] +$ $M[i - 1, j - 1] + M[i - 1,j] + M[i - 1,j + 1] + M[i,j - 2] + M[i,j - 1] + M[i,j] +$ $M[i,j + 1] + M[i,j + 2] + M[i + 1,j - 1] + M[i + 1,j] + M[i + 1,j + 1]$. Then we replace one of these four rows with the M-row $i + 2$ to add to the sum the element $M[i + 2,j]$. Then we must displace another M-row to install the row i of M' so we may assign this complete sum to $M'[i,j]$. In order to enable us to be more specific, assume that we use the **least recently used** (LRU) replacement strategy that most virtual memory management systems employ. (This means the page or block that has not been used for the longest time is replaced by the new page to be installed.) Thus, in our example, we first replace the M-row $i - 2$ and then the M-row $i - 1$. We now have in memory the M-rows $i, i + 1$, and $i + 2$ and the M'-row i. To compute the next element, namely $M'[i,j + 1]$, we again need the M-rows $i - 2, i - 1, i, i + 1$, and $i + 2$.

Under the LRU policy, since M-rows $i - 2$ and $i - 1$ are not present, they must be installed, replacing M-rows i and $i + 1$. Then the just-removed M-row i must be reinstalled, replacing M'-row i; subsequently M-row $i + 1$ must be reinstalled, replacing M-row $i + 2$. Now, the just-removed M-row $i + 2$ is reinstalled, replacing M-row $i - 2$. Finally, M'-row i must be brought back, replacing M-row $i - 1$. It follows that of the six rows involved in the computation (five M-rows and one M'-row), each must be reinstalled when computing $M'[i,j + 1]$ after having computed $M'[i,j]$. While the situation for the border elements ($M[i,j]$ for $i = 1,2,n - 1,n$ or $j = 1,2,n - 1,n$) is slightly different, in general it follows that for each of the n^2 elements to be computed, six page transfers are required. Thus, the data movement is $3n$ times greater than the amount of data contained in the matrices.[17] In particular, most of the n^2 elements of the matrix M are transferred $5n$ times; since $n = 2^{18}$, each of these M elements is transferred about 1.3 million times. This clearly validates our assertion about the lack of effectiveness of this approach.

For the following, let us assume that we can specify explicitly which blocks we want to transfer. The above analysis implicitly assumed that the replacement operations are automatically determined. (After all, it is difficult to conceive of any programmer coming up with as hopelessly inefficient a

---

[17] Each matrix consists of n pages. In total, $6n^2$ pages are transferred. Since $6n^2/2n = 3n$, the claim follows.

strategy as the one we described, yet it was the direct consequence of seemingly rational decisions: LRU and a code fragment that looked entirely acceptable.) The following scheme allows us to compute the entire matrix **M'** (we assume that both **M** and **M'** are surrounded with 0s, so we do not get out of range problems). To compute **M'**[i,*]:

1. Fetch rows $i - 2$, $i - 1$, and i of **M** and compute in **M'**[i,*] the first three lines of the stencil.
2. Fetch rows $i + 1$ and $i + 2$ of **M**, replacing two existing rows of **M**, and compute the remaining two lines of the stencil.
3. Store **M'**[i,*] on disk.

Thus, for computing **M'**[i,*] we need to fetch five rows of **M** and store one row of **M'**. If we iterate this for every value of i, we will retrieve $5n$ rows and store n rows. If we are a bit more clever and recognize that we can reuse one of the old rows (specifically, in computing **M'**[i,*], in the second fetch operation we overwrite rows **M**[$i - 2$,*] and another one, so the row that is still there is useful in the computation of **M'**[$i + 1$,*]), this will reduce the block retrievals from $5n$ to $4n$. Thus, even though **M** and **M'** have only $2n$ rows, the I/O complexity is $5n$; in other words, we have data movement that is 250% of the amount of data manipulated, a dramatic reduction over the previous result.

1.6.2   Scenario 2

The problem in Scenario 1 was that we had to retrieve the rows corresponding to one stencil computation in two parts. Perhaps we can improve our performance if we devise a set-up in which stencil computations need not be split. Assume that each block is now of size 2^{16}, so we can fit 16 blocks into our available main memory. This should allow us to compute an entire stencil in one part.

We assume that each row consists of four blocks (we will refer to quarters of rows to identify the four blocks). In this case, our algorithm proceeds as follows:

1. Compute the first quarter of **M'**[1,*].
   1.1 Fetch the first and second block of **M**[1,*], **M**[2,*], and **M**[3,*] and compute the entire stencil in the first quarter of **M'**[1,*].
   1.2 Store the first quarter of **M'**[1,*] on disk.
   1.3 Calculate the first two elements of the second quarter of **M'**[1,*] and store it on disk   **(eight resident blocks)**.
2. Compute the first quarter of **M'**[2,*].
   2.1 Fetch the first and second block of **M**[4,*] and compute the entire stencil in the first quarter of **M'**[2,*].

2.2 Store the first quarter of **M'[2,*]** on disk.

2.3 Calculate the first two elements of the second quarter of **M'[2,*]** and store it on disk   **(10 resident blocks)**.

3. Compute the first quarter of **M'[3,*]**.

    3.1 Fetch the first and second block of **M[4,*]** and compute the entire stencil in the first quarter of **M'[3,*]**.

    3.2 Store the first quarter of **M'[3,*]** on disk.

    3.3 Calculate the first two elements of the second quarter of **M'[3,*]** and store it on disk   **(12 resident blocks)**.

4. For $i = 4$ to $n - 2$ compute the first quarter of **M'[i,*]**.

    4.1 Fetch the first and the second block of row $i + 2$ of **M**, overwriting the respective blocks of row $i - 3$, and compute the entire stencil in the first quarter of **M'[i,*]**.

    4.2 Store the first quarter of **M'[i,*]** on disk.

    4.3 Calculate the first two elements of the second quarter of **M'[i,*]** and store it on disk   **(12 resident blocks)**.

5. Compute the first quarter of **M'[n - 1,*]**.

    5.1 Compute the entire stencil in the first quarter of **M'[n - 1,*]** and store it on disk.

    5.2 Calculate the first two elements of the second quarter of **M'[n - 1,*]** and store it on disk   **(10 resident blocks)**.

6. Compute the first quarter of **M'[n,*]**.

    6.1 Compute the entire stencil in the first quarter of **M'[n,*]** and store it on disk.

    6.2 Calculate the first two elements of the second quarter of **M'[n,*]** and store it on disk   **(eight resident blocks)**.

The second quarter of each **M'[i,*]** is calculated in a similar manner, except that we would go backwards, from $i = n$ to $i = 1$, which saves us initially fetching a few blocks that are already in memory; of course now we fetch the third quarter of each row, replacing all first quarters. Also, the second quarter of each **M**-row must be fetched from disk, because we will calculate all but the first two elements, which have already been computed in the previous round (first quarters). The third quarter is analogous (precomputing again the first two elements of each fourth quarter). Finally, the fourth quarter is computed similarly, but there is no precomputing of elements of the next round.

To calculate the I/O complexity of this second algorithm, we first note that we have space for 16 blocks. Computing the first quarter of **M[i,*]** requires us to have 10 blocks in memory, plus we need space (two blocks) for the first and second quarters of **M'[i,*]**. Therefore, the available memory is not exceeded. Adding up the fetches and stores in the first quarter round, we we need a total of $2n$ block retrievals (portions of **M**) and $2n$ block stores (portions of **M'**). For the second quarter round, we need $3n$ retrievals ($2n$ analogously to the first round, plus the retrieval of the second quarter of **M'**$[i,*]$, which had two elements precomputed in the first round) and $2n$ stores, and similarly for the third. For the fourth quarter round, we need $3n$ fetches and only n stores, since there is no precomputation in this round. The grand total is therefore $11n$ block fetches and $7n$ block stores, for an I/O complexity of $18n$ blocks of size 2^{16}. Since each matrix now requires $4n$ blocks, the data movement with this more complicated scheme is somewhat smaller: 225% of the size of the two matrices instead of the 250% of the much simpler scheme above.

This somewhat disappointing result (we seem to always need significantly more transfers than the structures require memory) raises the question of whether this is the best we can do.[18] Here is where the issue of lower bounds, to be taken up in Section 1.8, is of interest. We will return to this issue there and derive a much better lower bound.

We will return to the I/O complexity of a task in Part 2 in more detail. Here, we merely want to emphasize that important nontraditional measures of the performance of an algorithm are different from the usual time or space complexities. However, as we will see in Part 2, I/O performance is very intimately related to the time complexity of an algorithm when the memory space is not uniform.

1.7   On-Line versus Off-Line Algorithms

Algorithms can be classified according to the way in which they receive their input. If the entire input set is provided at the beginning of the algorithm, we say it is off-line. If input may be supplied during the computations of the algorithm, it is considered on-line. While most algorithms are off-line, because it often makes little sense to start solving the problem before all data are received, numerous problems are inherently on-line. For example, many algorithms occurring in operating systems are on-line, since an operating system deals with a dynamic situation where decisions must be continually made based on the information available at that time; once additional information is received, updates of the status are necessary. In general, on-line algorithms tend to be more difficult than off-line ones.

As an example, consider again the computation of the largest element of some set of integers. We have already seen an algorithm to solve this problem: the algorithm Max. Revisiting it makes it clear that this is a typical off-line algorithm. The entire input set V is assumed to be available before

---

[18] Of course, we are comparing the second approach with the out-of-core approach in Scenario 1. If we instead take the VMM approach in Scenario 1 as benchmark, all other techniques are marvelously efficient.

we start carrying out any computations. It is not unreasonable to consider an on-line algorithm for this purpose. We may have a continuous stream of input and would like to know, upon demand, what the maximum of the numbers seen up to this point was. It turns out that we can use Max without much modification; we simply treat each incoming new element as the next element with which we must compare our current TempMax and, if necessary, update it. It follows without great difficulty that the time complexity of this on-line version is still $O(n)$ if at some point we have received n integers as input. However, ordinarily one tends to report the time complexity of an on-line algorithm differently. Instead of giving a global answer ($O(n)$, where n is the number of inputs received), we might report the amount of work per input integer, because for each input, we have to do some work, so this amount of work should be attributed to the integer just received as input. Thus, we would report that per integer received, we must spend $O(1)$, or a constant amount of work. Also, in some on-line algorithms the question of how many input elements have been received at a certain point in time is not germane and might require an (extraneous) counter to enable us to know this.

Another example involves inserting elements into an ordered linear list with n elements. By adapting the analysis in Scenario 1 of Section 1.3, we see that one insertion requires on average $n/2$ probes, assuming all locations are equally likely.[19] Thus, carrying out m successive insertions in this way requires a total of $n/2 + (n + 1)/2 + ...(n + m - 1)/2$ probes, or $m \cdot n/2 + (m - 1) \cdot m/4$ probes. This is the on-line version. If we were able to batch these m insertions together, we could instead sort the m numbers (using HeapSort which requires no more than $3 \cdot m \cdot \log_2(m)$ comparisons; see Section 3.2.6) and then merge the two ordered structures (this requires about $m + n$ comparisons; see Section 3.2.4). Thus, this off-line process takes no more than $n + m \cdot [1 + 3 \cdot \log_2(m)]$. Since one probe is essentially one comparison, the off-line version is significantly more efficient. For example, if $m = n = 2^k$, then the on-line version requires asymptotically $2^k/(4 \cdot k)$ times more probes; for larger n, this is a dramatically increased number of probes.[20]

It should be clear that the complexity of an optimal on-line algorithm can never be better than that of an optimal off-line algorithm. If there were an on-line algorithm more efficient than the best off-line algorithm, we could simply use it on the data set of the off-line algorithm to obtain a more efficient off-line algorithm.

---

[19] More precisely, there are $n + 1$ places to insert x (we assume here that duplicates are permitted), namely before the first element, between elements 1 and 2, and so on until the $n + 1$st place, which is after the nth element. For the first place, we need one probe, for the second, two, through the nth place, which requires n; the last place ($n + 1$) requires no additional probe. Summing this up yields $n \cdot (n + 1)/2$; therefore, on average, we need $n/2$ probes.

[20] We have $n \cdot n/2 + (n - 1) \cdot n/4$ versus $n + n \cdot [1 + 3 \cdot \log_2(n)]$ probes. Thus, the asymptotic factor between on-line and off-line is $[n \cdot n/2 + (n - 1) \cdot n/4]/[n + n \cdot (1 + 3 \cdot \log_2(n))] = [3 \cdot n - 1]/[8 + 12 \cdot \log_2(n)] \approx n/(4 \cdot k)$. If $k = 8$, then $2^k/(4 \cdot k) = 8$; if $k = 16$, $2^k/(4 \cdot k) = 1024$; so for $k = 8$, about eight times more probes are required, and for $k = 16$, over a thousand times more probes are needed.

For the most part, we will concentrate on off-line algorithms. This does not mean we will ignore on-line algorithms completely since certain methods, notably search trees (including AVL trees, see 3.2.11) and hashing techniques (see 3.2.12), are essentially on-line algorithms (even though they are frequently presented as if they were off-line). On-line algorithms are also most amenable for amortized, or credit, analysis wherein lucky instances and bad instances of an algorithm are supposed to balance.

1.8   Amortized Analysis

If we execute an algorithm once, we can consider either its average or its worst-case complexity. If the difference between the two measures is small, we can ignore it. If it is large, we may want to know how likely it is that a bad instance will occur. This is particularly interesting if we execute the algorithm several times, since in this case we may be lucky in that a bad case (the algorithm approaches the worst-case situation) is balanced by a good case (the algorithm approaches an average or, even better, a best-case situation). If we carry out a complexity analysis taking repeated executions into consideration, this is called amortized, or credit, analysis. Not all algorithms lend themselves naturally to amortized analysis; on-line algorithms are usually most suitable for this approach. Obviously, when doing amortized analysis, one hopes that the bad cases are rare and the good cases frequent. While amortized analysis has attracted attention recently, it is not very different from average analysis. If one knows the probability of a case (also known as the potential in amortized analysis), the average complexity is simply the average, taken over all cases, of the product of the complexity of each case and its probability.

1.9   Lower Bounds and Their Significance

The complexity of an algorithm that solves a problem constitutes an *upper* bound on the complexity of that problem. In other words, we know we can solve the problem with that much effort, but this does not imply that there is not a better way. This is where the importance of *lower* bounds comes in. When determining a lower bound on the complexity of a problem, we determine a range between the lower bound and the complexity of a specific algorithm. If these two complexities are essentially the same (if they are equivalent in the terminology of Section 1.2), then our algorithm is asymptotically optimal. If the gap between the two complexities is great, we have two possibilities (both of which may be true): The lower bound is not very good and could be improved, or our algorithm is not very efficient and should be improved. There will be always cases where we are not able to improve either of the two complexities and yet the gap remains large. These are usually considered unpleasantly difficult problems.

Recall the example involving the I/O complexity of computing the stencil of a 2D matrix. We were concerned that the amount of block transfers between main memory and disk was much larger than the amount of memory required by the two matrices because we were using the idea of a lower bound; our lower bound on the number of block transfers was the number of blocks that the representation of the two matrices required. Since the two matrices altogether consist of 2^{37} elements, we expected the number of block transfers to contain about the same number of elements. Given the relatively limited amount of memory space in main memory, neither of our two attempts came close to this value.

Here is an argument that comes close to this obvious lower bound: Instead of attempting to compute $\mathbf{M'}[i,j]$ in its entirety, go through each row of $\mathbf{M}$ and accumulate in the appropriate $\mathbf{M'}$ elements the contributions of each $\mathbf{M}$ element. Assume as before that we split each row into four blocks. The element $\mathbf{M}[i,j]$ will affect $\mathbf{M'}$ elements in five rows. The first block of row $\mathbf{M}[i,*]$ requires the first blocks of the following $\mathbf{M'}$-rows to be present: $i - 2$, $i - 1$, i, $i + 1$, and $i + 2$. Thus, we need one block for $\mathbf{M}$ and five for $\mathbf{M'}$. However, of these five $\mathbf{M'}$ blocks, one will be completed once we are done with the $\mathbf{M}$ block, so we have to keep only four $\mathbf{M'}$ blocks around for further accumulation.

We can replace the first block of $\mathbf{M}[i,*]$ by its second block. Again, we need five $\mathbf{M'}$ blocks (plus the four we will need later). At the end of the second block of $\mathbf{M}[i,*]$, one of the five can be retired (stored) since its computations are completed. Now we have to keep eight $\mathbf{M'}$ blocks for further accumulation. We replace the second block of $\mathbf{M}[i,*]$ with its third and repeat. The final result is that we need 18 blocks at the high water mark of this approach, namely in the fourth quarter. We must keep around 12 old $\mathbf{M'}$ blocks plus the five currently computed ones, plus the $\mathbf{M}$ block that drives this process (the fourth quarter of $\mathbf{M}[i,*]$). It follows that we are 2 blocks short, since we have space for 16, not 18. This implies that we have to overwrite 2 of the 18, which must be first stored before they are overwritten and then fetched later. This introduces four more block transfers per row of $\mathbf{M}$. Since except for this problem, we would be optimal, that is, we would retrieve each block of $\mathbf{M}$ exactly once and store each block of $\mathbf{M'}$ exactly once, the problem is the difference between optimality (which would attain our lower bound) and an actual algorithm. This difference amounts to $4n$.

Consequently, the change in point of view (rather than computing each element of $\mathbf{M'}$ in its entirety, we view each element of $\mathbf{M'}$ as an accumulator) significantly improves the I/O performance. The gap between the naïve lower bound and the complexity of this algorithm is now only equal to the space occupied by one matrix (recall each row consists of four blocks). Thus, we now have data movement that is only 50% greater than the amount of data manipulated. While the gap is significantly reduced, it is still not clear whether the lower bound is effective, that is, whether there is an algorithm that attains it.

The situation is much clearer in the case of sorting n numbers by way of comparisons. This is the traditional lower bound example that is used almost universally, primarily because it is relatively easy to explain, as well as because of the significance of sorting in the global realm of computing. We will follow the crowd and present it as well, but it should be noted that for most problems, no nontrivial lower bounds are known.[21] There are only a few problems of practical significance for which one can determine attainable lower bounds; sorting by comparisons is one of them.

Since we are attempting to determine the complexity of a *problem*, not of a specific algorithm solving that problem, we cannot use properties of any specific algorithm, only properties of the problem. Thus, when sorting a given sequence of n integers using comparisons (if you prefer real numbers, replace integers by reals in the following), the only thing we know is that we can take two integers a and b and compare them. There are three possible outcomes of such a comparison, namely $a = b$, $a < b$, or $a > b$. For technical reasons, we would like to eliminate the possibility that $a = b$; this is easily achieved if we assume that the n numbers are pairwise different and that we never compare a number with itself. Thus, from now on when given any two different integers a and b, we assume we have two possible results of comparing them: $a < b$ or $a > b$.

Next we observe that any algorithm that sorts a sequence of n (pairwise distinct) integers by comparisons must consist of a sequence of comparisons of two numbers from the set, and once the algorithm terminates, it must tell us the exact order of these n integers. It follows that any algorithm can be represented by a decision tree; this is a binary tree[22] where each interior node corresponds to a comparison and each leaf corresponds to an outcome of the algorithm. A leaf represents a point in the algorithm where no more

---

[21] It is not entirely trivial to define what is nontrivial. However, if one is asked to compute N numbers, obviously $O(N)$ is a lower bound for this problem. We must expend at least some effort on each number. In most cases, this lower bound is trivial and cannot be attained. This is, for example, the situation for matrix multiplication. Given two (n,n)-matrices $\mathbf{A}$ and $\mathbf{B}$, compute the (n,n)-matrix $\mathbf{C}$ that is the product of $\mathbf{A}$ and $\mathbf{B}$. $\mathbf{C}$ contains $N = n^2$ numbers, and $O(N)$ turns out to be the best lower bound known for this problem. Few people believe that this bound is attainable (recall that the usual matrix multiplication scheme requires $O(N^{3/2})$ [or $O(n^3)$] time, although this *can* be improved – see Section 3.2.2), but nobody knows a better lower bound (as of 2005).

[22] Now it is clear why we wanted to eliminate the possibility $a = b$. We would need a ternary tree, where each node can have three children. (Clearly, to represent a ternary comparison requires two ordinary, binary ones. While this would not increase the asymptotic complexity, since it amounts to a factor of 2 and constant factors are routinely hidden, the exclusion of equality allows a much cleaner exposition.) Furthermore, since we are deriving a lower bound, and since each algorithm that works for the general case (i.e., where the numbers are *not* pairwise distinct) must also work for the case where the numbers *are* pairwise distinct, our lower bound for the special case is also one for the general case.

comparisons are needed because we know the exact order. Knowing the exact order, however, simply means that we know how to permute the original sequence of numbers — that is, we can sort.

Consider the case of three numbers: a, b, and c. Here is one decision tree (which represents one specific algorithm; a different algorithm would almost certainly result in an entirely different decision tree) for the problem of sorting these three numbers. Note that we record for any comparison $a < b$ whether it is true (T) ($a < b$) or false (F) ($b < a$) (since we excluded the case $a = b$).

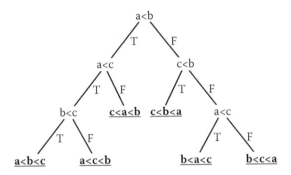

The outcomes of the algorithm are indicated in bold. Note that this is just one of many possible algorithms. Since we must make an argument that applies to *all* of them, we can only use properties of the general decision tree framework but not of specific trees. One such general property is that given n (pairwise distinct) integers, there are precisely $n!$ permutations of them; this means there are precisely $n!$ different outcomes of any sorting algorithm (since every permutation is a conceivable outcome, each algorithm must be able to provide every permutation as an answer). In our example, $n = 3$ and $3! = 6$, and indeed, our decision tree provided each of these six permutations: $a < b < c$, $a < c < b$, $b < a < c$, $b < c < a$, $c < a < b$, and $c < b < a$. Consequently, a decision tree that corresponds to an algorithm for sorting n numbers must have $n!$ leaves.[23]

What is the number of comparisons required to sort? Looking at our example, we can see that to reach $c < a < b$, we need two comparisons. However, we are interested in establishing a lower bound on the worst-case complexity,[24] so in our example, the most comparisons required to reach any of the six outcomes is three. In general, it is the height of the decision tree

---

[23] Actually, it must have at least n! leaves, since nothing in our decision tree approach precludes one permutation from being attached to more than one leaf.

[24] Lower bounds are almost always on worst-case complexities only. It usually makes little sense to look at anything else. Obviously, if the sequence of n numbers were already sorted, verifying this fact would require only $n - 1$ comparisons. This knowledge, however, is quite useless if they are not sorted (and usually they are not).

that provides the maximal number of comparisons required to reach a leaf (a permutation).

This leads naturally to the final question we must answer: What is the height of any binary tree with $n!$ leaves? To obtain the answer, consider the converse question first: What is the maximal number of leaves of a binary tree of a given height, say h? Clearly, the complete binary tree of height h has 2^h leaves.[25] Any other binary tree of height h can be obtained from the complete one by deleting nodes (or subtrees); this immediately establishes that no such tree can have more than 2^h leaves. It follows that the minimal height of a tree with N leaves is at least $\log_2(N)$. Assume that this is not true; in other words, there is a binary tree with N leaves whose height, say s, is less than $\log_2(N)$. Then we apply the result just obtained: Any binary tree of height s cannot have more than 2^s leaves, but since $s < \log_2(N)$, $2^s < 2^{\log_2(N)}$, and since $2^{\log_2(N)} = N$, it follows that $2^s < N$. Therefore, we obtain a contradiction to our original assumption that the tree has N leaves. Consequently, the height of a binary tree with N leaves must be at least $\log_2(N)$. All that remains to be done is to substitute $n!$ for N in this result. Any decision tree that sorts n (pairwise distinct) numbers by comparisons must have at least a height of $\log_2(n!)$. To get a better handle on this value, recall that the logarithm of a product is the sum of the logarithms. Thus.

$$\log_2(n!) = \log_2(1) + \log_2(2) + \ldots + \log_2(n/2) +$$
$$\log_2(n/2 + 1) + \ldots + \log_2(n-1) + \log_2(n).$$

We drop the first $n/2$ terms in this sum to get

$$\log_2(n!) > \log_2(n/2 + 1) + \ldots + \log_2(n-1) + \log_2(n).$$

Finally, we observe that for each of the remaining terms we have

$$\log_2(n/2) < \log_2(n/2 + k) \text{ for all } k = 1, \ldots, n/2.$$

Combining this with the fact that $\log_2(n/2) = \log_2(n) - 1$, we get

$$\log_2(n!) > n/2 \, [\log_2(n) - 1].$$

This shows that $\log_2(n!) > c \cdot n \cdot \log_2(n)$ for some constant c. Similarly, we can show

$$\log_2(n!) < \log_2(n) + \log_2(n) + \ldots + \log_2(n) +$$

---

[25] For the proof, first observe that the complete binary tree T_1 of height $h = 1$ has two leaves. Inductively, a complete tree Th_{+1} of height $h + 1$ can be constructed by taking two complete binary trees T_h of height h and making them the left and right subtrees of a root. Since by inductive assumption each of the trees T_h has 2^h leaves, T_{h+1} must have twice that many leaves, namely 2^{h+1}.

$$\log_2(n) + \ldots + \log_2(n) + \log_2(n) = n \cdot \log_2(n).$$

It follows that

$$\log_2(n!) \equiv n \cdot \log_2(n).$$

The final conclusion is therefore that any decision tree with $n!$ leaves must have a height that is $O(n \cdot \log_2(n))$. Thus, the worst-case complexity of sorting n numbers by comparisons is $O(n \cdot \log_2(n))$.[26]

Note that we made no use of any properties of a specific algorithm. The only concrete given was that comparisons had to be sequenced so that a conclusion could be reached. This conclusion had to be a permutation of the original sequence of n numbers, regardless of what algorithm was used. It must also be noted that this lower bound of $O(n \cdot \log_2(n))$ applies only if we do indeed sort using comparisons; if we sort in some other way, the statement is not applicable.[27]

The lower bound we derived is clearly a nontrivial one, not just because it is somewhat complicated to obtain. It is an attainable lower bound, that is, we will see in Chapter 3 algorithms that sort n numbers in time $O(n \cdot \log_2(n))$.

What then is the ultimate significance of lower bounds? Recall that we started this chapter with the question of how to determine whether a given algorithm is good. This question forced us first to explore what it is we might want to measure. Once this was determined, we still had to come up with a benchmark of quality. Just because we have an algorithm and can measure whatever we want does not mean the algorithm is any good. Having a lower bound changes this situation dramatically. Now we can attempt to attain this lower bound (or else show a better[28] lower bound); in other words, we have a goal. Most important is the case where the lower bound can be attained by some algorithm. This immediately implies that this algorithm is *optimal*. Optimal algorithms are the holy grail of algorithm design since they are *provably* best (at least for the measure we concentrate on, usually worst-case time complexity). Unfortunately, optimal algorithms are fairly rare. In most cases, substantial gaps exist between the (best) lower bound and any algorithms that solve the problem.

---

[26] While this is the number of comparisons, it should be clear that using word complexity, each comparison can be carried out in time $O(1)$. Thus, the lower bound on the worst-case complexity in terms of comparisons is also the worst-case time complexity for this problem.

[27] Later (in Section 3.2.7) we will see an algorithm that does not use comparisons to sort, namely RadixSort. Its time complexity has no correlation with the lower bound just derived.

[28] Here, *better* means higher. We could, for instance, have started with a lower bound of $O(n)$ for our sorting example. Clearly, to sort n numbers, we must at least look at each, giving rise to the $O(n)$ lower bound. Just as clearly, this is not a very good lower bound, and attempting to attain it is guaranteed to fail. Note that we can say this now because we have established that $O(n \cdot \log_2(n))$ is a better lower bound.

1.10 Conclusion

We described several performance aspects of an algorithm and illustrated most of them. We contrasted time and space complexity, the most important performance measures of algorithms. Entirely orthogonal[29] to these concepts, we distinguished worst-case, best-case, and average complexities and indicated when and why each of these concepts may be useful in practice. Yet again orthogonal, we discussed bit and word complexities. The I/O complexity of an algorithm, although introduced in this chapter, will be revisited in Part 2 in more detail, as it provides the basis for a performance measure that takes into account nonuniformity of memory accesses. On-line and off-line algorithms were contrasted, although we will primarily cover off-line algorithms. Finally, we emphasized the significance of lower bounds; it is only through their use that we can obtain an objective indication of whether an algorithm is really good.

Bibliographical Notes

Most of the material covered in this chapter is standard algorithm analysis and as such, it is presented in virtually all good algorithm books. Historically, Knuth's *The Art of Computer Programming* delineates the starting point for much of this; Aho, Hopcroft, and Ullman: *The Design and Analysis of Computer Algorithms* is another classic. A more recent book is Kleinberg and Tardos: *Algorithm Design* (very comprehensive, written at a fairly high level). Also useful are Kingston: *Algorithms and Data Structures, Design, Correctness, Analysis* (not as advanced or as comprehensive as Kleinberg and Tardos): Purdom and Brown: *The Analysis of Algorithms*; as well as Gonnet: *Handbook of Algorithms and Data Structures*; and Levitin: *Introduction to the Design and Analysis of Algorithms*. By and large, this selection is a matter of personal taste. Numerous textbooks, written at varying levels, convey the majority of the material in this chapter. Readers should choose the one they feel most comfortable with.

Not covered in most textbooks is I/O complexity. The seminar paper here is McKellar and Coffman, 1969, "Organizing Matrices and Matrix Operations for Paged Memory Systems". Chapter 7 of Leiss: *Parallel and Vector Computing, A Practical Introduction*, gives an overview of I/O complexity and I/O management. This book also contains some comments about parallel complexity.

---

[29] We consider a concept orthogonal to another one if the two are independent of each other. We can talk about worst-case or average time complexity; we can talk about worst-case or average space complexity; we can throw bit and word complexity into the mix and have three independent dimensions to manipulate.

Exercises

Exercise 1

Statement counts of entire algorithms or programs are composed of statement counts of individual program statements. This exercise addresses the constructive aspects of such a process.

For each of the following program statements, determine the best case and the worst case complexity, assuming that each simple instruction si (condition, assignment) takes one unit of time. Give your answer as an interval [best, worst] in each case.

a. Straight-line code: $si_1;\ldots;si_n$

b. Conditional: **if** cond **then** $list_1$ **else** $list_2$, where cond is a simple condition and $list_i$ is a list of n_i simple instructions, i = 1,2

c. For-loop: **for** i:=k **to** l **by** m **do** list, where list is a list of n simple instructions

d. While-loop:

> $Qu:= [q_1;\ \ldots\ q_k]$; We assume that the elements qi are all taken from a universal set U, consisting of n elements.

while Qu not empty **do**

> {   remove the front element q of Qu;
>   compute a new element p in U, based on q;
>   if p has not yet been considered, append p to Qu
> }

One must make assumptions about two aspects: the amount of work required to compute p when given q and the test of whether p had been already considered. The first is entirely arbitrary, say N simple instructions, but the second is not. Since the universal set has n elements, the most effective way (assuming n is of manageable size) is to allocate a boolean array AU[1:n] that records whether item q_i has been considered by setting AU[i] to true (AU is initialized to false). This operation must be factored into the determination of the statement count for this code fragment.

e. Once these basis cases are established, we can combine them into more complicated statements. For example, consider:

> si1; **if** c_1 **then** $\{si_2;si_3\}$ **else if** c_2 **then** $\{si_4;si_5;si_6\}$ **else** si_7;
>
> **for** i:= k **to** l **by** m **do if** c_3 **then** $\{si_8;si_9\}$ **else** $\{si_{10};si_{11};si_{12}\}$

Exercise 2

Consider the instructions in Exercise 1, but now determine the average complexity. This requires making assumptions about the likelihood of certain conditions to hold true. Note that for any assumption, your answer must lie within the interval [best, worst]. Assume that:

a. Each condition has a 50% chance of being true.
b. Each condition has a 25% chance of being true.
c. Each condition has a probability of $1/n$ of being true.

Exercise 3

Consider the following statement counts, expressed as functions of the positive integer parameter n:

$$f_1(n) = n^2 + 5n + 10$$

$$f_2(n) = [f_1(n)/\log_2(n)] \cdot [n \cdot \log_2(n) + 3n - 2]$$

$$f_3(n) = f_2(n)/f_1(n)$$

$$f_4(n) = [n + \log_2(n)] \cdot f_3(n)$$

$$f_5(n) = f_4(n)/\log_2(n)$$

$$f_6(n) = f_4(n)/n$$

a. Determine for each of these six functions f_i the most appropriate complexity class φ_j, $j \in \{1,\ldots,8\}$. Also, determine whether $f_i \equiv \varphi_j$ for that complexity class.
b. Show that the following assertions are all false: $f_1(n) \equiv n$; $f_2(n) \equiv n^2$; $f_4(n) \equiv n$; $f_5(n) \equiv n$.

Exercise 4

Formulate an algorithm and determine its best-case and worst-case complexities for the following problems:

a. Find the third largest of a set of n (≥ 3) numbers.
b. Find the first instance of an element that occurs at least three times in a sorted linear list with n elements.
c. Find the first instance of an element that occurs at least three times in an unsorted linear list with n elements.

    d. Find the first instance of an element that occurs exactly three times in a sorted linear list with n elements.

    e. Find the first instance of an element that occurs exactly three times in an unsorted linear list with n elements.

Exercise 5

Consider the questions in Exercise 4, but determine the average complexity under the following assumption: The elements in the linear list are all taken from a universal set with N elements, and the likelihood of an element being in any location in the list is $1/N$. Note that your answers will now depend not only on the number n of list elements, but also on N.

Exercise 6

Assume each block is of size 256 words, the active memory set size is 64, and the replacement strategy is pure LRU. Also assume that each array is mapped contiguously into the memory space and the first array element is the first element in its block. For each of the code fragments below, determine the number of blocks transferred between main memory and disk:

    a. **for** i:=1 **to** 65536 **do** A[i]:=A[65537-i]*A[i]
       (assuming the array A is of type [1:65536])

    b. **for** i:=1 **to** 1024 **do**
           for j:=1 **to** 1024 **do** C[i,j] := A[i,j] + B[i,j]
       (assuming the [1:1024,1:1024] arrays A, B, and C are mapped in column-major order)

    c. **for** i:=1 **to** 1024 **do**
           for j:=1 **to** 1024 **do** C[i,j] := A[i,j] + B[i,j]
       (assuming the [1:1024,1:1024] arrays A, B, and C are mapped in row-major order)

    d. **for** i:=1 **to** 1024 **do**
           for j:=1 **to** 1024 **do** C[i,j] := 0.0;
       for i:=1 **to** 1024 **do**
           for j:=1 **to** 1024 **do**
               for k:=1 **to** 1024 **do**
                  C[i,j] := C[i,j] + A[i,k]*B[k,j]
       (assuming the [1:1024,1:1024] arrays A, B, and C are mapped in column-major order)

    e. **for** i:=1 **to** 1024 **do**
           for j:=1 **to** 1024 **do** C[i,j] := 0.0;

```
for i:=1 to 1024 do
    for j:=1 to 1024 do
        for k:=1 to 1024 do
            C[i,j] := C[i,j] + A[i,k]*B[k,j]
```
(assuming the [1:1024,1:1024] arrays A, B, and C are mapped in row-major order)

f.
```
for i:=1 to 1024 do
    for j:=1 to 1024 do
        C[i,j] := C[j,i] + A[j,i]*B[j,i]
```
(assuming the [1:1024,1:1024] arrays A, B, and C are mapped in column-major order)

g.
```
for i:=1 to 1024 do
    for j:=1 to 1024 do
        C[i,j] := C[j,i] + A[j,i]*B[j,i]
```
(assuming the [1:1024,1:1024] arrays A, B, and C are mapped in row-major order)

Exercise 7

Determine for the following code how many pages are transferred between disk and main memory, assuming each page has 1024 words, the active memory set size is 300 (i.e., at any time no more than 300 pages may be in main memory), and the replacement strategy is LRU (the least recently used page is always replaced). Also assume that all 2D arrays are of size [1:1024, 1:1024], with each array element occupying one word, provided the [1:1024,1:1024] arrays A, B, and C are mapped into the main memory space: (a) in row-major order and (b) in column-major order:

```
for i := 1 to 1024 do
    for j :=1 to 1024 do
        { A[i,j]:=A[i,j]*B[i,j]; B[i,j]:=C[N-i+1,j]*A[i,j] }
```

Exercise 8

Reexamine the following algorithms that we analyzed using word complexity and determine their bit complexity, assuming that each element involved has m bits. Pay attention to the fact that operations such as comparing two elements and adding or multiplying two numbers no longer take $O(1)$ time, but that the time now depends on m.

a. Determining the largest of n elements (Section 1.2)

   b. The two scenarios of finding an element in a linear list, depending on probability assumptions (Section 1.3)

   c. Matrix multiplication of two [1:n,1:n] matrices

Exercise 9

Determine a lower bound on sorting n m-bit numbers by comparisons using bit complexity.

Exercise 10

Formulate a comprehensive algorithm that implements the argument made at the beginning of Section 1.9 to improve the computation of the stencil discussed at length in Section 1.6. Specifically, outline how under the stated assumption about the amount of available memory, the blocks should be sized and how the strategy for retrieving and storing back blocks is to be implemented. Then carefully analyze the number of block transfers, keeping in mind that only dirty blocks (blocks that have been written to since they were fetched from disk) need to be written back before they are replaced by other blocks.

Exercise 11

In the stencil example in Section 1.6, we assumed that there was a new matrix **M'** that we had to compute. It is frequently not necessary to have a second matrix. It might be acceptable to compute the result of applying the stencil in place, that is, using the same matrix **M** to store the new values. This creates problems since we must ensure that the old values of **M**, not the new ones, are used in the computations of the stencil. Thus, some temporary space must be allocated for this purpose, even though we do not need an entire matrix **M'** for this.

   Formulate an algorithm to incorporate this idea and determine its I/O complexity, along the lines of the argument advanced in Section 1.6.

2

Fundamental Assumptions Underlying Algorithmic Complexity

About This Chapter

In this chapter we formulate explicitly the assumptions underlying the complexity analysis introduced in the previous chapter. We discuss their implications and show that their effect is a significant simplification of determining desired performance measures of an algorithm. Many of the assumptions relate to some form of uniformity, be it uniformity in the way operations are counted, uniformity in accessing memory, or uniformity in the validity of mathematical identities. We also reexamine the asymptotic nature of the functions that result from determining complexities. While most of these aspects appear fairly innocuous, their discussion sets up the exploration in Part 2 of whether these assumptions remain valid when designing software based on the analyzed algorithms.

2.1 Introduction

In the previous chapter we established a conceptual framework for analyzing the performance of algorithms. In doing so we sidestepped several important issues and assumptions that are vital for the relative ease with which we manage to carry out this process. It is now appropriate to examine these assumptions in greater detail.

2.2 Assumptions Inherent in the Determination of Statement Counts

The first leap of faith we had to make when developing the theory of operation or statement counts had to do with the assertion that all statements are comparable in complexity. This obscured a number of rather thorny issues, which we attempt to clarify here. First at issue is the question of what operations can be considered atomic. Closely related is the area of memory access, in particular, its random access property that is implicitly assumed whenever we deal with algorithms.

At the heart of the assumptions of this section is the equivalence of atomic operations and statements. Recall that our treatment in Chapter 1 suggested that a statement essentially consists of no more than a constant number of atomic operations. Since the asymptotic nature of our performance measures allows us to hide constant factors, the fact that one statement may consist of several atomic operations may be conveniently swept under the rug — provided we can ascertain that the number of operations involved in a statement is indeed a constant; that is, it must be independent of the data structure to which the operations are applied. This is neither obvious, nor is it always true. Therefore, we must delve a bit deeper into this question.

First we must clarify what we mean by *atomic operation*. We have already obfuscated a bit by introducing two notions of complexity: bit and word complexity. An atomic operation in bit complexity is simply an operation that involves a single bit of each of its operands. Note that we usually assume that operations are binary, so there would be two bits involved, one from each of the two operands. However, there are also unary operations (for instance negation) as well as operations with more than two operands. At any rate, an atomic operation (in either bit or word complexity) can have only a fixed constant number of operands. An analogous definition applies to word complexity, but now the operation applies to a word rather than a single bit of each operand. As indicated, this is somewhat confused because the word length is not necessarily fixed across different architectures. On the one hand, there are 16-bit words, 32-bit words, and 64-bit words in different architectures; on the other hand, by its very nature, word complexity will assume that the word is long enough to accommodate whatever space is needed for a given data item, say an integer or a real number.

As we pointed out in Section 1.4, we need at least $\lceil \log_2(n) \rceil$ bits to represent n different numbers, but in word complexity, the space for such a number is simply considered one word, and an atomic operation on such words is assumed to take one unit of time. This is where the two complexity measures differ; if we have words of length m, an operation such as comparison of two words (numbers) takes one unit of time using word complexity, but m units of time using bit complexity. For other operations, such as multiplication of numbers, the difference is even greater. Thus, an operation that would be considered atomic within the context of word complexity might not be viewed as atomic under the rules of bit complexity. Therefore, it is very important to be aware of the context (bit or word complexity), as the atomicity of an operation depends on it.

It is instructive to contrast this with the mathematical operation of adding two-dimensional (2D) matrices. This operation is not atomic under the rules of either bit or word complexity. Ultimately, the reason is that the size of the matrices affects the amount of work required to carry out this computation. Clearly, if the two matrices are [2,2], less work is required to add them than if they are of size [1000,1000]. In general, if the two matrices are of size [1:n,1:n], we need n^2 additions of two scalar numbers, so even under word complexity rules, the time complexity is $O(n^2)$. Under bit complexity rules, the length of the scalars must also be considered. Assuming it is m (and ordinarily $m > \log_2(n)$, as there are 2·n^2 scalars[1]), the time complexity becomes $O(m·n^2)$. Note that m here is *not* a constant that can be hidden in the order-of notation, simply because it is not a constant — it generally depends on n (increasing n requires increasing m).

Now we are ready to tackle statements. As long as a statement contains only a fixed number of atomic operations, the equivalence (up to a constant factor) of operations and statements is valid. This applies to both bit and word complexity since it hinges on the atomicity of the operations (which depends on the context). Typical statements might be

$$X := 2*X + 1,$$

where X is a scalar (valid for word or bit complexity, as long as X is a scalar within the word or bit context) or

$$C[i,j] := C[i,j] + A[i,k]*B[k,j],$$

where A, B, and C are 2D matrices (of arbitrary size; for bit complexity with bit matrices and for word complexity with word matrices). The first statement involves one multiplication, one addition, and one assignment. As we pointed out, we consider atomic operations to be comparable as far as their time requirements are concerned. This is a reasonable assumption because in virtually all computer architectures, the time for a scalar multiplication is only a few times, perhaps five times, longer than the time of an addition.[2] In general, one may assume that the basic arithmetic operations are comparable; that is, the effort required to do the slowest is only a small constant times the effort to do the fastest.

---

[1] Boolean matrices are frequently represented as integer matrices. They would be an exception to this rule of $m > \log_2(n)$. Boolean matrices are, for example, used to represent graphs.
[2] This uses the fact that the word length is limited to 16, or 32, or 64 bits. This is of course true for all of today's commercial architectures (as of 2005). However, this statement would no longer be valid if arbitrarily long words were supported by a specific architecture.

Assignment is much more complicated. The converse of assignment, retrieval, is equally thorny. The issue is one of access to memory, whether we want to retrieve data or store data. Ordinarily, this issue is avoided since we concentrate on operations, without worrying where the values come from or where the results are stored. Underlying this lack of concern is the fundamental assumption of algorithm analysis that memory accesses are simple, cheap, and fast. Consequently, one invariably assumes that retrieval of arguments and storing of results can be subsumed in the time required to carry out the operations at hand; in other words, retrieving and storing is considered equivalent to carrying out an atomic operation (under either bit or word rules). This is an assumption that bears careful examination.

We will distinguish between access to simple variables, such as the variable X in the first statement above, and access to elements of more complicated structures, such as the array elements in the second statement. To simplify the presentation, let us assume that we are considering word complexity only.

In virtually all commercial computer architectures, access to a unit of memory takes an amount of time that is comparable to (i.e., within a relatively small constant factor of) the time required to carry out an atomic arithmetic operation, provided the unit resides in main memory. This holds because main memory possesses the *random access property* (RAP). This means that any unit in main memory has a unique index, that specifying this index provides access to the content of the unit thus indexed, and that the time to carry out this access is independent of the value of that index. Whether the value of the index is large or small makes no difference in the access time. Thus, the RAP is crucial for uniform memory access. It is the primary reason why it is justified to treat retrieval of a value from main memory and storage of a value in a unit in main memory as atomic operations. Since access to simple variables in main memory conforms to this paradigm, it follows that both retrieving the value of a simple variable and storing the value of a simple variable requires an amount of time that is comparable to that required by any other atomic operation.

Main memory *possesses* the RAP, but not all data structures *preserve* it. Even though all of our data structures may reside in main memory, whether a structure preserves the RAP depends on the nature of the structure. For example, a linear list does not preserve the RAP. Access to the first element of a linear list is direct, but access to the 50th element is not. We must first visit the first element, then proceed from it to the second, from there to the third, and so on, visiting every one of the preceding 49 elements of the linear list before we finally reach the 50th. Most seriously, access to the last element of a linear list with n elements requires time that is proportional to the size of the linear list. Access to the nth element takes $O(n)$ time even though the linear list resides in main memory (which does have the RAP) and we have a concrete index for the element we wish to access. Many data structures do not preserve the RAP, for example all trees, stacks, and queues, making it an important aspect of a data structure if it does preserve this property. In particular, it is very relevant for many applications that multidimensional arrays resident in main memory do preserve the RAP, provided the mapping into the memory space is carried out appropriately.

Any data structure must ultimately be mapped into main memory; otherwise it cannot be used in a program since memory space must be allocated in some way. In the following we will assume that the available main memory is sufficiently large to accommodate all the data that must be manipulated by an algorithm, including not just the input and output data sets, but also any intermediate sets that arise. Even if this assumption is satisfied,[3] we still have to verify that the structure can be mapped into the main memory space in a way that preserves the RAP. It is not too difficult to see that preserving the RAP is equivalent to the following: When mapping the structure into main memory, we effectively have to provide a method for computing the index of each element in the data structure in main memory. As the example of the linear list illustrates, this computation (namely, following a number of links) need not be simple, or independent of the size of the structure. Thus, we must further stipulate that the time complexity of computing this index has to be $O(1)$ for all elements; in other words, only a fixed (bounded) number of atomic operations are permissible for the calculation of the index of any element of the structure, regardless of its position in that structure (e.g., first, middle, or last – easy for an array, difficult for a linear list) and regardless of the size of that structure (e.g., computing the index of $A[i,j]$ must take the same amount of time whether A is a [5,5] or a [5000,5000] matrix).

Here is why multidimensional arrays preserve the random access property. Consider a k-dimensional array **A** of type $[1{:}n_1, 1{:}n_2, ..., 1{:}n_k]$, for $k \geq 1$.[4] Two standard memory mappings take a k-dimensional array and map it into the one-dimensional (1D) main memory space, namely row-major and column-major. To carry out a mapping of a k-dimensional space into a 1D space, it suffices to show how every k-tuple $I = (i_1, i_2, ..., i_k)$ of indices satisfying $1 \leq i_j \leq n_j$ for all $j = 1,..., k$, is assigned a single index value v_I such that the following holds:

If I and J are different k-tuples, then $v_I \neq v_J$.[5]

In other words, different array elements are assigned different indices in the main memory space.

$\{ v_I \mid I$ ranges over all valid k-tuples $\} = \{1,..., n_1 {\cdot} n_2 {\cdot} ... {\cdot} n_k\}$.[6]

---

[3] In Part 2 we will discuss at length what happens if this is not a valid assumption.
[4] We assume that the lower bound in each dimension is 1. Changing this to an arbitrary integer value, positive, negative or 0, does not change the complexity of the formulas below.
[5] This means the mapping is injective.
[6] This means the mapping is surjective. A mapping that is both injective and surjective is called bijective. We are therefore stipulating that our mapping be a bijection between the set of all valid k-tuples and the set of all integers from 1 through $n_1 {\cdot} n_2 {\cdot} ... {\cdot} n_k$.

In other words, the array has $n_1 \cdot n_2 \cdot \ldots \cdot n_k$ elements, and each of the values from 1 to $n_1 \cdot n_2 \cdot \ldots \cdot n_k$ occurs as the unique index of a uniquely determined array element. This implies that the mapping is as economical as possible, since there are no gaps in the index set; every value between 1 and $n_1 \cdot n_2 \cdot \ldots \cdot n_k$ represents some array element.

Let us first formulate the row-major mapping. We assume we are given the valid k-tuple $I = (i_1, i_2, \ldots, i_k)$,[7] then the index v_I corresponding to the k-tuple I is defined as follows:

$$
\begin{aligned}
v_{I,row} = \ &(i_1-1) \cdot n_2 \cdot \ldots \cdot n_k + \\
&(i_2-1) \cdot n_3 \cdot \ldots \cdot n_k + \\
&(i_3-1) \cdot n_4 \cdot \ldots \cdot n_k + \\
&\ldots \\
&(i_{k-2}-1) \cdot n_{k-1} \cdot n_k + \\
&(i_{k-1}-1) \cdot n_k + \\
&i_k.
\end{aligned}
$$

The corresponding formula for the column-major mapping is as follows:

$$
\begin{aligned}
v_{I,col} = \ &(i_k-1) \cdot n_1 \cdot \ldots \cdot n_{k-1} + \\
&(i_{k-1}-1) \cdot n_1 \cdot \ldots \cdot n_{k-2} + \\
&(i_{k-2}-1) \cdot n_1 \cdot \ldots \cdot n_{k-3} + \\
&\ldots \\
&(i_3-1) \cdot n_1 \cdot n_2 + \\
&(i_2-1) \cdot n_1 + \\
&i_1.
\end{aligned}
$$

It can be verified that both formulas satisfy the two requirements listed above. In both schemes, the k-tuple $[1,1,\ldots,1]$ is assigned the value 1 and the k-tuple $[n_1, n_2, \ldots, n_k]$ the value $n_1 \cdot n_2 \cdot \ldots \cdot n_k$, but for other k-tuples I, $v_{I,row}$ and $v_{I,col}$ are usually different.

Note that we are ignoring the offset of the array. In general, the memory space allocated to an array will not start at 1, but at its offset. Consequently, when carrying out the mapping, everything must be appropriately shifted according to the offset. In these formulas, we are also ignoring what happens if there is not enough main memory available; in this case the mapping specified by the formula is between the elements of the data structure and the logical memory space (which knows no physical limitations, as it is not physical), which must then be mapped separately into the available main memory. This last mapping between logical memory space and main memory might, for instance, be carried out by virtual memory management.

As an illustration, let $k = 4$ and $n_1 = n_2 = n_3 = n_4 = 2$. Then there are 16 valid 4-tuples. Here are the two mappings:

---

[7] A k-tuple is valid if all indices fall within their proper ranges, that is, $1 \le i_j \le n_j$ for all $j = 1, \ldots, k$.

$I =$	(i_1,i_2,i_3,i_4)	$V_{I,row}$	$V_{I,col}$
	1 1 1 1	1	1
	1 1 1 2	2	9
	1 1 2 1	3	5
	1 1 2 2	4	13
	1 2 1 1	5	3
	1 2 1 2	6	11
	1 2 2 1	7	7
	1 2 2 2	8	15
	2 1 1 1	9	2
	2 1 1 2	10	10
	2 1 2 1	11	6
	2 1 2 2	12	14
	2 2 1 1	13	4
	2 2 1 2	14	12
	2 2 2 1	15	8
	2 2 2 2	16	16

We now verify that each of these two general mappings preserves the random access property. This amounts to showing that the formulas can be computed in constant time. Let us look first at the row-major scheme. As written, there are k lines. In the first line, we have exactly $k + 1$ arithmetic (atomic) operations (1 subtraction, 1 addition, and $1 + k - 2$ multiplications, where $k - 2$ of them are needed for the product of the n_j's). The second through the penultimate line all have the same pattern, except that the product of the n_j's is progressively smaller and therefore needs fewer multiplications. Thus, line s requires $k + 2 - s$ operations, $s = 1, ..., k - 1$. The last line requires no operation. Adding all this up, we obtain $(k^2 + 3k - 4)/2$ or $O(k^2)$ operations. This can be improved if one observes that the most significant contribution comes from the computation of the product of the n_j's, which can be drastically reduced if we reorder the calculations by starting with the penultimate line and working our way up to the first line. In this scheme, we can obtain the product $n_s \cdot n_{s+1} \cdot ... \cdot n_k$ for any s from the product $n_{s+1} \cdot ... \cdot n_k$ (which had been calculated in the previous line) by way of a single multiplication (by n_s). Summing the operation counts up for this backward calculation results in $4k - 5$ arithmetic operations, for $k > 1$, which is $O(k)$.

A similar analysis of the time complexity can be carried out for the column-major scheme. This also results in a time complexity of $O(k)$.

These results seem to present a problem: For both schemes, the time complexity is dependent on k. However, a dependence on k is acceptable, since the value of k does not affect the size of the k-dimensional array. In other words, for a given value of k, either formula requires a number of operations that is independent of the size of the array (even though it does depend on k). Thus, k is considered fixed and is treated as a constant; for the entire universe of k-dimensional arrays, the same number of operations is needed to compute the index. Therefore, either of the two schemes (row- or column-major) preserves the random access property of the main memory. Consequently, k-dimensional arrays preserve the RAP, as claimed.

Now we can return to looking at the second of our two statements above, namely,

$$C[i,j] := C[i,j] + A[i,k]*B[k,j].$$

Assume that each of the three 2D arrays **A**, **B**, and **C** is of type $[1:n,1:n]$. Also assume that the mapping function is done using row-major. Then each array reference requires a constant number of arithmetic operations: a fixed number of arithmetic operations to compute the index into the main memory space and, thanks to the RAP, a single direct access to the memory location thus specified. Therefore, it is legitimate to consider such a statement to consist of a constant number of atomic operations. So, we can finally conclude that this statement, within the rules of our game that allow us to hide constant factors in the order of notation, can be viewed as requiring one unit of time.

The upshot of this discussion is that we can properly view not only atomic operations, but any simple statement to be of constant time complexity. We must qualify this with the word *simple* since statements such as while loops and do loops must be excluded, as they violate the goal of permitting execution in time $O(1)$.

In Part 2 we will discuss in some detail how the programmer's world differs from the ideal world of the algorithm designer. Here we summarize the latter's salient features. All operations are comparable in complexity, all simple statements are comparable in complexity, and, most importantly, there is complete uniformity of access to memory. Most significantly, the uniformity of memory access will turn out to be due primarily to our earlier assumption that we have enough main memory available to do whatever we want to do.

2.3   All Mathematical Identities Hold

It may appear that we are belaboring the obvious, but this is the proper place to emphasize a fundamental assumption when designing algorithms, namely that all mathematical identities remain valid. This includes basic properties of numbers, such as:

1. **Commutativity:** $a + b = b + a$ and $a*b = b*a$ for any numbers a and b.
2. **Associativity:** $a + (b + c) = (a + b) + c$ and $a*(b*c) = (a*b)*c$ for any numbers a, b, and c.

3. **Distributivity:** $a*(b + c) = a*b + a*c$ for any numbers a, b, and c.

This is primarily of interest when one talks about word complexity since in essence these properties hold precisely because we are assuming that limitations owing to word length are ignored.[8] A direct consequence of this assumption is the absence of rounding errors and overflow and underflow conditions; it is often even acceptable to ignore otherwise fatal occurrences such as division by zero when designing algorithms, as long as the general gist of the algorithm is not affected.

It should be clear that this simplifies the design and analysis of algorithms. It stems from the more mathematical nature of algorithms, which places it in opposition to programs. We will return in Part 2 to the significant difficulties that this aspect of algorithm design can cause for the designer of software.

2.4   Revisiting the Asymptotic Nature of Complexity Analysis

An important aspect of the discussion in Section 2.2 about the equivalence of operations and statements is the inherently asymptotic nature of complexity analysis. It should be clear that there are large differences between the time required to carry out different operations or statements. To illustrate this graphically, for the purpose of complexity analysis, the following two statements are both assumed to take one unit of time:

$$X:=1;$$

$$A[i,j,k,m] := B[i-1,T[j],k,m] + B[i,T[j],k,m] + B[i+1,T[j],k,m],$$

where X is a simple variable, **A** and **B** are 4D arrays of type $[1{:}n,1{:}n,1{:}n,1{:}n]$, and T is a 1D integer array of type $[1{:}n]$. This is true even though examination reveals that the second statement is composed of over 50 operations, while the first has only a single one — the point being that 50 is a fixed constant. More extreme examples are easily concocted.

It is of course true that in a typical algorithm, there are far more statements of the first kind than of the second, so on average, the 50-operation outlier

---

[8] In the case of bit complexity, we are always aware of the limitations, but only to the extent that they force us to extend the length of the numbers. Thus, for bit complexity, overflow conditions do not exist. They simply mean that the length of the sequences used to represent numbers increases, which presents no problem because this length is a parameter in the analysis in the first place. An overflow condition occurs if the result of an operation is too large to be representable using the given number of bits. For example, if we have 16-bit words, adding 1111000011110000 and 1111000011110000 yields overflow since the result is a 17-bit number (11110000111100000), which cannot be represented as an integer using 16 bits.

is smoothed out by the preponderance of very cheap statements. Again on average, we may have somewhere between four and six atomic operations per statement in a typical algorithm. Still, this is a constant of a significant size that is being hidden in our order of notation. Moreover, this is almost unavoidable — unless we want to expend dramatically more effort on determining the computational complexity of our algorithms. This is usually quite undesirable, especially in the case of algorithms, where even using all the simplifications that these assumptions afford us, the difficulty of arriving at an acceptable asymptotic complexity is nontrivial. [9]

It is important to realize that even for worst-case complexities, the asymptotic nature of our analyses introduces an averaging effect. Make no mistake — the reason we are able to get away with this is the constant-hiding ability that we acquired in going to asymptotics. Moreover, while the difference between average and worst-case complexities frequently amounts to more than a constant factor gap, the peculiar way in which we determine time, through counting statements that seemingly are wildly different in complexity, guarantees us (always assuming we are somewhat circumspect in making sure that our statements are indeed simple) that we will never be off by more than a constant factor.[10] This is the ultimate elegance that asymptotic complexity of algorithm analysis bestows on us.

2.5   Conclusion

Much of this chapter lays the groundwork for an examination of the differences between the ideal world inhabited by algorithm designers and the real world of software production. This investigation will take place in Part 2. It is important to be aware of the idealizing assumptions that algorithm designers are able to exploit.

First is the uniformity of memory access. This goes well beyond the preservation of the random access property enjoyed by main memory and creates an almost idyllic situation where memory hierarchies are completely absent. One may be tempted to argue that memory hierarchies could be dealt with in the same way in which we dealt with the significantly different kinds of statements we contrasted in the previous section. However, on closer inspection this will turn out to be impractical.

---

[9] It may also be counterproductive, since different architectures with their instruction sets may demonstrate substantial differences in performance. We may have two simple statements S1 and S2 in an algorithm, and in architecture AR1, S1 might take 10 times as long as S2, but in AR2, the two statements take the same amount of time. Being too precise in looking at simple statements (that is, making distinctions between slow and fast simple statements) is thus shown to be quite unhelpful.

[10] As one might suspect, how big this constant factor is will depend on the target platform (architecture plus instruction set).

A second advantage enjoyed by algorithms is the equivalence of statements and operations. This is almost exclusively due to the asymptotic nature of our complexity analysis, which allows us to hide substantial, but bounded, differences in the underlying notation.

A third advantage stems from the fact that certain properties and identities carry over from mathematics. This is because algorithms ignore length limitations in the representation of numbers without problems. In the case of bit complexity, the length of the representation is a parameter and thus gets factored into the analysis if it needs to be increased. In the case of word complexity, we assume that words, by definition, are long enough so that whatever we want to do can be done without concern for errors or over- and underflow conditions.

Bibliographical Notes

The same books that were cited for Chapter 1 are applicable here. After all, Chapter 2 deals with fairly common aspects of algorithm analysis. The one exception might be the mapping from arrays to the main memory space; it and the discussion of the random access property can be found in most compiler text books, for example in Aho, Sethi, and Ullman: *Principles of Compiler Design*; Muchnik: *Advanced Compiler Design and Implementation*; and Zima and Chapman: *Supercompilers for Parallel and Vector Computers*. What is different here is our stress on the difference between the algorithm designer's world and the world of the programmer. While these textbooks are aware of the assumptions, they do not pay a great deal of attention to them, since they are the standard assumptions underlying all algorithm design.

Exercises

Exercise 1

Determine the exact number of atomic operations (arithmetic operations and memory accesses) required to execute the following statements:

a. $X := X + 1$

b. $A[i] := B[j]*C[k]$, where **A**, **B**, and **C** are 1D arrays of type $[1:n]$ and offsets off$_A$, off$_B$, and off$_C$, respectively.

c. $A[i,j] := A[i,j] + B[i,k]*A[k,j]$, where **A** and **B** are 2D arrays of type $[1:n,1:n]$ and offsets off$_A$ and off$_B$, respectively.

   d. **A**[i,j,k,m] := **A**[i,j,k,m] + **B**[i,k,j,m]*__A__[k,j,i,m], where **A** and **B** are 4D
     arrays of type [1:n,1:n,1:n,1:n] and offsets off$_A$ and off$_B$, respectively.

Exercise 2

Repeat Exercise 1, but now determine the bit complexity of each of the
statements (instead of the word complexity, which was effectively calculated
in Exercise 1). Assume that the array elements use m bits and assume that
the indices use the minimum number of bits required to represent them (that
is, $\lfloor \log_2(n) \rfloor + 1$; note that this number and m are independent of each other,
as m could be 1, reflecting that we deal with Boolean matrices). Also, pay
attention to the number of bits required to compute the indices into the
memory space. Finally, remember that the arithmetic operations involved in
the index calculations have a bit complexity substantially higher than $O(1)$.

Exercise 3

Determine with concrete examples which of the three basic properties of
numbers listed in Section 2.3 (commutativity, associativity, and distributivity) hold for:

   a. Fixed-point numbers (integers)
   b. Floating-point numbers (reals)
   c. Boolean numbers

3

Examples of Complexity Analysis

About This Chapter

We begin with a review of techniques for determining complexity functions. Then we apply these techniques to a number of standard algorithms, among others representatives of the techniques of divide-and-conquer and dynamic programming, as well as algorithms for sorting, searching, and graph operations. We also illustrate on-line and off-line algorithms.

This chapter concentrates on techniques for determining complexity measures and how to apply them to a number of standard algorithms. Readers who have substantial knowledge of algorithm complexity may skip this chapter without major consequences. We first review approaches to finding the operation or statement count of a given algorithm. These range from simple inspection of the statements to much more sophisticated recursion-based arguments. Then we examine a number of standard algorithms that should be known to all computer scientists and determine their complexity measures, mostly time complexity and usually worst-case.

3.1 General Techniques for Determining Complexity

Suppose we are given an algorithm and want to determine its complexity. How should we do this? If the algorithm were given as a linear sequence of simple statements (so-called straight-line code where every statement is executed once), the answer would be trivial: Count the number of statements — this is its time complexity. Of course, such an algorithm would be utterly trivial. Virtually all algorithms of any interest contain more complex statements; in particular, there are statements that define iteration (for loops, while loops, repeat loops), statements that connote alternatives (if statements, case statements), and function calls, including those involving recursion.

Iteration: The most important aspect is to determine the number of times the body of the iterative statement is executed. In the case of *for* loops, we may be able to do this exactly. In other cases, we may only be able to determine an upper bound on, or some other type of estimate of, the number of iterations that will be performed. The quality of this upper bound or estimate will affect the quality of our analysis; a tight upper bound will usually give us a better complexity measure than a loose one. Once we have determined or estimated the number iterations, the statement count of the loop is then that number of iterations times the statement count of the body of the iteration statement. It is usually necessary to factor into this process the type of complexity we are interested in. If we want worst-case, then we must determine an upper bound; for average complexity, a good estimate may be preferable.

Alternatives: Again, this depends on the desired type of complexity. For worst-case complexity, we must determine the complexities of all the alternatives and take the maximum of them; for average complexity, we use the average of these complexities. (Recall our discussion of average in Chapter 1; it is important to be aware of what exactly average means within the context of a given algorithm.[1])

Function calls: If no recursion is present, we simply determine the complexity of executing the function in dependence of its arguments, that is, using (one or more of) the function's arguments as parameters for our measures. Then we must integrate this into the overall complexity analysis of the algorithm. If recursion is involved in the function call, more powerful techniques are needed.

Recursion: A function F is called recursive if its body contains a call to itself. An important aspect of recursion is that it has to terminate; this implies that the argument[2] must change for this to be achieved. Intuitively, that argument must evolve toward one of possibly several basis cases, and for each of these basis cases, the recursion stops, that is, no more calls to F occur. In most practical situations, the argument of F decreases until it hits a threshold when F returns without further recursive calls. The way in which this decrease happens is crucial for our task of determining the complexity of the call to the recursive function.

---

[1] Thus, for the statement **if** cond **then** s_1 **else** s_2, the probability of cond to be true determines how likely s_1 is executed in preference over s_2. One should not automatically assume that cond is true 50% of the time (merely because true is one of two possible values cond may take on; but see the discussion in Section 6.6 about initialization).

[2] We assume here for the sake of simplicity that our function F has just one argument or parameter; if more arguments are present, an analogous statement must hold. Typically, this single argument is a function of the size of the input set.

Let us make this a bit more concrete. Let F(n) be the function, with the argument n being the size of the input set. Thus, n is an integer and $n \geq 0$. Let us assume that for all values of n, at most n_0, no recursion, occurs; in other words, for all $n \leq n_0$, we have basis cases. Here, n_0 is some fixed nonnegative integer. Conversely, for all $n > n_0$, one or more recursive calls to F occur in F's body. Let us assume that there are exactly r recursive calls, for $r \geq 1$, a fixed value. It should be clear that in this formulation, termination of the call F(n) is assured precisely if the argument of each of these r recursive calls to F is *strictly* less than n.[3] n. In determining the complexity of F with argument n, it is crucial to know the decrease of the argument in each of these recursive calls. Let us write down schematically what we need to know of F:

F(n)
   If n $\leq$ n$_0$ then do basis case
   Else
      {...; F(n$_1$)   (first recursive call to F, with argument $n_1 < n$)
      ...; F(n$_2$)   (second recursive call to F, with argument $n_2 < n$)
      ...; F(n$_r$)   (rth recursive call to F, with argument $n_r < n$)

      ...

   }

We must now distinguish several cases according to the number r of calls and according to the nature of the decrease of the argument n.

Case 1

Each of the n_j is equal to $n - c$, where c is a fixed integer constant, for all $j = 1, ..., r$: Then for $r > 1$, the (worst-case time) complexity of computing F(n) is at least $r^{O(n)}$; that is, it is at least the number r raised to a linear function of n.[4] If $r = 1$, then the complexity of computing F(n) is at least O(n).[5] In each of these situations, what complicates things is the elided stuff (the "..." in the schematic above). If these statements together have a complexity that is

---

[3] We use here that n is an integer; otherwise this statement about termination is no longer true, as the following counter example indicates: Consider the function
F(x): if $x > 0$, then do basis case else F($x/2$).
When called with an argument $x > 0$, the function call F(x) does not terminate *as an algorithm*, since the argument x will never be equal to 0. Successive division by 2 of a positive value will always result in another positive value. However, it would terminate when implemented *as a program*, since eventually the argument will be so small that it will be set equal to 0 (by rounding error), but the number of recursion calls is unpredictable and clearly dependent on the word length of the parameter x.

[4] Let $T(n)$ be the time required to execute the algorithm, assuming the elided statements take O(1) time. Then we can write: $T(n) = r \cdot T(n - c) + O(1)$ for all $n > n_0$, and $T(n) = C_0$ otherwise, for C_0 some constant. From this, one shows by induction on n that $T(n) = r^{\lfloor (n-n_0)/c + O(1) \rfloor}$, which proves the claim.

[5] Let $T(n)$ be the time required to execute the algorithm, assuming the elided statements take O(1) time. Then we can write $T(n) = T(n - c) + O(1)$ for all $n > n_0$, and $T(n) = C_0$ otherwise, for C_0 some constant. From this follows the claim.

$O(1)$, the complexities are exactly $r^{O(n)}$ (for $r > 1$) and exactly $O(n)$ (for $r = 1$). If the complexity of the elided statements is greater than $O(1)$, then the resulting complexity may increase accordingly.

Typical examples of these situations are the Towers of Hanoï,[6] where $r = 2$, and computing the factorial function[7] $n!$ recursively ($r = 1$).

A similar result is obtained if the constant c depends on j, that is if $n_j = n - c_j$, where c_j is a constant, for all $j = 1, ..., r$. Specifically, the (worst-case time) complexity remains at least $r^{O(n)}$ if $r > 1$ and at least $O(n)$ if $r = 1$. A typical example is provided by the Fibonacci numbers.[8]

Case 2

A more interesting case happens when for all $j = 1, ..., r$, the n_j are not reduced by some constant subtrahend, but each n_j is a fraction of n. More specifically, assume that the elided statements have a time complexity of $b \cdot n$, where b is a positive constant. Also assume that for all $j = 1, ..., r$, $n_j = n/c$, where c is another positive constant, with $c > 1$. Finally, we assume that the basis case (i.e., when there is no recursive call) is of complexity b (the same b as before)[9] and that $n_0 = 1$.[10] In this case, we can formulate the time complexity of F as follows. Let $T(n)$ be the time complexity of $F(n)$. Then we can write:

$$T(1) = b$$

---

[6] The Towers of Hanoï is a famous game. We are given n disks of different sizes and three pegs. The n disks reside initially on the **St**art peg. The task consists of moving the n disks to the **De**stination peg, using the **Au**xiliary peg. Movements are constrained as follows: (1) We may move only one disk at a time. This disk must be the top disk on a peg; it may be moved to any other peg, subject to: (2) No larger disk may ever be placed on top of a smaller disk. Here is an algorithm that solves the problem of moving the n disks from **St** to **De**:
Basis case: If n=1, move disk 1 from **St** to **De** else
Recursion: { move recursively the smallest n-1 disks from **St** to **Au**;
      move the largest disk n from **St** to **De**;
      move recursively the n-1 smallest disks from **Au** to **De**
     }
The complexity of the Towers of Hanoï problem is $O(2^n)$ since precisely $2^n - 1$ moves must be carried out to get the n disks from **St** to **De**.
[7] Here is the algorithm for nonnegative n: If n=0 then n!=1 else n!=n·(n-1)! .
[8] The Fibonacci f_n numbers are defined as follows: $f_1 = 1$, $f_2 = 2$, $f_n = f_{n-1} + f_{n-2}$ for $n > 2$. Here $r = 2$, $c_1 = 1$, and $c_2 = 2$. While it is not properly part of this discussion, we cannot resist pointing out that just because we *can* do something recursively does not mean it is always a good idea. In fact, it is a truly terrible idea to compute the Fibonacci numbers recursively. (A similar statement holds for the recursive computation of the factorial function.) The reason should be obvious: As the above theory indicates, the complexity of doing this is exponential in n. It is a no-brainer that the Fibonacci numbers can be computed in linear time in n. (As a first cut, use an array with an element for each of the n numbers. Initialize the first two elements with f_1 and f_2 and then compute each of the subsequent elements by adding up the two previous ones. This then can be modified to use only three simple variables instead of the array.) There is a fairly convoluted formula that permits the computation of f_n directly, resulting in a time complexity of $O(\log_2(n))$.
[9] Really, we require that the time complexity of the basis cases be some constant b'. If b' is different from b, then we replace b' as well as b by $\max(b,b')$ and everything goes through nicely.

$$T(n) = r \cdot T(n/c) + b \cdot n,$$

reflecting that the problem T(n) is split into r problems of size n/c.[11] Then we can state for all values of n that are a power of c:

$$T(n) = O(n) \quad \text{if } r < c$$

$$T(n) = O(n \cdot \log_2(n)) \quad \text{if } r = c$$

$$T(n) = O(n^{\log c(r)}) \quad \text{if } r > c.$$

While the statement is technically valid only for powers of c, one usually assumes that for all other values of n, corresponding results are obtained by interpolation. Thus, assuming some degree of smoothness (which is ordinarily quite appropriate), one tends to omit the qualifier "n a power of c" and acts as if this statement is true for all values of n.[12]

3.2 Selected Examples: Determining the Complexity of Standard Algorithms

In order to get some facility in applying the techniques of the previous section, we examine a few standard algorithms and determine their complexity; for the most part, we are interested in their worst-case time complexity. We first deal with two examples of *divide-and-conquer* algorithms; these are techniques where one large problem is replaced by a sequence of smaller instances of the same problem, plus some additional work. Specifically, we look at better algorithms for the multiplication of two m-bit integers (using bit complexity) and of two [1:n,1:n] matrices (using word complexity).

---

[10] This means we have exactly one basis case, namely $n = 1$. It also means we are guaranteed to reach the basis case starting with a value 1 for n. Note that in this formulation, it is no longer crucial that the n_i's be integers; if the n_i's really need to be integers, this can be achieved through rounding n/c.

[11] The statement can be generalized. As stated, the additional work $b \cdot n$ in our formulation $T(n) = r \cdot T(n/c) + b \cdot n$ is linear in n. One can replace this with any complexity that is smaller than the resulting complexity that is claimed for $T(n)$. For example, if $r = 16$ and $c = 2$, the claim for $T(n)$ is $O(n^4)$; therefore, the additional work $b \cdot n$ can be increased to anything less than $O(n^4)$.

[12] Here is the proof of the three cases: If n is a power of c, then by repeated substitution of the expression for $T(n)$ we obtain $T(n) = b \cdot n \cdot \Sigma_{i=0,\ldots,\log c(n)} (r/c)^i$. Now if $r/c < 1$, then $\Sigma_{i=0,\ldots,} (r/c)^i$ converges to a constant, proving the first statement. If $r/c = 1$, then $\Sigma_{i=0,\ldots,\log c(n)} (r/c)^i = \Sigma_{i=0,\ldots,\log c(n)} 1^i = \log_c(n) + 1$, proving the second statement. Finally, if $r/c > 1$, $b \cdot n \cdot \Sigma_{i=0,\ldots,\log c(n)} (r/c)^i = b \cdot n \cdot [(r/c)^{1+\log c(n)} - 1] / (r/c - 1) = O(r^{\log c(n)}) = O(n^{\log c(r)})$, proving the third statement. The last equality, $r^{\log c(n)} = n^{\log c(r)}$, can be verified as follows: Let $n = c^s$ for some $s \geq 1$; then $r^{\log c(n)} = r^{s \cdot \log c(c)} = r^s$ and $n^{\log c(r)} = (c^s)^{\log c(r)} = c^{s \cdot \log c(r)} = (c^{\log c(r)})^s = r^s$.

3.2.1 Multiplying Two m-Bit Numbers

Consider the two m-bit integers x and y. We want to compute their product. Assume that m is a power of 2. Instead of the technique sketched in Section 1.4, which has a time (bit) complexity $O(m^2)$, consider the following approach: Break x and y into two halves each, $x = a.b$ and $y = c.d$, where a, b, c, and d each have $m/2$ bits. Clearly,

$$x \cdot y = (a \cdot 2^{m/2} + b) \cdot (c \cdot 2^{m/2} + d) = a \cdot c \cdot 2^m + (a \cdot d + b \cdot c) \cdot 2^{m/2} + b \cdot d.$$

Thus, this approach to multiplying two m-bit numbers requires four multiplications and three additions of $m/2$-bit integers, plus two shift operations. Now consider the following operations:

$$u = (a + b) \cdot (c + d);$$

$$v = a \cdot c;$$

$$w = b \cdot d;$$

$$z = v \cdot 2^m + (u-v-w) \cdot 2^{m/2} + w.$$

Note that the computation of u, v, w, and z requires a total of three multiplications of $m/2$-bit integers,[13] plus six additions of $m/2$-bit integers and two shift operations. The additions and the shifts require $O(m)$ time. Thus, we have the following expression for the time complexity of this method:

$$T(m) = k \qquad\qquad \text{for } m = 1;$$

$$T(m) = 3 \cdot T(m/2) + k \cdot m \quad \text{for } m>1,$$

where k is a suitable constant. Now we can apply the result of Scenario 2 in Section 3.1, which yields

$$T(m) = O(m^{\log_2(3)}) = O(m^{1.59}).[14]$$

Thus, this technique of multiplying two m-bit integers requires significantly less time than the traditional approach. This appears to be counterintuitive since the $O(m^{1.59})$ method uses eight additional operations, whereas the traditional method uses only five. It is therefore important to understand

---

[13] We are fudging a bit here, as the multiplication $(a + b) \cdot (c + d)$ involves integers that could be of length $m/2 + 1$, but this additional bit can be accommodated with only a small additional complication.

[14] We are not suggesting that $\log_2(3) = 1.59$, nor that $O(m^{\log_2(3)}) \equiv O(m^{1.59})$. The equal sign between the last two is simply a matter of convenience that expresses an approximate equality. It can be shown that for any > 0, m^{a+} is never $O(m^a)$, for all constants $a > 0$.

that this additional effort pales in comparison with the savings that we obtain. The crucial issue is that the resulting method for multiplying two *m*-bit integers, and even more so the original starting point, which was $O(m^2)$, has a complexity that is much larger than linear.

3.2.2 Multiplying Two Square Matrices

Consider the two [1:*n*,1:*n*] matrices **A** and **B**; we want to compute their product, for instance, in the matrix **C**. The traditional method consists of three nested loops:

```
for i:=1,...,n
   for j:=1,...,n
      {   C[i,j] := 0;
          for k:=1,...,n
             C[i,j] := C[i,j] + A[i,k]*B[k,j]
      }
```

The *k*-loop contains one simple statement, and the *j*-loop contains one simple statement and the *k*-loop; therefore, the total number of simple statements to be executed is $n^3 + n^2$.[15] Thus, the time (word) complexity of this approach is $O(n^3)$.

While one might be convinced that this cannot be improved upon, one would be very wrong. Consider the following, seemingly irrationally, convoluted approach. Let *n* be a power of 2. Represent the three matrices **A**, **B**, and **C** by their four quarters:

$$A = \begin{pmatrix} A_{11} & A_{12} \\ A_{21} & A_{22} \end{pmatrix} \quad B = \begin{pmatrix} B_{11} & B_{12} \\ B_{21} & B_{22} \end{pmatrix} \quad C = \begin{pmatrix} C_{11} & C_{12} \\ C_{21} & C_{22} \end{pmatrix}$$

Thus, the traditional scheme of multiplying matrices would correspond to the following computations:

$$C_{11} := A_{11}{}^*B_{11} + A_{12}{}^*B_{21} \quad C_{12} := A_{11}{}^*B_{12} + A_{12}{}^*B_{22};$$

$$C_{21} := A_{21}{}^*B_{11} + A_{22}{}^*B_{21} \quad C_{22} := A_{21}{}^*B_{12} + A_{22}{}^*B_{22},$$

---

[15] It is traditional to ignore the work associated with loop control (incrementing the loop indices and comparing them against their upper and lower bounds). We follow this tradition here; it is justified by the fact that constant factors are hidden in the order of notation, since clearly the innermost loop dominates (as long as it does contain at least one simple statement that is executed).

which consists of eight multiplications and four additions of quarter matrices (matrices of type $[1{:}n/2,1{:}n/2]$).

Instead of this traditional scheme, consider the following computations:

$$S_1 := A_{21}+A_{22} \qquad S_2 := S_1 - A_{11} \qquad S_3 := A_{11} - A_{21} \qquad S_4 := A_{12} - S_2;$$

$$S_5 := B_{12} - B_{11} \qquad S_6 := B_{22} - S_5 \qquad S_7 := B_{22} - B_{12} \qquad S_8 := S_6 - B_{21};$$

$$M_1 := S_2{*}S_6 \qquad M_2 := A_{11}{*}B_{11} \qquad M_3 := A_{12}{*}B_{21} \qquad M_4 := S_3{*}S_7;$$

$$M_5 := S_1{*}S_5 \qquad M_6 := S_4{*}B_{22} \qquad M_7 := A_{22}{*}S_8;$$

$$T_1 := M_1 + M_2 \qquad T_2 := T_1 + M_4.$$

Now one can verify (with considerable effort, but involving only elementary arithmetic) that the following holds:

$$C_{11} := M_2 + M_3 \qquad C_{12} := T_1 + M_5 + M_6 \qquad C_{21} := T_2 - M_7 \qquad C_{22} := T_2 + M_5.$$

We conclude that instead of carrying out eight multiplications (plus four additions) of matrices of size $n/2$ by $n/2$, which the traditional approach would have us do, this new approach requires seven multiplications of quarter matrices (the computations of the 7 M_i's), plus 15 additions and subtractions of quarter matrices. Let us determine the time complexity $T(n)$ of this approach. Since we are replacing the problem of multiplying two matrices of measure n by multiplying seven matrices of measure $n/2$, plus additional work that is no larger than $O(n^2)$, we can state:

$$T(n) = b \qquad\qquad \text{for } n = 1;$$

$$T(n) = 7{\cdot}T(n/2) + 15{\cdot}(n/2)^2 \qquad \text{for } n>1.$$

Applying a slight generalization of Case 2 in Section 3.1 (see the first footnote on page 53), we obtain the following (word) complexity:

$$T(n) = O(n^{\log_2(7)}) = O(n^{2.81}).\text{[16]}$$

It is important to understand that $O(n^{2.81})$ is much better than $O(n^3)$, even though the additional work, hidden in the constant, is larger. Thus, from a theoretical point of view, the $O(n^{2.81})$ algorithm is far superior to the traditional one. Whether this is also true from a practical point of view will be examined in Part 2.

---

[16] A caveat analogous to second footnote on page 54 applies.

Our next example is a representative of *dynamic programming*. This is a general technique for designing algorithms in which intermediate results are computed at one stage and combined to determine the intermediate results for the next stage. While network flow would probably be a more appropriate example, it tends to be fairly complicated to develop the algorithm. (Note that Dijkstra's algorithm, covered in Section 3.2.13.1, is also of this type.) For this reason, we examine instead the (practically much less important) question of determining an optimal computation order when multiplying matrices.

3.2.3 Optimally Sequencing Matrix Multiplications

While most matrix multiplication is concerned with square matrices, matrix multiplication is much more general. We can multiply a matrix of type $[1:p,1:q]$ with one of type $[1:s,1:t]$, provided $q = s$; these matrices are compatible.[17] Let us denote by $M_{p,q}$ a matrix of type $[1:p,1:q]$. Multiplying the matrices $\mathbf{M}_{p,q}$ and $\mathbf{M}_{q,r}$ by the traditional method (three nested loops) requires $p \cdot q \cdot r$ scalar multiplications (as well as a comparable number of additions). We will use the number of scalar multiplications as a proxy for the time complexity of this problem. Matrix multiplication is associative, that is $(\mathbf{A}*\mathbf{B})*\mathbf{C} = \mathbf{A}*(\mathbf{B}*\mathbf{C})$ for all compatible matrices $\mathbf{A}$, $\mathbf{B}$, and $\mathbf{C}$. Therefore, given a sequence of compatible matrices, this sequence can be multiplied in different ways. For example, the product $\mathbf{M}_{5,3}*\mathbf{M}_{3,1}*\mathbf{M}_{1,4}*\mathbf{M}_{4,6}$ can be parenthesized as $[\mathbf{M}_{5,3}*(\mathbf{M}_{3,1}*\mathbf{M}_{1,4})]*\mathbf{M}_{4,6}$ or $(\mathbf{M}_{5,3}*\mathbf{M}_{3,1})*(\mathbf{M}_{1,4}*\mathbf{M}_{4,6})$, among other ways, all of which yield the same result (owing to associativity). Interestingly, it turns out that different evaluation orders require different numbers of scalar multiplications; that is, they have different time complexities. In our example, the first order requires 192 scalar multiplications ($3 \cdot 1 \cdot 4 + 5 \cdot 3 \cdot 4 + 5 \cdot 4 \cdot 6$), reflecting the operation $\mathbf{M}_{3,1}*\mathbf{M}_{1,4}$, which results in a matrix of type $\mathbf{M}_{3,4}$ and requires $3 \cdot 1 \cdot 4$ multiplications, followed by the operation $\mathbf{M}_{5,3}*\mathbf{M}_{3,4}$, which results in a matrix of type $\mathbf{M}_{5,4}$ and requires $5 \cdot 3 \cdot 4$ multiplications, and concluding with the operation $\mathbf{M}_{5,4}*\mathbf{M}_{4,6}$, which yields the final result of type $\mathbf{M}_{5,6}$ and requires $5 \cdot 4 \cdot 6$ multiplications), while the second evaluation order requires only 69 ($5 \cdot 3 \cdot 1 + 1 \cdot 4 \cdot 6 + 5 \cdot 1 \cdot 6$). This immediately raises the question of determining the best evaluation order when asked to multiply a sequence of n compatible matrices:

$$M_{p_1,p_2}, M_{p_2,p_3}, \ldots, M_{p_n,p_{n+1}}.$$

One approach consists of trying out all possible orders. This would result in a time complexity that is exponential in the number of matrices. A better way is to set up an array $\mathbf{S}$ of type $[1:n,1:n]$ and store in the element $S[i,j]$

---

[17] Unfortunately, if the matrices are not square, no nifty multiplication algorithm like the one given in Section 3.2.2 is known. Thus, we are stuck with the traditional method (three nested loops) of multiplying matrices.

the optimal number of scalar multiplications required to compute the product $\mathbf{M}_{p_i p_{i+1}} * \ldots * \mathbf{M}_{p_j p_{j+1}}$.[18] This makes sense only for $i \leq j$. For $i = j$, that number is 0; also, if $i = j - 1$, there is nothing to be decided, as only two (adjacent) matrices are involved and the optimal number of scalar multiplications needed for this is $p_i p_{i+1} p_{i+2}$. It follows that for $i = j$ and for $i = j - 1$, we can initialize our matrix S:

$$i: = 1, \ldots, n: S[i,i]: = 0$$

$$i: = 1, \ldots, n-1: S[i,i+1]: = p_i p_{i+1} p_{i+2}.$$

One can now see quite easily that for general i and j, $S[i,j]$ is determined as follows:

$$S[i,j] = \min_{i \leq k \leq j-1} \{ p_i p_{k+1} p_{j+1} + S[i,k] + S[k+1,j] \} \text{ for all } i < j+1$$

which reflects the following argument: The optimal number is the minimum of all possible ways of splitting the product of matrices i through j into two portions; these two portions correspond to the last multiplication that is carried out to produce the product of the matrices i through j. The first portion consists of matrices i through k and requires $S[i,k]$ scalar multiplications. The second portion corresponds to the remainder, namely matrices $k + 1$ through j and requires $S[k + 1,j]$ scalar multiplications. Finally, the term $p_i p_{k+1} p_{j+1}$ reflects the work necessary for the product of these two portions. Clearly, we want to get the value of k for which this attains a minimum. It follows that $S[1,n]$ provides the desired answer, namely the minimum number of scalar multiplications required to compute the product of the n matrices.

Now for the complexity analysis of this scheme. Starting from the initialization (the main diagonal $i = j$ and the diagonal above it, $i = j - 1$), we must compute the requisite values, in diagonal form ($i = j - 2$, then $i = j - 3$, etc.), until the area above the main diagonal is filled. There are $n \cdot (n + 1)/2$ elements to be filled in. How much effort is needed to compute each of them? The key observation is the formula for $S[i,j]$ where the minimum must be taken over all k from i through $j - 1$. We claim that this range is $O(n)$ for $O(n^2)$ pairs $[i,j]$. For example, consider all pairs $[i,j]$ where $i - j$ $n/2$. How many such pairs are there? These pairs correspond to the diagonals above the main one with numbers $n/2 + 1$, $n/2 + 2$, through n. Thus, there are $(n/2 \cdot n/2)/2$ or $n^2/8$ such pairs. Therefore, for each of these $O(n^2)$ pairs, $O(n)$ values of k must be examined; each examination takes $O(1)$ time. Therefore, altogether $O(n^3)$ scalar multiplications are needed for just these $n^2/8$ pairs.

---

[18] While multiplication is associative, it is not commutative. This is why we may not interchange left and right factors; we may only parenthesize in different ways.

Consequently, the overall time complexity of this scheme is $O(n^3)$ since the other pairs do not increase this.

The next group of algorithms is related to sorting. Recall that in Section 1.9 we established that sorting n numbers by comparisons requires at least $O(n \cdot \log_2(n))$ comparisons. Now, we want to show that this lower bound is attainable, that is, that there exist algorithms for sorting n numbers whose time complexity is $O(n \cdot \log_2(n))$. We will examine three methods, namely MergeSort, QuickSort, and HeapSort. The situation turns out to be unexpectedly complex in that the algorithm that is fastest on average has a surprisingly large worst-case time complexity; thus, there is no obvious winner. We also analyze a fourth method for sorting, RadixSort, that uses no comparisons at all.

3.2.4   MergeSort

Assume we are given an array **A** of type [1:n] containing n numbers that we want to sort in ascending order. For simplicity of presentation, assume n is a power of 2, $n = 2^k$. Consider the following approach based on the operation of merging two subarrays. Given two *sorted* subarrays **A**[p:q] and $A[q + 1$:$r]$,[19] we can obtain a single sorted subarray **B**[p:r] (of another array **B**) by the following approach that consists of merging the two sorted subarrays:

```
P1:=p; P2:=q+1; P3:=p;
while P1 q and P2 r do
    {
        if A[P1]<A[P2]   then {B[P3]:=A[P1]; P1:=P1+1; P3:=P3+1}
                         else {B[P3]:=A[P2]; P2:=P2+1; P3:=P3+1}
    }
    if P1>q then assign the elements of A[P2:r] to B[P3:r];
    if P2>r then assign the elements of A[P1:q] to B[P3:r];
```

Then the algorithm of sorting the n numbers in **A**[1:n] is given by the following statements (recall that $n = 2^k$):

```
for s:=1, 2, 4, 8, 16, ..., 2^k-1 do
    {
        merge the two subarrays A[p:p+s−1], A[p+s:p+2s−1] of
            consecutive subarrays of length s into the arrays
            B[p: p+2s−1], for all
            p:=1, 2s+1, 4s+1,..., n−2s+1;
        interchange the arrays A and B
    }
```

---

[19] Note that the two sorted subarrays are adjacent. In general, merging can be formulated without this assumption; however, this is not needed for MergeSort.

For the complexity analysis, we first directly observe that merging two sorted arrays of sizes s_1 and s_2 into one sorted array of size $s_1 + s_2$ requires no more than $s_1 + s_2$ comparisons; thus, merging has a time (word) complexity of $O(s_1 + s_2)$. Proceeding to the MergeSort algorithm, we observe that the process is completed in stages, with the first stage corresponding to the lengths of the subarrays to be merged being 2^0 (1), the second stage to lengths 2^1 (2), in general the ith stage corresponding to lengths 2^{i-1}, until in the last stage, the subarrays are of length 2^{k-1}. It follows now that in stage i, there are exactly 2^{k-i} pairs, since the entire 2^k (n) elements are subdivided into pairs of subarrays of length 2^{i-1}. Since in stage i merging has time complexity $O(2^i)$ and there are 2^{k-i} pairs, the complexity of stage i is $O(2^k)$ or $O(n)$, independent of the value of i. Now there are exactly k values of i, from 0 through $k - 1$. Therefore, the overall complexity is $O(k \cdot n)$, but since $k = \log_2(n)$, this is exactly $O(n \cdot \log_2(n))$. Thus, MergeSort attains the lower bound on the number of comparisons; MergeSort is optimal in the number of comparisons in the worst case. Note that the only difference between worst-case and average behavior could occur in merging. Since the possible gap is small,[20] it follows that the average time (word) complexity is also $O(n \cdot \log_2(n))$. Since we need an additional array **B** to carry out this scheme, the space (word) complexity is n (worst-case, average, and best-case).[21]

Because of its space complexity, MergeSort is usually not considered a practical algorithm, in spite of its optimal time complexity. We will examine this assertion and its basis more carefully in Part 2.

3.2.5   QuickSort

QuickSort has good press; it is generally considered the fastest known sorting algorithm, that is, if one is interested in the average time performance. Its worst-case time performance is surprisingly bad.

Again, we start with an array **A**[1:n] of n numbers that we want to sort in ascending order. The key idea in QuickSort is partitioning these numbers around a pivot element x so that all elements to the left of x are x and all elements to the right of x are x. Here is how this partitioning of the subarray **A**[lo:hi] is carried out. Note that in contrast to MergeSort, everything is done in place, that is, no additional array is needed.

---

[20] Specifically, the best-case time complexity of merging two sorted arrays of sizes s_1 and s_2 into one sorted array of size $s_1 + s_2$ requires $\min(s_1, s_2)$ comparisons; the average time complexity must lie between the best-case and the worst-case complexities, that is, between $\min(s_1, s_2)$ and $s_1 + s_2$ comparisons. Since $s_1 = s_2$ in this context, $\min(s_1, s_2) = s_1$, and $s_1 + s_2 = 2s_1$; therefore, $\min(s_1, s_2) = O(s_1 + s_2)$, and the claim follows.

[21] While we have applied word complexity usually to time complexity, it can also be used within the context of space complexity, where it simply means that one word holds one number, regardless of how many bits this number requires for its representation.

Partitioning **A**[lo:hi] around *x*, returning *i* and *j*:
i:=lo; j:=hi;
repeat
    {
        while A[i]<x do i:=i+1; find candidate for exchange (too large, x)
        while A[j]>x do j:=j–1; find candidate for exchange (too small, x)
        if i ≤ j do
            {exchange A[i] and A[j]; i:=i+1; j:=j–1 }
    } until i>j

Note that the place of the element x in the subarray may change during this process since the element x can be a candidate for exchange (see "too large" or "too small," above). However, upon completion, the value of the pivot element x is guaranteed to be in all elements of **A**[j:i].[22] Then QuickSort can be stated as follows:

QuickSort(A[lo:hi])
    {
        Choose a pivot x=A[r] with r between lo and hi;
        Partition A[lo:hi] around x;
        If lo<j then QuickSort(A[lo:j]);
        If i<hi then QuickSort(A[i:hi])
    }

Thus, once we have split the array **A**[lo:hi] into two portions, with the left portion, namely **A**[lo:j], containing elements x and the right portion, namely **A**[j:hi], containing elements x, we call QuickSort recursively for each of these two portions. The choice of the pivot element x is arbitrary; any element in the array **A**[lo:hi] will do. Typical choices are the first, the last, or the middle element. Clearly, to sort **A**[1:n], we call QuickSort(**A**[1:n]).

First we determine the time (word) complexity of the partitioning operation. Since the value of i increases from lo and that of j decreases down from hi until they cross and since the exchange operation has complexity $O(1)$, partitioning has a time complexity (best, average, and worst) of O(hi–lo).

Next we determine the best-case complexity of QuickSort. It is not difficult to see that the best case occurs when the two portions **A**[lo:j] and **A**[j:hi] are always of equal size $n/2$. In this case, we have essentially MergeSort in reverse order; that is, each subarray is split into two equal-sized halves until the resulting subarrays are of size 1, which is the basis case. How many times can the array **A**[1:n] be recursively cut into two equal halves before the basis case is obtained? Clearly, not more often than $\lceil \log_2(n) \rceil$. Let us visualize the recursive process of QuickSort in stages, so that the process is shown for the entire array **A**[1:n]. Then we can see that the complexity of

---

[22] Since $i > j$ is the termination condition, there is at least one element in **A**[j:i]. Furthermore, if there are two or more, then x must be in all of them; note that there is no prohibition of repeated elements.

partitioning the various portions of the array $A[1:n]$ in any stage, which is the sum of the complexities taken over all the portions of $A[1:n]$ in that stage, is $O(n)$. (This is true for all partitionings, whether the resulting portions are of equal size or not.) Furthermore, in the best case, there are $\lceil \log_2(n) \rceil$ stages; therefore, the overall time (word) complexity in the best case is $O(n \cdot \log_2(n))$.

Let us now consider the worst-case time complexity. It is not difficult to see that the worst case is one where the partitioning results in two portions, one of which contains one element and the other contains all the remaining elements. If this case occurs consistently for every partitioning (of the larger portion), then it follows that we will end up with $n - 1$ stages. In stage 1 we have two portions, one of size 1, the other of size $n - 1$. In stage 2 we partition the portion of size $n - 1$ into two, one of size 1, the other of size $n - 2$, and so on. Note that the only work that is carried out happens in the partitioning operations. Summing up the complexities for the worst case, we obtain

$$O(n) + O(n-1) + O(n-2) + \ldots + O(2) = O(n^2).$$

Thus, the worst-case time complexity of QuickSort is $O(n^2)$.

It turns out that the worst-case situation is quite rare; one can show that the average time complexity is only a small constant factor times the best-case time complexity (assuming each permutation of the numbers 1 through n is equally likely). Since the only work carried out is in the partitionings, which is very little, QuickSort is on average the fastest sorting method known.

What about the space complexity? As presented here, QuickSort is recursive. While nonrecursive formulations exist, keeping track of the boundaries of the various partitionings of the original array $A[1:n]$ requires either space in the recursion stack (for the recursive version) or space in some other date structure (list or stack for the nonrecursive version). In either case, the amount of space necessary is proportional to the number of stages. Thus, in the best case, and similarly in the average case, this additional space is $O(\log_2(n))$. In the worst case the additional space needed for the management of the boundaries becomes $O(n)$. We will revisit this issue in more detail in Part 2.

3.2.6 HeapSort

This is another in-place sorting method, meaning that no additional array is needed. HeapSort is often considered inferior to QuickSort, we think unfairly so. While its average time complexity is somewhat worse than that of QuickSort, its worst-case complexity is dramatically better. Moreover, it is inherently nonrecursive and has a much better space complexity. It is, however, a more complicated algorithm, which may be off-putting to some.

The key concept in HeapSort is the heap. This is an array[23] $A[lo:hi]$ of numbers with the property that for all i, $lo \leq i \leq \lceil hi/2 \rceil$, $A[i] \geq A[2 \cdot i]$ and

A[i] ≥ A[2·i + 1], as long as the array elements exist. Heaps have a number of interesting properties; one of them is that the first element, A[lo], of any heap A[lo:hi] is the maximum of all elements in the heap. Another is that heaps are surprisingly efficient to construct.

Here is how one can construct a heap A[lo:hi]. We first observe that the second half of the heap, A[⌈(lo + hi)/2⌉:hi], always complies with the heap condition. We then proceed to "insert" the remaining elements of the array one by one, starting with the one in position ⌈(lo + hi)/2⌉ −1, then that in position ⌈(lo + hi)/2⌉ − 2, and so on, until we get to the element in position lo. Our insertion process is such that after the insertion of the element in position i, the resulting array A[i:hi] satisfies the heap condition for all i = (lo + hi)/2⌉ − 1,..., lo + 1,lo. Here is the first algorithm for the insertion of A[i] into A[i:hi], assuming A[i + 1:hi] satisfied the heap condition:

```
HeapInsert A[i:hi]
    { Compare A[i] with A[2·i] and A[2·i+1] if they exist;
        if A[i] ≥ max{A[2·i],A[2·i+1]}, do nothing – insertion successfully
            completed
        otherwise
        if A[2·i]<A[2·i+1] then
            { interchange A[i] and A[2·i+1]; repeat insertion process with
                A[2·i+1] }
        else { interchange A[i] and A[2·i]; repeat insertion process with
            A[2·i] }
    }
```

Then we use this to construct an entire heap, given the array A[lo:hi]:

```
For i := ⌈(lo+hi)/2⌉-1, ⌈(lo+hi)/2⌉-2,...,lo do
    HeapInsert A[i:hi]
```

We apply this to the array A[1:n]. Once we have the heap A[1:n], we know that its first element, A[1], contains the maximal element of the heap, so we exchange it with the element in position n and insert the element that now sits in position 1 into the array A[1:n − 1] so that it becomes a heap. In general, we grow the sorted array from the back, making sure that the displaced element in position j is properly inserted in the shrinking heap A[1:j − 1], for j = n,n − 1,n − 2,...,2,1. Obviously, when j = 1, the remnant heap is of size 1 and the remainder of the array, A[2:n], contains all elements larger than A[1] in sorted order. Now we can formulate the HeapSort algorithm:

---

[23] Heaps can be formulated using binary trees as well, in which case the two children of the node corresponding to A[i] correspond to A[2·i] and A[2·i + 1]. It follows from this that the binary tree corresponding to a heap is always a complete binary tree, in which only the last row of nodes may be incomplete (more specifically, the last row of nodes is contiguous, except the nodes on the right may be missing). It follows therefore that a tree representing a heap with n nodes is exactly of height ⌈$\log_2(n + 1) − 1$⌉, which is bounded from above by $\log_2(n)$.

```
HeapSort (A[1:n])
  { Construct a heap: for i :=⌈(1+n)/2⌉-1,…,1 insert A[i] into the heap A[i:n].
    For j:=n,n-1,…,2,1 do
      {
        interchange A[j] and A[1];
        insert the element in position 1 into the heap A[1:j-1]
      }
  }
```

We now come to the complexity analysis of HeapSort. We first look at HeapInsert. Given a heap $A[j:hi]$ with $m = hi - j + 1$ elements, there are at most $\lceil \log_2(m) \rceil$ iterated insertions (insertions that are the consequence of extracting the larger of $A[2j]$ and $A[2j + 1]$ and interchanging it with $A[j]$). Thus, the complexity of HeapInsert $A[j:hi]$ is $O(\lceil \log_2(hi - j + 1) \rceil)$. When constructing the heap $A[1:n]$, this complexity is bounded from above by $O(\log_2(n))$, and since there are only about $n/2$ elements that must be processed using HeapInsert, the complexity of constructing the heap $A[1:n]$ is $O(n \cdot \log_2(n))$.[24] Then we must examine the process of taking the element in position 1 (which is always the maximum of the remnant heap $A[1:j]$) and exchanging it with that in position j; each of these operations entails one HeapInsert with a heap of size $n - j$. Again, we bound the complexity of this operation by $O(\log_2(n))$, and since there are n elements altogether, this part of HeapSort requires $O(n \cdot \log_2(n))$ time. Thus, the total time (word) complexity of HeapSort is $O(n \cdot \log_2(n))$.

This analysis is for the worst case that can occur. However, it should be clear that any gap between worst-case and best-case analysis is minimal. The first part of HeapSort (the construction of a heap) can be done in linear time (see footnote 25) and this is the same for worst case and best case; the second part consists of inserting elements that necessarily will be small (loosely speaking, in any heap, the last positions contain the small elements, the first positions, the large elements). This implies that there will be numerous interchanges, indicating that the upper bound of $O(\log_2(n))$ for the insertion operations is close to optimal. Since the average complexity will always fall between the best-case and the worst-case complexity (regardless of how we define *average*), HeapSort's complexity is $O(n \cdot \log_2(n))$ in all cases — average, worst, and best.

The space complexity of HeapSort is much easier to determine. There is no recursion, and the iterations that occur require only simple loop variables.

---

[24] It turns out that we are overly generous in this analysis; a finer analysis shows that the complexity of constructing a heap with n elements is only $O(n)$. This is because about $n/2$ elements need not be inserted at all (the half with the higher position numbers), so $n/4$ elements need at most one interchange, $n/8$ need at most 2, and in general, $^n/_2 r$ elements need at most $r - 1$ interchanges ($r = 1,…,\log_2(n) - 1$) when doing the repeated insertions in the heap. Summing this up yields $O(n)$ (see the first footnote on page 12 of Chapter 1). However, since the second part of HeapSort requires time greater than linear (otherwise it would be a contradiction to the lower bound we derived in Section 1.9), it is not particularly urgent to carry out the most exacting analysis for the construction of a heap.

Also, no other additional space is needed to carry out the algorithm, except for interchanging elements, which can be done in constant space. Therefore, the space complexity of HeapSort is constant. This should be contrasted with MergeSort and QuickSort, which require significantly greater space complexity.

3.2.7 RadixSort

This is the odd man out in our list of sorting methods. It does not use any comparisons at all and it seems to contradict the lower bound we derived in Section 1.9. Furthermore, its performance is usually measured in word complexity, but the algorithm itself is distinctly bit- or digit-oriented. Specifically, it uses the positional representation of integers and relies on the fact that there is a fixed number D of digits; in the case of binary numbers, we have $D = 2$; in the case of decimal numbers, $D = 10$.[25] Conceptually, in RadixSort there exists a "bucket" that can accommodate numbers for each digit (it is also known as BucketSort for this reason). If the numbers involved have m digits, with position m the least significant and position 1 the most significant, RadixSort proceeds as follows:

Initially in stage m, we have the given n numbers $N_1, \ldots, N_n$, each with m digits.

```
for j:=m,m-1,...,2,1 do
   { for each number N in the order as listed in Stage j, examine its jth digit
     q and place N into the bucket with number q;
     Create Stage j-1 by sequencing the numbers as follows: first all the
     numbers in Bucket 0, then all the numbers in Bucket 1, etc., until last
     come all the numbers in Bucket D-1.
   }
Stage 0 contains the given n numbers sorted in ascending order.
```

To determine the time complexity, we observe that in each stage we examine each number and place the number into the bucket indicated by a digit of the number; this operation requires constant time for each number, provided we manipulate pointers to the numbers rather than the entire numbers themselves. Therefore, the work to be carried out in one stage is $O(n)$. There are m stages; consequently, the overall time (word) complexity is $O(m \cdot n)$. There is no difference between worst-case, best-case, or average time complexity. The space complexity is $O(D)$, provided we do not count the pointer to the numbers (if we do consider the space for the pointers, the space complexity is $O(\max\{D, n\})$).

---

[25] RadixSort can also be applied to words over an alphabet A, in which case the letters in the underlying alphabet A take the place of the digits. However, while words are sorted in a similar way as numbers, in that the first letter or digit is most significant for the order and the last letter or digit is least significant, words tend to have differing lengths, while we assume here that all numbers have the same number of digits. This would be appropriate for numbers represented by a fixed number of bytes, which is the paradigm of word complexity.

Let us examine the time complexity more closely. Since m is fixed, $O(m \cdot n)$ is faster than $O(n \cdot \log_2(n))$; therefore, RadixSort appears to contradict the lower bound on sorting we derived in Section 1.9. There are two responses to this. The first one is of a technical nature: The lower bound in Section 1.9 was on the number of comparisons *when sorting by comparing two numbers*. This, however, is not how RadixSort sorts. There is not a single comparison in the entire algorithm and therefore the lower bound cannot be applied at all. However, in a way this answer misses the point. Implicitly, we took the lower bound in Section 1.9 to be much more universal; we really assumed that the $O(n \cdot \log_2(n))$ time complexity implied by the comparison argument was applicable to *all* sorting methods. While this is technically incorrect (the argument applied only to comparisons), RadixSort nevertheless does *not* provide a counterexample. This can be seen as follows.

Recall that m is the number of digits. In Section 1.4, when we discussed bit and word complexity, we made the argument that it is inappropriate to assume that the number of bits (or digits) is independent of n, the number of elements to be sorted. Specifically, we indicated that in order to represent n different elements, we need at least $\lceil \log_2(n) \rceil$ bits; this generalizes for numbers in base D to $\lceil \log_D(n) \rceil$ digits. Thus, m and n are *not* independent; m must always be at least $\lceil \log_D(n) \rceil$. This brings us back to the lower bound; given the relationship between m and n, it now follows that RadixSort has a complexity that is very much like $O(n \cdot \log_2(n))$.

The next group of problems we examine centers around searching. There are two different aspects of this notion. We may search for a given element in a collection of elements or we may have some kind of index and want to retrieve the element with that index. Typical examples are looking up a word in a dictionary (first aspect) and finding the smallest number of a set of numbers (second aspect).

Searching for a given element x in a set of elements is interesting from the point of view of complexity, because the problem displays very different behaviors depending on how the set is represented. Let us assume that the elements are contained in an array $\mathbf{A}[1:n]$. In Section 1.3 we analyzed one facet of this problem, namely the case where the array is not sorted.[26] As we pointed out there, in this case a significant gap arises between average and worst-case complexity (using most realistic definitions of *average*). Still, searching for a given element in an unordered array containing n elements requires $O(n)$ time. This *linear* or *sequential search* is very unattractive, especially if several such searches are to be performed. The situation changes dramatically if the array is sorted.

---

[26] It is true that our analysis in Section 1.3 assumed a linear list instead of an array, but for the approach we examined, the random access property of the array does not imply any advantage over the sequential access associated with a linear list. Therefore, we use an array to preserve the uniformity of our presentation. Furthermore, when we turn to binary search, the random access property of the set representation is indispensable.

3.2.8 Binary Search

Assume that the array $A[1:n]$ containing n elements is sorted; our task is to determine whether a given element x is in A, and if so, what its index is. The key idea of binary search is the following: Given a search space $A[lo:hi]$, we first determine the element in the middle, namely $A[m]$ with $m = $ (hi − lo + 1)/2 (if hi − lo + 1 is odd, use one of the two adjacent integers); if $A[m]$ = x, then we have found x in location m; otherwise we repeat our search in the smaller search space $A[lo:m − 1]$ if $A[m] < x$ or $A[m + 1:hi]$ if $A[m] > x$. Termination then is achieved either if x is found in a specific position (successful search) or if the search space is so small that x cannot be in it, that is, if lo > hi (unsuccessful search).

The complexity of this algorithm is directly related to the number of search space reductions that can occur when starting with the search space $A[1:n]$. Each such reduction cuts the size of the search space in half; thus, no more than $\lceil \log_2(n) \rceil$ such reductions (halvings) can occur before the search space size is less than 1 (which means that x cannot be found in it). Since the amount of work required to carry out one reduction is constant, it follows that binary search requires $O(\log_2(n))$ time. While this is the worst-case complexity, the average time complexity is about the same. It is especially interesting to note that binary search retains its efficiency if the search is unsuccessful. The space complexity of binary search is $O(1)$ since we only need space to keep track of the upper and lower bounds of the current search space. Note that no recursion is required; the search is entirely iterative.

It is important to realize the enormous improvement in the performance of searching for an element that is caused by the assumption of order. If $A[1:n]$ is sorted, the time complexity is $O(\log_2(n))$, but if it is not, it is exponentially slower, namely $O(n)$. Thus, if one is to do several searches on the same data set, very often it pays to invest in sorting the array $A[1:n]$ first, an unproductive activity with a high cost of $O(n \cdot \log_2(n))$, and then do s searches at a cost of $O(\log_2(n))$ each. Contrast this with the cost of s searches based on an unsorted array. Clearly, sorting is more economical if

$$O(n \cdot \log_2(n)) + s \cdot O(\log_2(n)) < s \cdot O(n).$$

This is precisely the case for all $s > O(\log_2(n))$.

Let us now turn to the other aspect of searching, namely finding an element with a given index in a list of numbers.[27] Specifically, assume we are given an array $A[1:n]$ and an integer K with $1 \le K \le n$. Our task consists of

---

[27] Strictly speaking, it can be applied to any type of element that has a total ordering. In other words, given two such elements a and b, with $a \ne b$, either a precedes b or b precedes a. Numbers have this property, as do words using the lexicographical ordering. Subsets of a set S do not; if S = {x,y,z} and a = {x,y} and b = {x,z}, then a does not contain b and b does not contain a. Note that linear search requires only testing for equality, while binary search requires a total order as well, because otherwise the array could not be sorted. Since finding the Kth largest element does not rely explicitly on sorting, it is prudent to point out that a total order is nevertheless required.

determining the Kth-largest of these n elements. There are certain specific values of K for which this problem is particularly important. If $K = 1$, we want to find the maximum (which we have already discussed). For $K = 2$, we might first find the maximum and then the maximum of the remaining elements. If K is large, this process is not particularly attractive. For example, if $K = O(n)$,[28] it would lead to an algorithm with a time complexity of $O(n^2)$,[29] a truly awful performance since we could just sort the array (in time $O(n \cdot \log_2(n))$) and then access the Kth-largest element in constant time (since the array permits direct access to the element with index $n - K + 1$ and accessing the element with that index, by virtue of the array's random access property requires $O(1)$ time). It is therefore interesting the see that solving our problem can be done much more efficiently than resorting to sorting.

3.2.9   Finding the *K*th Largest Element

Consider the following recursive approach; note that **A** is not assumed to be sorted:

Select(A[1:n],K)

1. Randomly choose a pivot element *m*.
2. Use *m* to construct the sets L, E, and G of those elements that are strictly smaller, equal, and strictly greater than *m*, respectively:

   For i:=1,...,n do
       if A[i]=m then add A[i] to E
           else if A[i]<m then add A[i] to L else add A[i] to G

   During the construction of **L**, **E**, and **G**, also count their elements c_L, c_E, and c_G, respectively.
3. If $c_G \geq K$, then return Select (G,K).

       else if $c_G + c_E \geq K$ then return m
           else return Select (L,K-($c_G + c_E$))

This algorithm splits the search space **A**[1:*n*] around the pivot element *m* and then determines the three sets **L**, **E**, and **G**. If there are at least *K* elements in **G**, then we call Select recursively to determine the *K*th largest element in **G**. Otherwise we see whether **G**∪**E** contains at least *K* elements; if so, *m* is

---

[28] A very common value is $K = n/2$, in which case the problem is finding the *median* of the set. Informally, the median of a set is the element with the property that half of the elements of the set are larger and half of the elements are smaller than the median.

[29] We would spend $O(t)$ time to find the maximum of an array of size t; first $t = n$ (find the maximum of the entire set), then $t = n - 1$ (find the maximum of the remaining $n - 1$ elements), and so on, until $t = n - K + 1$. Summing this work up yields a quadratic time complexity.

the desired *K*th largest element. Finally, if none of these cases applies, we call Select recursively again, but now with the set **L**, and instead of finding its *K*th largest element, we find **L**'s element with the number $K - (c_G + c_E)$, reflecting that we removed **G** and **E** from the search space and therefore K has to be reduced accordingly by the number of the removed elements in **G** and **E**.

The most important factor in the determination of the complexity is the recursive calls to Select, and more specifically, the size of the sets involved in these calls. Initially, our search space size is n; in the single recursive call in step 3, the search space size is either c_G or c_L (note that there is no more than one recursive call, as at most one of the two cases with recursion can apply). It is not difficult to see that the worst case occurs if $\max\{c_G, c_L\} = n - 1$. If this occurs in every recursive call, we have the situation of Scenario 1 of Section 3.1, with the proviso that the additional work (namely the construction of the sets **L**, **E**, and **G**) takes $O(n)$ time; consequently, the worst-case time complexity is a pathetic $O(n^2)$.[30]

What would be a desirable situation? Recall that in binary search, the search space was split into two equal halves. Can we achieve something similar here? Suppose *m* were the median of the search space; then we would mirror binary search, except for step 3, which is concerned with keeping track of the index *K*. Of course, we do not know how to get *m* to be the median,[31] but we can get very close. Here is how.

Replace step 1 in Select with the following steps:

1.1 Split the search space **A**[1:*n*] into groups of five elements each and sort each of these sets.

1.2 Determine **M** to be the set of all the medians of these five-element sets.

1.3 *m*:=Select(**M**,È*n*/10˘).

We will refer to steps 1.1, 1.2, 1.3, 2, and 3 as the *modified Select algorithm*. While it is clear that any choice of *m* will work, and hence the *m* determined in steps 1.1, 1.2, and 1.3 will also work, it is not so clear what this convoluted construction buys us. Step 1.1 groups the search space into five-element sets and sorts each of them. This requires $O(n)$ time, since the grouping operation implies one scan of the search space and sorting five elements can be done in a constant number of comparisons (seven comparisons are sufficient to sort five numbers). Also, we can incorporate step 1.2 into this process — just take the middle element of each five-element (by now sorted) set and add it to **M**. How large is **M**? Since we have about $n/5$ five-element sets and we

---

[30] To see this directly, consider that in the first call, we need $O(n)$ time. In the second call, we need $O(n - 1)$ time. In general, in the *i*th call, we need $O(n - i + 1)$ time, for $i = 1, \ldots, n$. Summing this up yields the claim of $O(n^2)$.

[31] The best way we know at this point of finding the median is to find the *K*th largest element with $K = n/2$. Since we are still struggling with this problem, looking for the median is not exactly promising.

take one element from each, **M** has about $n/5$ elements. Step 1.3 then consists of determining, again recursively, the median of the set **M**, that is, the median of the medians of the five-element sets.[32]

With this specific choice of m, let us revisit the question of how large are the sets **L** and **G** determined in step 2. Let us first determine which elements cannot possibly be in L. Clearly, m cannot be in **L**, and since m is the median of **M**, half of the elements in **M** are $\geq m$, so they cannot be in **L** either. Moreover, each of these elements is the median of its five-element set, so in each such set there are two more elements that are $\geq m$, namely the elements greater than or equal to its set's median. Summing all this up, we reach the conclusion that there are at least $n/10 + 2 \cdot n/10$, or $3 \cdot n/10$, elements $\geq m$; therefore, none of them can be in **L**, and hence c_L cannot be larger than $7 \cdot n/10$. By a similar argument, one sees that there are at least $3 \cdot n/10$ elements in $A[1:n]$ that are $\leq m$, so none of them can be in **G**, and hence $c_G \leq 7 \cdot n/10$. It follows therefore that in step 3, the search space for either of the two recursive calls is no larger than $7 \cdot n/10$.

Let $T(n)$ be the time the modified Select algorithm requires for a search space with n elements. Then the recursive call in step 1.3 requires time $T(n/5)$, and the (single) recursive call in step 1.3 requires time at most $T(7 \cdot n/10)$. Since $7 \cdot n/10 < 3 \cdot n/4$, we can bound $T(7 \cdot n/10)$ from above by $T(3 \cdot n/4)$. (Clearly, T is monotonically increasing, that is, if $s < t$, then $T(s) < T(t)$.) Our final expression for $T(n)$ is therefore

$$T(n) \leq T(n/5) + T(3 \cdot n/4) + C \cdot n,$$

where $C \cdot n$ reflects the work to be done in steps 1.1, 1.2, and 2. It follows now that

$$T(n) = 20 \cdot C \cdot n$$

satisfies this relation. The worst-case time complexity of the modified Select algorithm for finding the Kth largest element in the set $A[1:n]$ of n elements is therefore $O(n)$.[33] Furthermore, the space complexity is $O[\log_2(n)]$ since the recursive calls require space proportional to the depth of the recursion. Since in the worst case, the modified Select algorithm reduces the search space size by a factor of $7/10$, such a reduction can take place at most $\lceil \log_{10/7}(n) \rceil$ times before the search space is reduced to nothing, and that is $O(\log_2(n))$

---

[32] In modified Select, we used five-element sets. There is nothing magic about the number 5; any odd number (>4) would do (it should be odd to keep the arguments for L and G symmetric). However, 5 turns out to be most effective for the analysis.

[33] We assume a suitable termination condition for Select; typically something like: if $n \leq 50$ then sort directly and return the desired element. (Here, 50 plays the role of n_0, a value of n so small that it has little significance for the asymptotic complexity of how one deals with the cases where $n \leq n_0$.) Under this assumption, we write $T(n) = T(n/5) + T(3 \cdot n/4) + C \cdot n$ and show by direct substitution that $T(n) = 20 \cdot C \cdot n$ satisfies the equality. On the right-hand side we get $20 \cdot C \cdot n/5 + 20 \cdot C \cdot 3 \cdot n/4 + C \cdot n$, which adds up to exactly $20 \cdot C \cdot n$.

times. Hence, the worst-case space complexity of modified Select is $O(\log_2(n))$.[34]

In comparing the initial version and the modified version of Select, one is struck by the fact that the modification, even though far more complicated, has a guaranteed worst-case complexity far superior to that of the original. However, what this statement hides is the enormous constant that afflicts its linear complexity. On average, the original Select tends to be much faster, even though one does run the risk of a truly horrible worst-case complexity.

It is tempting to improve QuickSort by employing modified Select to determine its pivot. Specifically, we might want to use modified select to determine the pivot x as the median of the subarray to be sorted. While this would certainly guarantee that the worst-case complexity equals the best-case complexity of the resulting version of QuickSort, it would also convert QuickSort into something like ComatoseSort. The constant factor attached to such a sort would make it at least one, if not two, orders of magnitude slower than HeapSort.

So far, all the algorithms we have explored were essentially off-line. In other words, we expected the input to be completely specified before we started any work toward a solution. This may not be the most practicable approach to some problems, especially to problems where the underlying data sets are not static, but change dynamically. For example, an on-line telephone directory should be up to date: It should reflect at any time all current subscribers and should purge former customers or entries. This requires the continual ability to update the directory. Were we to use an unsorted linear list to represent the directory, adding to the list would be cheap, but looking up a number would be a prohibitive $O(n)$ if there were n entries. Thus, we would like to be able to use a scheme that is at least as efficient as binary search — which requires the array to be sorted. However, it would be clearly impractical to sort the entire array whenever we want to insert or delete an entry. Here is where search trees come into their own.

3.2.10 Search Trees

A search tree is a binary tree in which each node N contains information I(N).[35] Thus, each node consists of three components, a pointer R(N) to its left subtree rooted in N_L, a pointer L(N) to its right subtree rooted in N_R, and I(N). Note that one or both subtrees of the node N can be empty. However, whenever they exist, the information associated with each node N_L in the left subtree, $I(N_L)$, must be strictly smaller than I(N), and the information associated with each node N_R in the right subtree, $I(N_R)$, must

---

[34] The worst-case space complexity of the original Select algorithm was $O(n)$, since $O(n)$ recursive calls would occur if the search space is reduced by one element for each recursion step.
[35] Again, we require that we have a total order imposed on the information. Ultimately, anything that can be sorted can also be accommodated in search trees.

be strictly larger than I(N).[36] One direct consequence of this definition is that no search tree can contain duplicate information.[37]

Below we will show how search trees can be used to insert, delete, and find an element. While testing whether a given binary tree with n nodes in which each node N contains information I(N) is a search tree can be done in time $O(n)$,[38] search trees are usually constructed by inserting elements successively. Since insertion and deletion are based on search, we start with this operation.

3.2.10.1   *Finding an Element in a Search Tree*

The key observation is that in any search tree, there is a unique location for any element x, whether x occurs in the tree or not. We assume that p is a pointer to the root of the search tree we examine; if p is not null (i.e., does not point to an empty tree), we will also use p to denote the node p points to. Furthermore, if p is not null, L(p) is a pointer to the left child of (the node pointed to by) p, and R(p) points to the right child.

```
Find(p,x)
    If p is null then return – x not in search tree
    Else if x=I(p) then return p – x is in the node p points to
        else if x<I(p) then call Find(L(p),x) else call Find(R(p),x)
```

---

[36] It is tempting to replace this global test (for each node, all nodes in its left subtree must be examined, and all nodes in its right subtree must be examined) with a local variant, something like this: For each node N, the information of the left child of N must be strictly smaller than I(N), and the information of the right child of N must be strictly larger than I(N). However, this definition does not result in search trees, as this tree indicates 5, which satisfies the local variant but not the global definition of a search tree:

[37] Assume that two different nodes contain x. Find the smallest subtree that contains both nodes; let N be the root of that subtree. Either I(N) = x or one of the two nodes with x is in N's left subtree and the other in its right subtree. (If both were in the left subtree, the tree rooted in N would not be smallest — use N's left subtree; the same situation would exist if they both were in the right subtree.) In the first case, compare I(N) with the other node containing x. If it is in N's left subtree, the definition requires it to be strictly smaller than I(N); the same situation would exist if it is in the right subtree. An analogous argument applies if one occurrence of x occurs in the left subtree of N and the other in the right subtree.

[38] Applying the definition directly implies a complexity of $O(n^2)$ because for each of the n nodes, the definition requires us to inspect all the nodes of its left and right subtrees. However, $O(n^2)$ time is by no means optimal. A lower bound on the time complexity is $O(n)$, since each node must be inspected. This lower bound can be attained: Do an in-order traversal of the tree (this requires linear time; see Section 3.2.10.4), write the information into an array in the order in which it is encountered during the traversal (time $O(n)$), and finally determine whether this array is sorted (also linear time). One can verify that this array is sorted if and only if the tree is a search tree.

This formulation is recursive. However, since it is obviously tail recursion, it can be mechanically converted to iteration, without requiring space for the recursion stack.[39] This immediately answers the question about the space complexity; the nonrecursive version has space complexity $O(1)$. The recursive version has a space complexity that is proportional to the depth of the recursion, which in turn is bounded from above by the height of the tree.[40] This is also the time complexity of Find(p,x) (regardless of which version we use). In the worst case we search for information attached to a leaf of maximal distance from the root of the search tree; this is precisely the definition of the height of a tree. Since in each recursive call (in each iteration), $O(1)$ work is done, the height of the tree is an upper bound on the complexity. Unfortunately, a search tree with n nodes may have a height equal to $n - 1$ in the worst case (clearly, a linear list can be viewed as a pathological binary tree); thus, the worst-case time (word) complexity of Find(p,x) is *O(n)*.

3.2.10.2 Inserting an Element into a Search Tree

Once we understand Find(p,x), this operation is quite trivial. Essentially, we pretend to search for x. If we find it, the attempted insertion is illegal since x is already in the search tree. If we do not find it, it is because we encounter an empty pointer to the place where x *should* be; all we have to do now is put x there.

---

[39] Tail recursion means that at most one recursive call is executed and the function returns immediately after that recursive call. Thus, we have the following schema for the function F with n parameters:

F(x1,...,xn)
{ if basis-case   then StatementGroup1 else { StatementGroup2; F(y1,...,yn) }
}

This recursive function with tail recursion can be equivalently replaced by the following nonrecursive function F′ (this assumes that the passing of the parameters is by value and that the vector assignment ::= is carried out correctly):

F′(x1,...,xn)
{ while not basis-case do { StatementGroup2; [x1,...,xn]::=[y1,...,yn] };
StatementGroup1
}

It is obvious that the nonrecursive version F′ does not require additional space; also, the time complexities of F and F′ are identical.

Note: The vector assignment ::= implies that all values of the variables $y1$ through yn are determined *before* the assignment to $x1$ through xn is carried out. To see why this is important consider the following recursive call: $F(x1 - 2, x1 - x2)$; were one to do $x1: = x1 - 2; x2: = x1 - x2$ instead of $[x1,x2] ::= [x1 - 2, x1 - x2]$, wrong values would be assigned.

[40] This assumes that we do *not* take into consideration the space required for the left and right pointers for each node. While this is the usual convention, it is a questionable assumption. The input is really only the set of n numbers, yet the space for the pointers is clearly *O(n)*. Thus, it would be much more appropriate to consider the space complexity to be the space required by the function *plus* the space required for the representation of the tree (since this latter space has nothing to do with the input provided).

```
Insert(p,x)
   If p is null then
      create a node N with I(N)=x, L(N)=R(N)=null, and p pointing to N
      else if x=I(p) then return – x already in the search tree :: illegal
      insertion
         else if x<I(p) then call Insert(L(p),x) else call Insert(R(p),x)
```

The comments made about Find apply here as well. In particular, the space complexity is bounded from above by the height of the tree for the recursive version and $O(1)$ for the nonrecursive one; the space complexity is also bounded from above by the height of the search tree (for both recursive and nonrecursive versions). Again, since the height of a tree with n nodes is $n - 1$ in the worst case, the worst-case time complexity is $O(n)$.

3.2.10.3   Deleting an Element from a Search Tree

Deletion is trickier. We first find the element x to be deleted, but in general we cannot just erase its node N. Instead we must distinguish two cases, if at least one subtree of N is empty (this is the easy case) and if both subtrees of N are nonempty.

In the easy case, we *can* simply remove the node N. If both subtrees of N are empty, we set to null the pointer from N's parent to N (this makes N disappear, since it can no longer be accessed; in Section 6.3, we will discuss this issue and its implications in greater detail). If only one subtree of N is empty, let N' be the root of the nonempty subtree of N; then have the pointer from N's parent (which used to point to N) point to N's only child, N'. It is easy to see that this deletion operation maintains the property of being a search tree, but the node N has disappeared, and with it the element x.

What do we do if both subtrees of N are nonempty? We cannot remove the node N, but we can replace x, the information attached to N, with some suitable other information, thereby effectively deleting x. There are two suitable candidates, namely the smallest element of all elements larger than x and the largest element of all elements smaller than x. The idea is to locate the replacement y, put y as I(N) where N is x's node, and then delete N', y's node.

We must be concerned about two things: Does this operation preserve the property of being a search tree, and if so, how do we delete N'? If y is the smallest of all larger elements, then putting y at N maintains all smaller elements to N's left and all larger elements to N's right (even though N now holds y instead of x). The same is true if y is the largest of all smaller elements. Thus, this operation preserves the search tree property.

Now, for the deletion of N'. Let y be the smallest of the elements larger than x. Clearly, y is obtained by taking the right pointer from N (everything larger is to the right), and from that node on always the left pointer (everything to the left is smaller), until we reach a node whose left subtree is empty. That node is N', and I(N') is y. Most importantly, when we are deleting y, N' is one of the easy nodes to delete because its left subtree is guaranteed to be empty. A similar argument applies if y is the largest of the elements smaller than x. Here is the algorithm:

```
Delete(p,x)
    if p=null then error – x not in search tree
    else if l(p)<x then Delete(R(p),x)
    else if l(p)>x then Delete(L(p),x)
    else { ** l(p)=x**
        let N' be the parent of (the node of) x;
        let q be the pointer from N' to x;
        if L(p)=null then set q to R(p)
        else if R(p)=null then set q to L(p)
        else if
            { **both subtrees of p are nonempty**
            r:=R(p);
            while L(r)≠ null do r:=L(r); l(p):=l(r);
            **now r points to y, the smallest of all elements larger than x**
            Let N" be the parent of r and let t be the pointer of N" to r;
            Set t to R(r).
            }
    }⁴¹
```

For the complexity analysis, it should be clear that the sum of the work involved in finding x and then y is bounded from above by the height of the search tree. Thus, everything we derived for Find and Insert applies here as well: Given a search tree with n nodes, Delete(p,x) has a worst-case time complexity of $O(n)$; the worst-case space complexity of the recursive version is also $O(n)$. However, closer inspection of the algorithm indicates that we again have tail recursion, so the space complexity of the iterative version is $O(1)$.

In summary, we determined that the three operations Find, Insert, and Delete on search trees all have the same worst-case time complexity, namely $O(h)$, where h is the height of the tree. The problem with this result is that h can grow unacceptably large for general search trees. This calls for a modification of the notion of a search tree.

Before we do this, we want to relate search trees to sorting. More specifically, we want to use a search tree to obtain the contents of all its nodes sorted in ascending order. This can be achieved by traversing the search tree.

---

⁴¹ Alternatively, if we want y to be the largest of all elements smaller than x, we replace the last six lines with:
r:=L(p); while R(r) π null do r:=R(r);
now r points to y, the largest of all elements smaller than x
l(p):=l(r); Let N" be the parent of r and let t be the pointer of N" to r; Set t to L(r).

3.2.10.4   *Traversing a Search Tree*

This is a fundamentally recursive technique. It first prints out all the information of the left subtree, then the information of the root, and then all the information in the right subtree.[42] Since everything to the left is smaller and everything to the right is larger than the information in the root, the resulting output is sorted:

```
Traverse(p)
    If p≠ null then {Traverse(L(p)); print(I(p)); Traverse(R(p)) }
```

The complexity analysis is as follows: For time, we visit each node in the search tree once, and the work done at each node is constant. Therefore, the time complexity is $O(n)$ for a tree with n nodes. For space, we again observe that the depth of the recursion is equal to the height of the search tree; in the best case this will be $O(\log_2(n))$, but in the worst case, the height of the tree, and therefore the space complexity of Traverse(p), is $O(n)$.

The main reason a search tree with n nodes can have a height of $O(n)$ is imbalance. If the tree were an optimal binary tree with n nodes, its height would be exactly $\lceil \log_2(n + 1) - 1 \rceil$. However, it is not clear whether the optimal use of binary trees is compatible with the property of being a search tree. Moreover, we would like to retain efficient search, insertion, and deletion operations. All of this can be achieved through the use of AVL trees, named after the initials of their inventors (Adelson-Velskii and Landis).

3.2.11   AVL Trees

An AVL tree is a search tree with the property that for each node N, the height of its left subtree and the height of its right subtree differ by at most 1. The height of an empty tree is assumed to be –1, and the height of a nonempty tree is 1 plus the maximum of the heights of its subtrees. We assume that each node N has four components: the three of the search tree (the information field I(N), the pointer to its left child L(N), and the pointer to its right child R(N)) plus an additional one, H(N), to capture the height of the tree rooted in N.[43] We show how to implement search, insertion, and deletion using this type of search tree.

3.2.11.1   *Finding an Element in an AVL Tree*

Since an AVL tree is a search tree and the function Find(p,x) does not modify the tree, the identical function Find will work for AVL trees as well. The

---

[42] Strictly speaking, this is in-order traversal, since the content of the node is printed out *between* the contents of the left subtree and those of the right subtree. Similarly, one defines preorder (postorder) traversal wherein the content of the node is printed out *before* (*after*) the contents of the left subtree and those of the right subtree are printed out.

complexity analysis is also the same; the worst-case time complexity is $O(h)$, where h is the height of the AVL tree. The only difference here is that for AVL trees, the height is bounded, as we show below.

3.2.11.2   *Inserting an Element into an AVL Tree*

This is where things become more interesting. The key notion is *rotation*. If inserting an element in its proper place in the search tree (no change here — it is still a search tree, and therefore there is a unique place for any given element in that tree) results in a violation of the balance condition, we have to rebalance the tree. In order to allow testing for the balance condition, height information must be managed throughout. Here is the basic scheme:

```
InsertAVL(p,x)
    If p is null then
        create a node N with I(N)=x, L(N)=R(N)=null, H(N)=0,
        and p pointing to N
    else if x=I(N(p)) then return
                        – x is already in the search tree :: illegal insertion
        else
        { If x<I(p) then call InsertAVL(L(p),x)
                        else call InsertAVL(R(p),x).
            If H(L(p)) and H(R(p)) differ by more than 1
                then {Rebalance(p); exit }
                Else if H(p) ≠ 1 + max{H(L(p)),H(R(p))}
                        then update H(p) else exit
        }
```

The differences between Insert and InsertAVL occur exclusively after the creation of the node for the element to be inserted. Apart from setting the height field of that node to 0, all the action occurs when the successive recursive calls to InsertAVL return. We distinguish three cases based on the heights involved. In the first case if the left and the right subtree of the current node $N(p)$ differ by more than 1, we have to rebalance. We describe this algorithm below and note here that a rebalancing operation does not change the height of the tree that is rebalanced. Therefore, no more

---

[43] It is possible to formulate the algorithms for AVL trees using only a three-valued balance tag for each node N. However, since the additional space of a search tree with n nodes over and beyond the n words for the input is already $O(n)$ owing to the left and right pointers, the difference in space between using two bits for the balance tag and the word for representing the height is quite negligible.

For those who are really interested in the precise additional space required by the height field, it is no more than $n \cdot \lceil \log_2(1.45 \cdot \log_2(n)) \rceil$ bits. As we will see, the height of an AVL tree with n nodes is at most $1.45 \cdot \log_2(n)$; thus, the log of that is sufficient to represent the height of any subtree. So, for each of the n nodes, we need at most that many bits to record the height. Consequently, the difference between the algorithms using a three-valued balance tag and ours that use a height field is $\lceil \log_2(1.45 \cdot \log_2(n)) \rceil - 3$. To make this more concrete, for all $n \leq 2^{44}$ (that is for all n less than about 17 trillion), 6 bits are sufficient. However, the algorithms with the height field are much more intuitive.

rebalancing further up the tree is required (remember, the tree into which we insert is assumed to be an AVL tree) and no more updating of the heights of any nodes further up is necessary either.[44] This is why we have an exit statement; its meaning is that we abort any further orderly returning of the recursive calls (since no more work is needed further up in the tree). The second case applies if we have to update the height of the node N(p). In this case H(p) is set to 1 + max{H(L(p)),H(R(p))} and recursion must return orderly since this update of the height may require additional height updates further up in the tree. However, if no height update is required for this node, the third case, then no height updates will be required further up the tree — hence the exit statement, which avoids any further unnecessary checks for updates.

We now have to formulate the rotation operation. Recall that we started with an AVL tree and messed it up (violating the balance condition) by inserting an element x into it. Furthermore, keep in mind that we check whether to apply a rotation going up from the inserted node toward the root of the AVL tree (this is the reverse path from the root to the inserted element), testing at each node whether the height condition is violated. Assume we find a node N for which the height condition is violated (note that we may never find a violation, in which case we only update the height information, but do no rotation; if we do find such a node, it is the first time that the height condition is violated on the path from x to the root of the AVL tree). We distinguish several cases:

Case 1

$H(L(N)) = H(R(N)) - 2$; that is, the left subtree of N has a height smaller by 2 than its right subtree.[45] We distinguish two cases, namely whether the element x was inserted into the right subtree of R(N) or into the left subtree of R(N).

Case 1.1

The value x was inserted into the right subtree of R(N). Clearly, x was inserted into R(N)'s right subtree precisely if $H(R(R(N))) > H(L(R(N)))$. We do a *single left rotation* on N:

1. Let q be the pointer from N's parent to N (if N is the root of the AVL tree, q is the root pointer).
2. Make the left pointer of R(N) point to N.
3. Make the right pointer of N point to L(R(N)).[46]
4. Make q point to R(N).

---

[44] This implies that when inserting, at most one rotation (rebalancing operation) will occur.
[45] Because the tree was an AVL tree before the insertion of a single element, it is impossible for the difference in the heights to exceed 2.
[46] L(R(N)) is the root of the subtree RL in the diagram.

5. Keep all other pointers unchanged.

6. Update the height fields of the reconfigured nodes L(N(q)) and N(q).[47]

This corresponds to the following diagram:

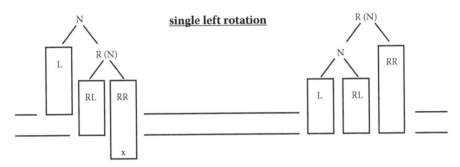

single left rotation

It is easily verified that the resulting tree is a search tree and that the height of this tree is equal to the height of the tree rooted in N *before* the insertion of x. Note that the insertion of x necessarily increased the height of the subtree RR into which is was inserted; if it had not, then there would not be a violation of the height condition at N.

Case 1.2

The value x was inserted into the left subtree of R(N). Clearly, x was inserted into R(N)'s left subtree precisely if H(R(R(N))) < H(L(R(N))). We do a *double left rotation* on N:

1. Let q be the pointer from N's parent to N (if N is the root of the AVL tree, q is the root pointer).

2. Make the left pointer of R(N) point to R(L(R(N))).[48]

3. Make the right pointer of N point to L(L(R(N))).[49]

4. Make the left pointer of L(R(N)) point to N.

5. Make the right pointer of L(R(N)) point to R(N).

6. Make q point to L(R(N)).

7. Keep all other pointers unchanged.

---

[47] This is done (in this order) by using the relation $H(N) = 1 + \max\{H(N_L),H(N_R)\}$ for any node N and its children N_L and N_R (if they exist; otherwise the height is -1). Thus, for the new nodes N and R(N) in the diagram, we have
$H(N) = 1 + \max\{H(L),H(RL)\}$ and $H(R(N)) = 1 + \max\{H(N),H(RR)\}$.

[48] R(L(R(N))) is the root of the subtree RLR in the diagram.

[49] L(L(R(N))) is the root of the subtree RLL in the diagram.

8. Update the height fields of the reconfigured nodes L(N(q)), R(N(q)), and N(q).[50]

This corresponds to the following diagram where the two occurrences of *x* indicate the two places where *x* might have been inserted (*x* occurs in exactly one of these two places):

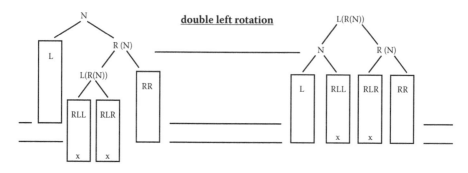

Case 2

$H(L(N)) = H(R(N)) + 2$; that is, the left subtree of N has a height greater by 2 than its right subtree. This situation is the exact mirror image of the situation covered in Case 1; the algorithms for single rotation and double rotation are obtained by systematically replacing every occurrence of right by left, and of left by right in the above algorithms.

Single right rotation on N:

1. Let q be the pointer from N's parent to N (if N is the root of the AVL tree, q is the root pointer).
2. Make the right pointer of L(N) point to N.
3. Make the left pointer of N point to R(L(N)).
4. Make q point to L(N).
5. Keep all other pointers unchanged.
6. Update the height fields of the reconfigured nodes R(N(q)) and N(q).

Double right rotation on N:

1. Let q be the pointer from N's parent to N (if N is the root of the AVL tree, q is the root pointer).
2. Make the right pointer of L(N) point to L(R(L(N))).
3. Make the left pointer of N point to R(R(L(N))).

---

[50] This is done analogously to the height updates for the single left rotation, but now it is applied to the three nodes N, R(N), and L(R(N)) in the diagram.

4. Make the right pointer of R(L(N)) point to N.
5. Make the left pointer of R(L(N)) point to L(N).
6. Make q point to R(L(N)).
7. Keep all other pointers unchanged.
8. Update the height fields of the reconfigured nodes R(N(q)), L(N(q)), and N(q).

The operation Rebalance(p) mentioned in our algorithm InsertAVL is precisely this group of rotation algorithms. One of these four will apply in any situation that requires rebalancing:

```
Rebalance(p)
  If H(L(N))=H(R(N)) – 2 then
     {
        if H(R(R(N)))>H(L(R(N)))   then Single left
                                   rotation on N
                                   else Double left
                                   rotation on N

     }
     else
     { **H(L(N))=H(R(N))+2**
        if H(L(L(N)))>H(R(L(N)))   then Single right
                                   rotation on N
                                   else Double right
                                   rotation on N

  }.
```

We now come to the complexity analysis of the operation InsertAVL. Assume we have an AVL tree with n nodes. Inspecting the algorithm for InsertAVL reveals that it is almost identical to the algorithm Insert for general search trees, except that we perform a rebalance operation *once* and updates of the height field, possibly for every node on the path from the root to the node inserted. The height updates take $O(1)$ time per node visited. Also, since at most one rebalance operation will occur in an insertion and each of the four possible candidates consists of a very small number of simple instructions (eight in the case of double rotations, five for single rotations), it follows that the upper bound on the time complexity of our insertion operation is still the height of the tree. Thus, $O(h)$ is the worst-case time complexity of InsertAVL. Because of the recursive nature of the insertion process, the (worst-case) space complexity is also $O(h)$.

This seems to suggest that we have not gained anything. Both Insert and InsertAVL have a time and a space complexity of $O(h)$, where h is the height of the search tree. However, the fundamental difference is that the worst-case height of an AVL tree is guaranteed to be much smaller than the worst-case height of a general search tree. We will show that in the worst case, the height of an AVL tree with n nodes is less than $1.45 \cdot \log_2(n)$.

What is the greatest height of an AVL tree with n nodes? According to the definition of an AVL tree, the difference of the heights the two subtrees of any node must not exceed 1. So, let us construct worst possible trees by making sure the difference is always exactly 1. Here is the recipe:

1. The empty tree T_{-1} has zero nodes and has height -1, which is maximal (simply because it is unique).

2. The tree T_0 of height 0 with one node, the root, is clearly the tree with one node that has the greatest height (again, it is unique).

3. To construct a tree T_h of height h for $h \geq 1$ with the minimal number of nodes, take a tree T_{h-1} of height $h - 1$ with the least number of nodes, take a tree T_{h-2} of height $h - 2$ with the least number of nodes, and make T_{h-1} the left subtree and T_{h-2} the right subtree of the root of T_h.

One can verify that this construction yields trees of any height $h \geq 0$ with the least number of nodes.[51] How many nodes does T_h have? If M_h is the number of nodes of T_h for $h \geq 0$, we can write

$$M_0 = 1,\ M_1 = 2,\ \text{and for all } h > 1,\ M_h = 1 + M_{h-1} + M_{h-2}.$$

We claim that M_h grows exponentially. In other words, there exists a constant C such that $M_h \geq C^{O(h)}$. Define C to be $(1 + \sqrt{5})/2$. It follows that $M_h \geq C^h$.[52] Since $C > 1.618$, it follows that

$$M_h \geq 1.618^h.$$

We use this result to obtain an upper bound on the height of any AVL tree with n nodes. Since M_h is the minimum number of nodes of any AVL tree of height h, any AVL tree of height h must have at least M_h nodes. It follows

---

[51] Assume the contrary, namely that there exists an AVL tree of height h with fewer nodes. Since there cannot be a contradiction to our claim for $h = -1$ and $h = 0$, there must be a smallest value, say $g \geq 1$, such that an AVL tree of height g has fewer nodes than the T_g constructed by our recipe. Let T be such a tree of height g that has the smallest number of nodes (in particular, by assumption T has fewer nodes than T_g). Now consider the left and right subtrees T_l and T_r of the root of T: Their heights must differ by exactly 1 (if they were equal, we could replace one of them with an AVL tree of lesser height, which would also have fewer nodes, contradicting our assumption that T has the least number of nodes). However, it follows now that T_l and T_r have heights less than g and therefore cannot have fewer nodes than T_{g-1} and T_{g-2}, respectively, as g is the smallest height where our recipe is assumed not to deliver an AVL tree with the smallest number of nodes. This results in a contradiction, since the nodes of T are obviously the root of T plus all the nodes of T_l and all of T_r.

[52] First one verifies directly that $1 + C = C^2$. Then we obtain by induction on h: $M_h = 1 + M_{h-1} + M_{h-2} \geq 1 + C^{h-1} + C^{h-2} = 1 + C^{h-2} \cdot (C + 1) = 1 + C^{h-2} \cdot C^2 = 1 + C^h > C^h$; the claim follows since the two (required) basis cases M_0 and M_1 are trivially verified.

from this that in the worst case, the height h of an AVL tree with n nodes is bounded from above by $1.45 \cdot \log_2(n)$.[53] Thus, in the worst case, the height of an AVL tree with n nodes is no greater than 45% more than the height of an optimal tree.

Now we return to the complexity of InsertAVL. Since we have bounded the height of an AVL tree with n nodes by $O(\log_2(n))$, the worst-case time and space complexity are therefore $O(\log_2(n))$. This is in marked contrast to the general search tree insertion whose worst-case time complexity is $O(n)$.

3.2.11.3   *Deleting an Element from an AVL Tree*

Deletion from an AVL tree proceeds essentially in the same way as it did in a general search tree, except that we have to verify the balance condition when returning along the path from the deleted element (the one whose node disappears) to the root, and if necessary carry out appropriate rebalance operations. Rebalancing is done by carrying out the appropriate rotation algorithm. Note that it is the physical removal of a node, not the overwriting of a value (x by y), that may affect the balance of the tree. Another issue of note here is that it may be necessary to rebalance for each node along the path; this is in contrast to insertion, where a single rebalancing operation suffices to balance the tree. To see that this may indeed occur, consider the tree T_h of height h with the minimal number of nodes. Deleting any element in the smaller subtree of the root will necessarily decrease that subtree's height (by definition it is the smallest AVL tree of that height, so reducing its number of nodes by one implies that the height shrinks after rebalancing). We can now iterate this process. The node to be deleted from T_{h-2} will be deleted from its smaller subtree, which is T_{h-4}. Within that T_{h-4}, we delete from its T_{h-6}, and so on, until we get to a T_2 or a T_1. Consequently, for the root of every subtree that occurs on the path from the deleted node to the root of the AVL tree, a rebalancing operation is required, since in each case the right subtree has a height that differs by 2 from the height of the left subtree. However, since each of the rotations has constant time complexity and since the length of the path is bounded from above by the height of the AVL tree, which in turn is bounded from above by $1.45 \cdot \log_2(n)$, the worst-case time complexity of deleting an element in an AVL tree with n nodes is $O(\log_2(n))$. This is also the worst-case space complexity of deletion in AVL trees.

Let us summarize the situation of AVL trees compared with general search trees. In both cases the height of the tree is the upper bound on the complexity of searching, inserting, and deleting. The fundamental difference is that for general search trees with n nodes, the height may grow as large as $n - 1$, while for AVL trees with n nodes, the height is always smaller than $1.45 \cdot \log_2(n)$. Therefore, the complexity, time and space, of the three operations when applied to AVL trees is $O(\log_2(n))$. This is *exponentially* better than the

---

[53] For any n and h in an AVL tree, we know that $n \geq C^h$; from this we get $\log_C(n) \geq h$, and since $\log_C(n) = \log_C(2) \cdot \log_2(n)$, the claim follows.

$O(n)$ of general search trees. Consequently, the height balance condition of AVL trees is a very powerful condition that has enormous practical implications.

So far, we have used various types of searches to locate information. Common to all was that a certain order relation existed. This was reflected in the dramatic improvement in performance resulting from sorting the search space. One may be tempted to assume that order is paramount in locating information. This is quite wrong; a method that seemingly thrives on chaos is more efficient (on average and under certain conditions) than anything exploiting order. This is hashing. While its rigorous complexity analysis is either too complicated to give here or is obtained using simulation, we want to mention it since it is an extremely important technique.

3.2.12 Hashing

In contrast to the previously discussed methods, hashing does not depend on any ordering relationship on its search space. The only test we must be able to carry out is one for equality. Hashing is useful primarily if we want to carry out insertions and searches. Other operations tend to be difficult (e.g., deletions) or impossible within the underlying setting (e.g., finding the median or the maximum, assuming there is an order relation).

There is a large set **S** of elements, called keys, any one of which might have to be stored. The storage structure is a one-dimensional (1D) array **H** of type $[0:h-1]$. It is crucial that h, the size of the storage array, is much smaller than the set **S** of all possible keys. While the search techniques described in previous sections rely on order, hashing uses a hash function σ to map (elements of) S to (locations in) **H**. Thus, σ maps the set **S** to the set $\{0, 1, ..., h-1\}$, so that for every key K in **S**, $\sigma(K)$ is a number between 0 and $h-1$. The intention is to place K into $H[\sigma(K)]$. However, since S has many more elements than **H** has locations, *collisions* are inevitable. A collision occurs if two keys K_1 and K_2 are mapped by σ to the same location in **H**, $\sigma(K_1) = \sigma(K_2)$.

Therefore, a collision resolution strategy must be applied. We assume that the array **H** indicates for each location whether or not that location is occupied by a key. With every key K, a fixed sequence of probes $a_{0,K}, a_{1,K}, a_{2,K}, ...$ is associated, where the first element, $a_{0,K}$, is equal to $\sigma(K)$, and subsequent elements in this sequence of probes are inspected if the previous probe indicated that the location in **H** corresponding to it was occupied by a key other than K. Thus, we first check $H[a_{0,K}]$; if it is empty (not occupied by any key), we place K there if we want to insert and we conclude that K is not in the hash table if we want to search for K. If $H[a_{0,K}]$ contains K, then for insertion we report that K already exists in **H** (hashing does not permit duplicates, so this is an error), while for searching we report that K is found. Finally, if $H[a_{0,K}]$ is occupied by a key other than K, we proceed to the next element in the sequence of probes, namely $a_{1,K}$, and repeat this process.

It follows from this very brief sketch that it is highly desirable that the sequence of probes visit all the locations of **H** in as few probes as possible; this means that we want $\{a_{0,K}, a_{1,K}, a_{2,K}, \ldots, a_{h-1,K}\}$ to be equal to $\{0, 1, \ldots, h-1\}$.[54] The crucial observation is that for both inserting and searching for a specific key K, the same sequence of probes is used; therefore, we either encounter K in one of the probes in $\mathbf{H}[a_{i,K}]$ or we hit an empty location. Getting to the (first) empty location while doing the probes signals that K is nowhere in the entire hash table. This follows since K would have to be placed into a location in **H** according to this process of successive probes, and if during an insertion attempt, an empty slot had been encountered, K would have been placed there.

Note that up until now we have not said anything about the computation of the sequence of probes $a_{0,K}, a_{1,K}, a_{2,K}, \ldots$ — for good reason, since any sequence will do as long as it satisfies, for every key K, the requirement $\{a_{0,K}, a_{1,K}, a_{2,K}, \ldots, a_{h-1,K}\} = \{0, 1, \ldots, h-1\}$. Quite counterintuitively, the more random this sequence is, the better the performance. While complete randomness would result in the best possible performance, it is obviously not feasible, since we must be able to compute the probe sequences. There are several approaches in the literature, including linear probing ($a_{i,K} = (a_{i-1,K} + 1) \bmod(h)$ for all $i = 1, \ldots, h-1$) and quadratic probing ($a_{i,K} = (a_{i-1,K} + i) \bmod(h)$ for all $i = 1, \ldots, h-1$); however, double hashing is generally accepted to be a technique that reasonably approaches the desired ideal of randomness. In double hashing the increment (the summand that is added to get from $a_{i,K}$ to $a_{i+1,K}$) is the result of applying a second hash function $\sigma\sigma$ to K; $\sigma\sigma$ must be independent of the first one (σ).[55]

Thus, in double hashing we have for all keys K, $a_{0,K} = \sigma(K)$, and $a_{i,K} = (a_{i-1,K} + incr) \bmod(h)$ for all $i = 1, \ldots, h-1$, where incr is chosen as follows: If $\sigma\sigma(K)$ is different from 0 and if $\sigma\sigma(K)$ does not divide h (the size of the hash table **H**), then incr $= \sigma\sigma(K)$, else incr $= 1$. The intuitive objective is the following: Even if we have two keys K_1 and K_2 for which the first hash function hashes to the same location ($\sigma(K_1) = \sigma(K_2)$), our two probe sequences will not be identical if $\sigma\sigma(K_1) \neq \sigma\sigma(K_2)$. This will ensure that we will not retrace for K_1 the same probe sequence as for K_2.[56] It is important to stress the independence of the two hash functions; if they are not independent, this argumentation collapses. Also, we must comment on the

---

[54] If this was not satisfied, we might miss locations in **H**. At first glace, this might just lead to certain inefficiencies, especially if we do not know how long we should continue probing, but it may have more dire consequences. Note that in the case of insertion such a missed location may be the only empty location; thus, even though **H** is not completely full, we will not be able to insert the key.

[55] For large enough sets S, it is of course unavoidable (for any choice of σ and $\sigma\sigma$) that there are keys K_1 and K_2 such that $\sigma(K1) = \sigma(K_2)$ and $\sigma\sigma(K_1) = \sigma\sigma(K_2)$ – this will occur whenever S has at least $h^2 + 1$ elements. However, double hashing will reduce the likelihood of this occurring. And since hashing is based on probabilities at any rate, this is just what is needed.

[56] Consider for example the case $h = 4$ and assume the following situation: **H**[0] contains K1, **H**[2] contains K2 (with K1 = K2), and **H**[1] and **H**[3] are empty. Suppose for a K3 different from K1 and K2, $\sigma(K3) = 0$ and $\sigma\sigma(K3) = 2$; the probe sequence for K3 is 0, 2, 0, 2, and it is apparent that K3 will not find a place in **H**, even though half of **H** is unoccupied.

alternative definitions of the increment. If $\sigma\sigma(K) = 0$, then we must choose a different value for the increment; also if $\sigma\sigma(K)$ divides h, the probe sequence would not visit all locations in the hash table **H**.[57] This last point is why hash table sizes are frequently chosen to be prime numbers; if h is prime, then any value of $\sigma\sigma(K)$ will be acceptable as long as it is not 0.

The performance analysis of random hashing is quite involved; the performance of double hashing is usually determined by simulation. The most important notion is that the hash table must not be close to full; it is vital that a good number of slots be unoccupied. In fact, one defines the load factor α of a hash table to be the ratio of the number of occupied slots to the total number of slots, $\alpha = n/h$, where n is the number of keys that have been inserted and h is the size of the hash table. If α is no larger than 80% (this means at least one-fifth of the locations in **H** are wasted), the number of probes for insertion and for searching is about 2 on average. Note that this is independent of the size of the hash table; in other words, it makes no difference how many keys are stored in **H**. As long as at least 20% of all slots are empty, we need only two probes on average. Contrast this with any of the order-based techniques, such as binary search. Clearly, the more elements are stored, the longer the search takes.

Thus, hashing seems to be head and shoulders above all the other techniques for locating elements. This assessment is not entirely correct; hashing also has a few significant drawbacks. Deletion is not easily implemented,[58] and it is crucial to have a good idea beforehand of how many elements will have to be inserted.[59] The most significant problem, however, is the worst-case performance of hashing: If we are truly unlucky, we will need $n + 1$ probes to insert, or search for, a key into a hash table that contains n keys. In this case hashing is as bad as linear search. Worse, if we are consistently unlucky, inserting n keys into an initially empty hash table could take as

---

[57] The problem is that when deleting K, we cannot just declare its location to be unoccupied since this could affect the ability to find another element K' whose own probe sequence passed through this (formerly occupied) slot. Setting the slot of K to empty would indicate that K' is not in the hash table, since we would carry out the probe sequence of K' until we hit the empty slot, and then we would conclude that K' is not in **H** — even though it is. One way around this problem is to mark keys as deleted without actually emptying their slots until they can be replaced by a new key that is to be inserted into **H** and whose probe sequence passes through that slot.

[58] If one does not know this, the load factor might exceed 80% — with dire consequences for the performance. Worse, if one were to attempt to insert more than h keys, a completely new hash table with a larger size would have to be populated from scratch.

[59] Another searching method, again order-based, which is faster than BinarySearch but slower than hashing, on average, is interpolation search. Here, the key idea is that knowledge of the distribution of the entries should allow faster access. In the extreme, knowing the precise index of course yields access in a single probe. However, even if such specific information is not available, often some knowledge about the distribution is available. Note that BinarySearch uses no external information at all, but anyone who has used a dictionary would probably start probing at the beginning of the (single volume) book when looking for a word that starts with a letter at the beginning of the alphabet. This type of knowledge-driven probing is captured by interpolation search, which can attain an access complexity of $O(\log_2(\log_2(n)))$ probes given an ordered set of n entries, *provided* the knowledge is correct.

many as $O(n^2)$ probes. This is extremely unlikely, but this is what worst-case performance is concerned with.

In summary, hashing is an extremely attractive method for inserting and search, if one has a good idea of the number of elements to be accommodated, if one is not very pressed for space (so that the load factor can always be kept below 80%), and if one is exclusively interested in the average performance of inserting and searching.[60]

3.2.13 Graph Algorithms

The last group of algorithms we examine in this chapter deal with *graphs*. While many problems have regular structures and are therefore amenable to data structures that reflect this regularity, many other problems are quite unstructured. For example, while the roads of some cities have a regular checkerboard structure, the interstate highway network is not very regular. This type of structure can be represented by graphs.

A graph G consists of a finite set **V** of *vertices* or *nodes* and a set **E** of *edges*. An edge is a direct link between two nodes. One distinguishes between *directed* and *undirected* graphs. An edge $e \in$ **E** may unidirectional, that is, it goes from a node $u \in$ **V** to a node $v \in$ **V**, or it may be unidirectional. In the first case, we write e = (u,v), and in the second, e = {u,v}. If all edges $e \in$ **E** are unidirectional, the graph G = (**V,E**) is called directed; if all edges $e \in$ E are bidirectional, the graph G = (**V,E**) is undirected. An undirected graph can be viewed as a special case of a directed graph since we can simulate a bidirectional edge {u,v} in the undirected graph by the two unidirectional edges (u,v) and (v,u) in a directed graph with the same set V of nodes.[61] Since directed graphs are the more general concept, we will tacitly assume them from now on. Trees and linear lists, as well as stacks and queues, are all special cases of graphs.

There are two traditional ways of representing a graph G = (**V,E**), namely using *adjacency lists* and using an *incidence matrix*. If we enumerate all the neighbors[62] of a node $u \in$ **V** in a list L_u, then the set of all lists {L_u | $u \in$ V} is the adjacency list representation of G. Similarly, if we create a boolean matrix I_G with a row and a column for each node $u \in$ **V** such that $I_G[u,v]$ = true if and only if (u,v) is an edge, then I_G is the incidence matrix representation of

---

[60] In our example of the road map, a unidirectional edge would correspond to a one-way street, and a bidirectional edge, to a two-way street. A two-way street can be viewed as two one-way streets going in opposite directions, connecting the same locations.

[61] The node $v \in$ V is a neighbor of the node $u \in$ V if (u,v) $\in$ E.

[62] By inherently recursive we mean that an iterative process that achieves the same result must simulate the recursive process (as opposed to techniques that convert the recursion to iteration, such as the method for tail recursion we explained above). More specifically, any equivalent iterative process requires additional space that is proportional to the depth of the recursion of the recursive process. It may appear that the algorithm Depth(G,u) exhibits only tail recursion, but this is not so, because there may be several neighbors of a given node v, and after its first neighbor has been processed, the second must be taken up and so on until the last one has been considered. Therefore, there may be as many recursive calls in the body as there are neighbors of v.

G. It is important to understand the relationship between the number n of nodes and the number m of edges: Since any node u can have an edge to any node v, it follows that $m \leq n^2$. However, since we usually assume that edges (u,u) are not permitted, the relationship is normally given as $m \leq n \cdot (n-1)/2$. Also, we will always assume that our graphs are connected; that is, we assume that **V** cannot be split into two disjoint sets V_1 and V_2 with no edge from any node in one set to any node in the other set. Consequently, there is a lower bound on the number m of edges in terms of n, namely $m \geq n - 1$. For example, linear lists and trees attain this lower bound. The completely connected graph G = (**V**,**E**) with E = {(u ≠ v) | u,v∈ **V** with u = v} attains the upper bound. We summarize:

$$n-1 \leq m \leq n \cdot (n-1)/2.$$

Now it is clear that the space complexities of the two representations may differ; the incidence matrix will always have space n^2 (independent of m), while the adjacency list representation requires only $O(m)$ space. Thus, the adjacency lists will be more space economical than the incidence matrix if there are relatively few edges; however, in the worst case both have a space complexity of $O(n^2)$.

A common question of significant practical importance in graphs is whether we can reach a certain node v when starting in node u. Other questions of interest relate to bandwidth and throughput issues of networks. They lead to a host of related problems, some of which we will examine (and solve) below.

We will mainly consider reachability questions. The first of these asks which nodes can be accessed in one or more steps when starting in a given node u. Two fundamentally different solution methods answer this question, namely depth-first and breadth-first search.

3.2.13.1   Depth-First Search

The idea is to start at u and attempt to go as deep in G as possible by taking the first unvisited neighbor, v, of u and repeating this operation at v. However, in order to reach all possible nodes, we must allow for the same process to take place subsequently at u's second unvisited neighbor, and so on. This is an inherently recursive process that can be formulated as follows:

Let Visited be a boolean array with an entry Visited[v] for each node v∈ V.
Initially, all entries of Visited are false. Set Visited[u] to true.
Depth(G,u)
    For all neighbors v of u with Visited[v]=false do
        { Visited[v]:=true; Depth(G,v) }

When Depth(G,u) returns, the array Visited will record (with Visited[v] = true) all those nodes v (including u) that can be reached from u.

We must now determine the complexity of this algorithm. It is clear that there will never be more than n nodes that will be set to true in the array Visited. However, when checking the neighbors of a given node (already visited), we may have to carry out many more tests than there will be nodes that are to be processed. This is because several of the neighbors may have already been visited, but finding this out still requires work. Thus, in the worst case, we may have to check every *edge* in this process. Since the work for each edge is $O(1)$, it follows that the worst-case time complexity is $O(m)$ — or is it? Here is where the representation has significant impact. While it is true that each edge may have to be examined, finding out what is an edge is not entirely trivial, at least not for the incidence matrix representation. For the adjacency lists, getting the next neighbor (checking the next edge) is easy: Just take the next element in the list of neighbors. This takes $O(1)$ time.

For the incidence matrix representation, however, getting the next neighbor of v involves going through the row $I_G[v,*]$ starting from the last neighbor that we had processed and checking each row element until we get one, say $I_G[v,w]$, that has the value true; this means w is the next neighbor to be checked. The upshot of this is that we will have to traverse the entire row for v in order to find all its neighbors. Since each row in I_G has n elements, this amounts to time $O(n)$. Since we may have up to n nodes v that must be checked in this way, the overall time complexity for the incidence matrix representation is $O(n^2)$, even if there are very few edges. For the adjacency list representation, however, the time complexity is indeed proportional to the number of edges since the next neighbor is directly accessible. Since the space complexity depends on the depth of the recursion, which is equal to the length of the longest path determined by Depth(G,u) starting in u through G, the worst-case space complexity is $O(n)$ since no path can contain more than n nodes (note that any node can occur at most once; Visited[w] is set to true as soon as w is visited).

3.2.13.2 Breadth-First Search

Here we collect all neighbors of u not yet visited in a queue, and for each node in the queue, we again determine all its neighbors and append them to this queue if they have not yet been visited. In this way, we visit each reachable node in the shortest number of steps from u. Here is the algorithm:

```
Breadth(G,u)
Let Visited be a boolean array with an entry Visited[v] for each node v∈ V.
Initially, all entries of Visited are false.
Qu is a queue of nodes to be processed; initially Qu contains only u.

While Qu is nonempty
    {
        Remove the front element v of Qu. Set Visited[v] to true.
        For all neighbors w of v with Visited[w]=false append w to Qu.
    }
```

As with Depth(G,u), when Breadth(G,u) returns, the array Visited will record (with Visited[v] = true) all those nodes v (including u) that can be reached from u.

For the complexity analysis of Breadth(G,u), we first observe that a node v will appear at most once on the queue Qu; thus, the while loop will terminate after no more than n iterations. Then we see that the checking neighbors process is almost identical to that for Depth(G,u), except that here we append to the queue instead of calling the function Depth recursively. The upshot is that the worst-case time complexity of Breadth(G,u) is exactly the same as that for Depth(G,u). If the graph is represented by its incidence matrix I_G, then it is $O(n^2)$; if the graph is represented by its adjacency lists, it is $O(m)$.

The space complexity depends on the size of the queue Qu, which is bounded from above by n. Therefore, the worst-case space complexity of Breadth(G,u) is $O(n)$, regardless of how G is represented.

Note that both Depth(G,u) and Breadth(G,u) return the same array Visited, but the order in which the nodes are visited is very different. While Depth will always have a complete path from u to v in its recursion stack for every node v at the time is sets Visited[v] to true, Breadth only reflects the distance of v from u, but not a path from u to v. Breadth can be modified to record the distance of v from u directly, as follows (–1 indicates that the node has no recorded distance from u):

BreadthDist(G,u)
Let Visited be an integer array with an entry Visited[v] for each node v $\in$ V.
Initially, all entries of Visited are -1.
Qu is a queue of pairs of [node,distance] to be processed;
initially Qu contains only [u,0].

While Qu is nonempty
  {
    Remove the front pair [v,dist] of Qu. Set Visited[v] to dist.
    For all neighbors w of v with Visited[w]=-1 do
      append [w,dist+1] to Qu.
  }

Visited now records for each node v exactly its distance from u, with Visited[w] = –1 indicating that w cannot be reached from u.

The time and space complexities of this modification are the same as those of the original algorithm Breadth.

So far, we have implicitly assumed that all edges are of equal weight. Specifically, when determining the distance, we assumed that each edge has length 1. This may not be very realistic; for example, in the interstate highway network, different pairs of cities correspond to different distances. This leads one to assign to each edge e$\in$ E a *weight W(e)*. Weights should satisfy some properties; in particular, they must be nonnegative. Furthermore, we will assume that the weights on edges induce weights on paths: if $e_1 = (v_0,v_1)$, $e_2 = (v_1,v_2)$, $e_3 = (v_2,v_3)$, ..., $e_s = (v_{s-1},v_s)$ is a path from v_0 to v_s of length s, then the weight of that path is the sum of the weights of its edges:

$$W(e_1, ..., e_s) = W(e_1) + W(e_2) + ... + W(e_s).$$

Since we do not allow self-loops (edges $[v,v]$ for some node $v \in V$), a path ε_v starting in v and consisting of zero edges has a weight $W(\varepsilon_v) = 0$, for all nodes v. Note that cycles may occur in graphs. A path $e_1 = (v_0,v_1)$, $e_2 = (v_1,v_2)$, $e_3 = (v_2,v_3)$, ..., $e_s = (v_{s-1},v_s)$ is a cycle if $v_0 = v_s$. Obviously, the weight of cycles is usually nonzero.[63] Given this setup, we are now interested in finding a path with the minimum weight from a given node u to some node v. We may generalize this somewhat and ask to find the minimum weight of all paths from the node u to all other nodes v. This is known as a *single source problem*, reflecting that u is the only starting node. It can be solved by Dijkstra's algorithm.

3.2.13.3   *Dijkstra's Algorithm*

This turns out to be another representative of dynamic programming (see Section 3.2.3). It computes in the array **WT** for each node v the minimum weight $w(u,v)$ of a path from the single source u to v.

Given: A graph G=(V,E) with weight information W(e) for each edge e.
WT is an array with an entry for each node v. Initially, WT[v]= ∞ for all $v \in V$.
S is a set of nodes, initially empty.

WT[u]:=0
For each neighbor v of u: WT[v]:=W(u,v).
Add u to S.

While S ≠ V do
{
    select from V-S a node w such that WT[w] is minimal and add w to S.
    for each neighbor v of w that is in V-S
        set WT[v] := min{WT[v],WT[w]+W(w,v)}
}

---

[63] Another property one commonly assumes about weights (or distances or cost) is the *triangle inequality*. Given a path from a to b and a path from b to c the weight of the path from a to c should be no greater than the sum of the weights of the paths from a to b and from b to c: $W(a,c) \le W(a,b) + W(b,c)$ for all a, b, and c. This is a very reasonable assumption, which is, however, occasionally violated by the pricing approaches airlines apply when selling tickets. (To the best of my knowledge, this is the only practical scenario in the real world where the triangle inequality is not respected.)

We assume for the purpose of carrying out arithmetic in this algorithm that ∞ is treated as a number larger than any of the numbers occurring. Upon completion, **WT**[v] will contain either a positive number, indicating the actual weight of the path from u to v, or ∞, indicating that no path exists from u to v.

For the complexity analysis, note first that in each iteration of the while loop, one node from **V** is selected and placed in **S**, and no node is placed twice in **S**. Thus, there are $n - 1$ iterations of the while loop. The work inside the while loop is bounded by $O(n)$ time. In the selection of w, **V-S** must be inspected, and **V-S**, although steadily shrinking, is of size $O(n)$ for $O(n)$ number of iterations. The determination of neighbors of w and their processing also requires no more than $O(n)$ time. Therefore, the overall worst-case time complexity is $O(n^2)$. Note that in this algorithm, the representation (incidence matrix or adjacency lists) does not affect the time complexity.

The space complexity is $O(n)$ since we need to maintain the set **S**, which will grow to n elements, and we must calculate the array **WT**, which has n elements. The remaining space requirements are constant. This yields a total space requirement of $O(n)$ (worst case, best case, and average).

3.3   Conclusion

We have provided techniques for determining the complexity of algorithms, both nonrecursive and recursive, and discussed how they apply to specific algorithms. Then we gave a number of important algorithms and derived their complexities. These algorithms included representatives of dynamic programming, namely Dijkstra's algorithm and the algorithm for optimal sequencing matrix multiplications, divide-and-conquer methods, namely the $O(n^{2.81})$ square matrix multiplication method generally attributed to Viktor Strassen, the algorithm for finding the Kth largest element in an unordered set, and QuickSort, and on-line methods, namely searching, inserting, and deleting in search trees and, in particular, in AVL trees. We also discussed three other sorting methods: MergeSort, HeapSort, and RadixSort. Finally, we briefly reviewed hashing, a technique that allows locating elements in ways that are unrelated to any order information, as well as basic graph algorithms.

Bibliographical Notes

The algorithms discussed in this chapter are standard and can be found in standard algorithm textbooks, including those mentioned at the end of

Chapter 1. In particular, interpolation search can be found in Gonnet: *Handbook of Algorithms and Data Structures.*

Exercises

Exercise 1

Consider a recursive algorithm F(n) defined by

```
If n n₀ then do basis case
else
    {...; F(n₁), ...; F(n₂), ...; F(nᵣ),...
    }
```

a. Assume that $n_i = c_i n$ for $i = 1, \ldots, r$ and for all i, $c_i < 1$. What is the worst-case time complexity of F(n)? Formulate your result precisely and prove it.

b. Assume that for some of the i's, $n_i = c_i n$, and for all other i's, $n_i = n - d_i$, where all $c_i < 1$ and all d_i 1. What is the worst-case computational complexity of F(n)? Formulate your result precisely and prove it.

Exercise 2

Assume there are two types of commands:

- Insert(x), where x is a number
- Retrieve(k), where k is a positive integer; this returns the kth-largest of the numbers inserted if there were at least k insertions or otherwise an error indication. Assume that k may vary from command to command.

a. Design data structures that allow efficient implementation of this scenario. Note that repeated insertions of the same number result in this number being present with multiplicity >1.

b. For your data structures, give algorithms for Insert(x) and Retrieve(k).

c. Determine the time complexity (worst case; average under reasonable, stated assumptions) of your algorithms. You may assume that for each Insert command, there will be α Retrieve commands (not necessarily with the same value of k).

Exercise 3

The following questions apply to a (not necessarily balanced) binary search tree.

  a. Insert the following values into an initially empty search tree. Show the search tree after each insertion:

  1 3 2 4 6 5 8 7 10 9 11 12 13 14 15 16

  b. Delete the following elements from the search tree you constructed in (a):

  1 2 3 4 6 8 10

The following questions apply to a balanced binary search tree (AVL tree):

  a. Insert the following values into an initially empty AVL tree. Show the AVL tree after each insertion, indicating precisely the rotations used:

  1 3 2 4 6 5 8 7 10 9 11 12 13 14 15 16

  b. Delete the following elements from the AVL tree you constructed in (a). Be sure you rebalance as needed and show your AVL tree after each deletion, indicating precisely the rotations used:

  1 2 3 4 6 8 10

Exercise 4

  a. For a balanced search tree (AVL tree) of height h, determine the maximal number of rotations for a deletion. Hint: Start with an AVL tree of height h that has the minimal number of nodes; then consider a leaf closest to the root of the tree.

  b. Consider an AVL tree of height h with the least number of nodes. What is the least number of rotations that are required when deleting a leaf of that tree? Describe precisely that leaf whose deletion will achieve this minimum number of rotations. Is this leaf unique?

Exercise 5

For a balanced search tree (AVL tree) containing n elements, determine (in terms of n):

a. The length of a longest path from the root to a leaf.

b. The length of a shortest path from the root to a leaf.

Exercise 6

Assume you are given two matrices **A**, **B** of type $[1:n,1:n]$ and consider the problem of determining whether any element of **A** is an element of **B**.

a. Derive a lower bound for this problem.

b. Design an algorithm for this problem. Derive its time complexity. It should be as close to your lower bound as possible.

Exercise 7

Consider an extension of the problem in Exercise 2. Design an augmented AVL tree structure and specify algorithms with the following characteristics:

Insert(x): In time $O(\log_2(n))$ and space $O(1)$, where n is the number of elements in the structure at this time (i.e., the number of Insert operations minus the number of Delete operations up until now). Repetitions are allowed.

Delete(x): In time $O(\log_2(n))$ and space $O(1)$, where n is the number of elements in the structure at this time (i.e., the number of Insert operations minus the number of Delete operations up until now). If there are several instances of x, Delete(x) deletes one of these instances.

Find(k): In time $O(\log_2(n))$ and space $O(1)$, where n is the number of elements in the structure at this time (i.e., the number of Insert operations minus the number of Delete operations, up until now).

Exercise 8

Suppose that instead of doing the Find(k) operation of Exercise 2, with k an arbitrary positive integer that can vary from one Find to the next, we replace it with FindMedian, which returns the median of all elements that are currently stored in the structure. (Note that FindMedian is the same as

Find $(n/2)$ where n is the number of elements in the structure at this time. However, even though this value changes with insertions and deletions, it is clearly not as arbitrary as the general case.)

Can you devise a data structure and algorithms for

a. Insert(x)

b. Delete(x)

c. FindMedian

that improve over the Find(k) approach discussed in class. (Obviously, that approach will still apply, so we know all three operations can be done in time $O(\log_2(n))$ and space $O(1)$; however, the question to solve is: Can you do better?).

Carefully formulate your data structure, outline the three algorithms in some detail, and determine with care the time and space complexities of your three algorithms.

Exercise 9

Consider QuickSort on the array A[1:n] and assume that the pivot element x (used to split the array A[lo:hi] into two portions such that all elements in the left portion A[lo:m] are x and all elements in the right portion A[m:hi] are x) is the *second* element of the array to be split (i.e., A[lo + 1]). Assume $n = 8$. Assign integers between 0 and 7 to the eight array elements such that QuickSort, with the stated choice of pivot,

    a. Executes *optimally* (A[lo:m] and A[m:hi] are always of equal size)

    b. Executes in the *slowest* possible way

Exercise 10

Consider QuickSort on the array A[1:n] and assume that the pivot element x (used to split the array A[lo:hi] into two portions such that all elements in the left portion A[lo:m] are x and all elements in the right portion A[m:hi] are x) is the *first* element of the array to be split (i.e., A[lo + 1]). Assume $n = 8$. Assign the numbers 0 through 7 to the eight array elements such that QuickSort, with the stated choice of pivot,

    a. Executes *optimally* (A[lo:m] and A[m:hi] are always of equal size)

    b. Executes in the *slowest* possible way

Exercise 11

Consider HeapSort on the array A[1:n].

    a. Construct a heap for the following array of numbers: 1 8 2 5 6 3 4 7 9 10. Show the array after the insertion of each element into the heap.

    b. Use your heap to sort the array. Show the resulting heap after the extraction of each maximum.

Exercise 12

For the following product of rectangular matrices, determine the smallest number of multiplications required to carry out this product:

a. $M_{2,4}*M_{4,3}*M_{3,1}*M_{1,4}*M_{4,7}$

b. $M_{3,2}*M_{2,4}*M_{4,3}*M_{3,1}*M_{1,4}*M_{4,7}$

Part 2

The Software Side: Disappointments and How to Avoid Them

The second part of this book presents and examines the view of the programmer.

Software development tends to be dominated by software engineering aspects. However, there are somewhat lower-level details that often conspire against the programmer and her desire to produce efficient code. These details frequently occur at the interfaces between the various steps involved in software development. Here, our emphasis is on the transition between algorithms and their implementation.

To begin with, we firmly believe in the maxim "Don't reinvent the wheel; use a canned algorithm." This is the main reason we do not spend much time on the correctness of the algorithms in Chapter 3; we only provide some key insights that should hint at how correctness would be established. However, the complexity analysis is given because that is the way to decide which algorithm to use. If we have several correct, canned algorithms, it is imperative that we have tools to help us decide which of them to use. However, the term *use* requires some examination. When determining which algorithm to select, it is crucial to take into consideration not just the algorithm, but also its implementation together with constraints that are imposed by the target platform, the programming language to be used, and perhaps other considerations. In other words, we must be able to obtain a reasonable measure of the performance of the implementation if this selection is to have practical value.

If there were no problems in the transition from algorithm to software, there would be no need for this book. However, most practitioners are painfully aware of many instances where their performance expectations raised by algorithm analysis were seriously disappointed. To a large extent, this has discredited the study of algorithms in the eyes of many software developers. A primary objective of this book is to establish techniques and tools that help in overcoming this view. Our basic premise is that algorithm analysis has much to offer to programmers, provided they know how to use it.

To this end, we begin by listing the sources of disappointments that regularly arise when implementing algorithms in Chapter 4. While we must devote some attention to the question of correctness, we mainly consider it to the extent it may be affected by issues that affect performance even more. In other words, the algorithm is assumed to be correct, and we look only at things that can go wrong when translating it into code. We are much more interested in the question of why discrepancies can occur, some of them quite serious, between the theoretically derived performance of an algorithm and the observed performance of its seemingly faithful implementation. We also comment on possible sources of unpredictability — recognizing that unpredictability is unusual and often hides a lack of understanding of actions that are consequences of the interaction of the algorithm with the run-time support system and other intermediate agents that are of no concern for the algorithm analysis but may have a significant deleterious impact on the overall performance of the resulting code. Finally, we make a brief detour into the world of infeasibility and undecidability, concepts that are firmly rooted in complexity theory but may occasionally affect problems in the real world.

Many disappointments have their roots in the nonuniformity of memory accesses. In Chapter 5 we examine in considerable detail the surprisingly unpleasant consequences of this lack of uniformity; the problem lies in the fact that algorithms are developed assuming complete uniformity of memory accesses, while real memory systems consist of (frequently quite complicated) memory hierarchies. The implications of this difference are occasionally staggering, frequently nasty, and usually unexpected. One unwelcome but fundamental consequence is that the performance of a piece of software does not depend solely on the underlying algorithm; instead, it is frequently indispensable to have a firm grasp of the target platform's architecture, the system software involved, and the interplay between these three diverse actors. For example, generations of programmers have been raised in the belief that programs written in a higher-level programming language are portable. This usually tends to be true when it comes to correctness (it is very rare that a program written in a standard programming language that behaves correctly when executed on platform A will produce wrong results on a platform B that has equivalent system software), but it is distressingly often disproved when it comes to performance. The same program may run dramatically slower on platform B than it ran on platform A, even when ostensible differences in raw performance between the two platforms are taken into consideration.[1] This is quite impossible for an algorithm; essentially, the only architectural influence one might consider is the amount of time one assumes an *average* statement will take. However, it is extremely misguided to expect this type of hardware independence when the algorithm is implemented.

These and related topics are studied in Chapter 6, which is devoted to an examination of the influence of compiler and run-time support issues on the performance of a program. The difficulty usually lies in the fact that things cannot be studied in isolation; it is almost always the interplay of several agents that causes unexpected effects. Specifically, we will look at the importance of understanding memory mappings, passing parameters, and the effect of recursion on space complexity and examine some surprising consequences. We also explore the realm of dynamic structures, which are intimately related to the administration of a program's memory and to garbage collection (which is frequently a source of apparently unpredictably behavior). We consider issues related to optimization as it is carried out by high-performance compilers — ostensibly with the objective of producing the most efficient code possible but sometimes interfering with other components of the run-time environment and thereby producing code that effectively runs slower than unoptimized code. Finally, we take a look at language properties and their influence on performance. Many of these issues tend to be very subtle and are often ignored, but occasionally they are responsible for effects that are neither expected nor easily explained. We conclude this chapter with a few brief comments on the influence of parallelism, recognizing that in most modern processing systems, parallel processes are executed that the programmer is not aware of and has no influence over.

In Chapter 7 we focus on implicit assumptions. Algorithms are usually formulated assuming a rather forgiving approach; for example, one tends not to worry about exception handling and one may merely state certain assumptions under which the algorithm functions correctly. In a program, however, we must consider what to do when an exception is thrown. Also, if a specific assumption is necessary for the program to work properly, it is mandatory that this assumption be tested for. Both the code for the exception handling and the test of assumptions may have unpleasant implications for the program's performance. Moreover, alternative code must be provided if

---

[1] It is in the nature of human behavior that people rarely complain about the opposite: when the program executes much faster on platform B than on platform A. However, once one has accounted for the differences in raw execution speed and the program is still much faster on B than on A, the programmer should now ask why the program performed so poorly on A — instead of being happy about the performance improvement.

the test fails; otherwise the program might crash — a result that is unacceptable to most users.

Chapter 8 is concerned with consequences of the finiteness of number representation. While algorithm design does pay some attention to this issue (it is after all the chief motivation for the distinction between the word and bit complexities of algorithms), the consequences for software are distinct and deserve some review.

In Chapter 9 we return to the asymptotic nature of algorithms and weave it into the question of how to select an algorithm. We are mainly concerned with practical aspects and pay particular attention to the issue of crossover points; these are crucial in selecting algorithms whose implementation yields good performance.

Finally, in Chapter 10 we examine the implications of undecidability from a practical point of view: What can be done if a problem we want to solve is such that algorithmic theory tells us that it cannot be solved. In many cases this is the consequence of undue generalization rather than a futile attempt to square the circle. We also look at a related question, namely what to do when the time complexity of the algorithm is prohibitively large. Here, the issue is frequently the gap between the worst-case and the average time complexity, specifically, the question of what is average in a specific context. Also, we look at heuristics, which can be very helpful in obtaining efficient solutions for some problems with unmanageable complexity.

4

Sources of Disappointments

About This Chapter

We enumerate a litany of the most important woes that may befall a hapless programmer when transitioning from an algorithm to software. These woes include software that produces incorrect results, software whose performance differs significantly from that suggested by algorithm analysis, general unpredictability of performance, and problems related to undecidability and intractability.

Our starting point in this chapter is a correct algorithm for a specific problem whose complexity has been properly analyzed. We explore possible pitfalls that might occur in the translation of the algorithm into an executable program. We concentrate on explaining the problems; for the most part, solutions are addressed later. Thus, we focus on observed problems, one might say symptoms, and defer the comprehensive treatment of the underlying causes to subsequent chapters.

4.1 Incorrect Software

Given that we start with a correct algorithm, how is it possible to end up with wrong software, in spite of a careful translation of the abstract formulation into a concrete program? The most common explanation is that the programmer made some careless mistake, but even absent such careless mistakes, incorrect programs occur much more often than one would expect.

For the most part, the reason is that algorithms specify far less detail than is required for a competent implementation of a program. Here is a short list of contributing factors that conspire against the unwary programmer.

Exception handling: Algorithms do not concern themselves with minor details such as division by 0 or the lack of initialization of a variable. In this way algorithms can concentrate on the essentials and need not worry about being buried in extraneous details. However, software must address all these details adequately, and if it does not, incorrect code results.

Rounding errors: Most programmers view the issue of rounding errors as one exclusively related to numerical methods but sometimes non-numerical algorithms subtly involve the representation of numbers. A surprisingly difficult issue is testing for equality. In an algorithm, a test of whether two values are equal requires no further comment; in a program it may not be as obvious. If the two values are the result of floating point operations in a program, a test for equality may require a more elaborate condition than merely asking whether the two values are identical. For example, the test of whether the square of the square root of 2 is equal to 2, $\sqrt{2} \cdot \sqrt{2} = 2$, may fail in some programs (algorithmically, it is of course always true). Similarly, the mathematically *divergent* sum $1/2 + 1/3 + 1/4 + 1/5 + \ldots$ *converges* to a fixed constant in virtually all computer platforms.[1] In these situations algorithms tend to presuppose the mathematical interpretation, while programs typically behave according to the rules dictated by the finite representation of the numbers involved and the specific implementation of the arithmetic operations. The gap between these two approaches can result in software that does not produce the results promised by the algorithm; in practical terms, wrong software is obtained.

Stability: This concept is for the most part directly related to numerical aspects of computations. Some algorithms solve problems but are unsuitable to be implemented in code. Almost invariably this is due to the finite length of the numbers involved in the computations.

Passing parameters: Algorithms typically do not specify the interface between the calling program and the algorithm itself. This implies in particular that the question of how to pass the arguments is not addressed adequately in the abstract (algorithmic) formulation. Thus, what starts as an algorithm must now be encapsulated as a procedure or function, and this procedure or function must receive the arguments as parameters. The communication of these arguments to the function is known as parameter passing. There are several, fundamentally different, ways of passing parameters, and it is crucial to understand these methods, since using the wrong method of passing parameters to a function may result in code that produces completely wrong results.

---

[1] Even worse, that *constant* number may vary from platform to platform, since it depends on the specific type of arithmetic that a processor implements and the word length of the representation of the numbers (of both the fractions and the sum).

Implicit assumptions: Occasionally, in designing an algorithm we make very reasonable assumptions, which nevertheless may be violated by the resulting program under some circumstances. These tend to be quite subtle, but subtlety is cold comfort if the program turns out to be malfunctioning. An example might be the assumption that a sorting algorithm would not change the order of the elements of an array if that array was already sorted. This seems to be a truism, except that we did not consider that there could be duplicates in the array. (While search trees and hashing do not permit duplicates, there is nothing wrong in sorting an array with duplicate elements.) A sorting method considers only the keys that are to be sorted, and sorting algorithms may interchange the order of identical elements, but in many applications the key is just an entry point for the access to other information.[2] If a change in the original position of identical elements is undesirable, this would have to be stated explicitly, but this requirement may have been overlooked.

While it is somewhat unusual for the code derived from a correct algorithm to fail to produce the expected results, it occurs more often than desirable. Note that our discussion deals exclusively with sequential algorithms; parallel algorithms are much more likely to give rise to incorrect parallel programs, for a variety of reasons directly related to the parallel nature of the software.[3]

4.2 Performance Discrepancies

Discrepancies between the performance suggested by the analysis of the algorithm and the observed performance of the code obtained by translating the algorithm faithfully are much more common than outright wrong results. Occasionally, the reasons are similar. For example, choosing an inappropriate way of passing parameters may seriously affect the performance of the resulting program. A particularly egregious instance is provided by binary search, where the wrong parameter-passing mechanism can slow performance exponentially. Much more common causes are the memory hierarchy of modern computing architectures and the support systems (compilers,

---

[2] Sorting methods that guarantee that they will not interchange the order of identical elements are called *stable* sorting algorithms. The fact that a name was coined to differentiate them from those that might swap such elements indicates that this aspect is more important in applications than one might suspect if one focuses only on the sorting method itself.

[3] One of the most insidious problems of parallel and distributed software is so-called race conditions whereby two processes compete for some resource (e.g., access to memory, communication links, input/out (I/O) controllers). Sometimes one wins, and at other times the other wins, even though the starting configurations of the two instances are seemingly identical.

operating systems, run-time execution systems) that heavily influence how efficiently a program executes.

We have already hinted at the evil influence of virtual memory management (VMM); similar but less dramatic observations hold for caches. We have more to say about this in Chapter 5. The major problem is that VMM interacts fairly subtly with other aspects of a program. For example, consider the problem of adding two matrices:

$$C := A + B,$$

where **A**, **B**, and **C** are matrices of type [1:n,1:n], for n a number large enough that the matrix addition cannot be carried out in main memory (in-core). For the algorithm, this formulation would be fully sufficient; for a program, we need to specify a good deal more. A typical program fragment might look like this:

```
for i:=1 to n do
  for j:=1 to n do
    C[i,j] := A[i,j] + B[i,j]
```

Since main memory is one-dimensional, the two-dimensional arrays **A**, **B**, and **C** must be mapped into main memory. There are two standard mapping functions for this purpose: row-major and column-major, as we explained in Section 2.2. Since in this scenario we do not have enough main memory to accommodate the three matrices, the mapping function will map each array into the logical memory space, which in turn is divided into blocks. It is these blocks (pages) that are fetched from disk and stored to disk by VMM. To make this more concrete, let us assume that $n = 2^{13}$, that the size of a page is 2^{11} (words), and that our available main memory permits us to have 2^{10} pages in main memory. If the memory-mapping function is row-major, each row consists of four pages; if it is column-major, each column consists of four pages. Since the total amount of space required for the three matrices is about $3 \cdot 2^{26}$, but only 2^{10} pages are available, VMM will swap pages in and out of main memory as dictated by the code above.

Here is the first problem: Most programmers are not aware of the memory-mapping function used.[4] Therefore, they are unable to determine how many pages this very simple program fragment will swap in and out. The second problem is that most programmers are not particularly keen on understanding VMM.[5] For our explanations, we assume that the replacement policy is

---

[4] A rule of thumb is the following: A language directly based on Fortran uses column-major; all other languages use row-major memory mapping. However, it is always a good idea to make sure of this. Many programming languages do not specify which mapping function is to be used by the compiler, so this becomes a property of the compiler (thereby driving yet another nail into the coffin of portability).

[5] Indeed, for many programmers, the most important aspect of VMM is that it permits them to ignore I/O problems.

pure LRU (least recently used); this means the page that has been unused for the longest time will be the next to be swapped out if the need arises to bring in a page when all available memory space is occupied. Most common operating systems that support VMM implement some version of LRU.[6] [7]

An even greater problem is that most programmers believe all this information is of no relevance to writing good code. They would be correct if the three matrices fit into main memory.[8] However, they do not, and the difference between the numbers of pages swapped for one and for the other mapping function is staggering. Specifically, if the memory-mapping function is row-major, $3 \cdot 2^{15}$ pages are swapped in and out, but if it is column-major, it is $3 \cdot 2^{26}$ pages. In other words, one version swaps fewer than 100,000 pages, and the other swaps over 200 million. Thus, it is safe to assume that one version is about 2,000 times slower than the other. To be even more drastic, if the faster version takes 15 minutes to execute,[9] the slower would take about 3 weeks. Yet, from an algorithmic point of view, the two versions have identical performance.

Note that for an in-core version, nothing ugly would happen, regardless of which mapping strategy is used. It is only once VMM comes into play that all hell breaks lose.

It is instructive to determine an approximate running time for the in-core version (which is the algorithm, for all practical purposes). There are 2^{26} elements in each matrix; thus, the grand total of required memory for all three matrices is a bit over 200 million words (800 Mbytes, assuming one word has four bytes). There are about 67 million additions and 67 million assignments. It is probably quite conservative to assume that each of the 67 million elements of the matrix **C** can be computed in 50 nsec on a reasonably modern (circa 2005) processor assuming all elements reside in main memory.[10] Consequently, an in-core version might take about 3,356,000,000 nsec, or not even four seconds, for the computation. In practice, it will take much longer, since presumably even in an in-core version, the matrices **A** and **B**

---

[6] Not all operating systems support VMM; for example, Cray supercomputers have never provided VMM, for precisely the performance issues that we explain here.

[7] Typically, LRU is not implemented exactly, since this would require a good deal of space to store the age of each page. Instead, variants are preferred that use less space to provide information that approximates the age of a page.

[8] Because of the random access property of main memory, the performance of this code fragment would be independent of the memory-mapping function, provided all matrices are in main memory, that is, if the problem were in-core. Note that we are again ignoring complications caused by the use of caches.

[9] This is actually pushing it. It takes typically more than 10 msec to retrieve a page, so in 15 minutes fewer than 90,000 pages can be retrieved, assuming that nothing else happens.

[10] This is very conservative because we do not assume overlapping of computations or pipelining. Assume a clock cycle of 2 nsec (also conservative). Each of the two operands must be retrieved (we ignore the address calculation and concentrate on retrieving contiguous elements for main memory); we assume five clock cycles for each. The same holds for storing the result back. We will assume that the operation itself requires 10 clock cycles. The grand total comes to 25 clock cycles, or 50 nsec. Pipelining can result in a significant time reduction, since after an initial start-up period (priming the pipeline), it could churn out a result every clock cycle.

initially reside on disk and must first be fetched; similarly, the resulting matrix **C** most likely must be written to disk. These operations take significantly more time. Retrieving from or writing to disk one page takes more than 10 msec (that is, 10,000,000 nsec); since there are about 100,000 such page operations, this will take about 17 minutes.

We now have four scenarios with three very different timings:

1. 3 sec (in-core; for the computation alone, assuming **A** and **B** are in main memory and **C** stays there)
2. 17 minutes (in-core; assuming **A** and **B** must be fetched from disk and **C** must be written to disk)
3. 17 minutes (out-of-core; assuming **A** and **B** must be fetched from disk and **C** must be written to disk and assuming the memory-mapping function is row-major)
4. 3 weeks (out-of-core; assuming **A** and **B** must be fetched from disk and **C** must be written to disk and assuming the memory-mapping function is column-major)

Note that the fastest timing and the slowest timing are almost seven orders of magnitude apart. Algorithmic time complexity would suggest the fastest timing (computation of 67 million elements, each taking about 50 nsec), while actual observation might provide us with the slowest timing, namely 3 weeks.

In practice, no sane programmer would let a program execute for weeks if the running time predicted on the basis of the algorithm was a few seconds.[11] Instead, the programmer would assume after a while that something went wrong and abort execution. Thus, there might even be the possible interpretation that the code is wrong, so this issue could be listed in Section 4.1 as well.

We will see in the next chapter that some techniques permit a programmer to avoid such problems. It is fairly easy to change the code in such a way that the worst-case behavior above (out-of-core; **A** and **B** must be fetched from disk and **C** must be written to disk, and the memory-mapping function is column-major) can be avoided. More intriguingly yet, using optimization techniques as they are available to any good optimizing compiler, such code changes could even be done automatically.

The fundamental issue in this situation is the truly incomprehensible vastness of the gap between the time needed to access an item main memory or from disk. It takes a few nanoseconds to access an item in main memory, but it takes more than 10 msec to access this item on disk.[12] This gap is almost

---

[11] It is not even clear whether the system would stay up that long.

[12] I know of nothing in the physical world that comes even close to such a discrepancy. To wit, consider transportation: The slowest common way to get from A to B is probably walking, the fastest using a jet airplane. Yet the jet is only about 200 times faster than walking, or less than three orders of magnitude.

seven orders of magnitude. It clearly places a premium on keeping things local.

4.3 Unpredictability

Computational complexity is an important tool for predicting the resource demands of an algorithm and, by extension, of a program based on that algorithm. It is therefore disconcerting when the predictions obtained by analyzing the underlying algorithm are not borne out by the execution of the resulting software. This is particularly annoying if the observed performance of the software changes seemingly randomly from one run to the next, even though the input data are similar (or even identical).

Here is an illustration. We have developed an algorithm to solve a given problem. This algorithm has a certain time complexity $f(n)$ where n is the size of the input. Translating this algorithm into code results in a program that is being executed repeatedly with very similar data sets. When measuring the run time of the program, we find that even for identical input set sizes, very different timings are observed. Moreover, nothing in the time complexity analysis of the algorithm indicated that the range of $f(n)$ for a given value of n should be more than minimal. How can this discrepancy between time complexity and run time behavior be explained?

The issues of nonuniform memory access outlined in the previous section could be in play. However, if the amount of main memory available exceeds the space complexity of the algorithm and if the program is a reasonably faithful implementation of the algorithm, such issues do not explain how different runs of a program with identical memory requirements could have differing execution times. Instead, the culprit could be the management of dynamic data structures.

Many algorithms assume the availability of data structures that are used in the process of producing the desired result but have no further significance. For example, in MergeSort, we need an additional array to store intermediate results (consisting of sequences of sorted subarrays that are then to be merged to create larger sorted subarrays). This additional array is required by MergeSort during the process of sorting but can be discarded once sorting is completed. Similarly, when deleting an element from a binary search tree, the action of discarding a node is carried out by disconnecting the node from the tree, thereby making that node inaccessible. In both cases at some point memory is freed up; this means this memory can be used subsequently for other purposes. Thus, it should be clear that the space complexity of sorting m arrays of size n using MergeSort is $O(n)$ and not $O(m \cdot n)$. The intermediate array needed for the first sort can be reused in the next sort and so on. Similarly, a search tree with n nodes may be the result of many different insertions and deletions, say n_{ins} insertions and n_{del} deletions with $n = n_{ins} - n_{del}$. However, the space complexity of representing this search tree is always assumed to be $O(n)$, and not $O(n_{ins})$. Thus, the complexity analysis of the algorithm implicitly assumes an idealized world in which space that is no longer needed is automatically thrown back into a pool of available space, without anybody having to attend to this action.[13]

When transitioning from algorithm to software, an explicit mechanism must exist that allows the reuse of memory once it is freed. The invocation of such a mechanism may be imposed on the programmer or it may be automatic. Some programming languages require the programmer to attend explicitly to the freeing (deallocating, releasing) of freed-up memory and provide statements for this purpose; these statements for freeing memory are viewed as paired up with the statements that allocated the memory for the dynamic data structures earlier in the program execution. In particular, in this programming setting it is expected that the programmer provide statements that free no-longer-needed space. Other programming languages assume that the collection of freed-up space is carried out automatically by a process known as garbage collection.

In both cases unpredictability may result. Consider first the situation where the programmer must free memory explicitly. It is true that at the end of executing a program, all space allocated to that program is freed. This may suggest to a programmer that the tedious business of explicitly freeing memory during execution is not necessary. Alternatively, an inexperienced programmer may not even be aware of the need to write statements to free memory.[14] If this occurs in a programming environment where a fixed amount of memory space is allotted to a program, then exceeding that space would crash the program. This is not very likely to happen, since many computer systems provide virtual memory management. Thus, if the amount of freed space is not excessive, it is possible that VMM avoids crashing the program. However, as we pointed out above, VMM can seriously slow down the execution of a program, with the outcome that seemingly highly similar input sets result in vastly different paging requirements for VMM. Consequently, the timings can differ greatly as well.

Consider now the case where garbage collection is carried out automatically by the run-time support system. In this scenario it is the garbage collection system that decides autonomously when to do garbage collection. It is now not very difficult to see how unpredictability can arise. We simply do not know when garbage collection is carried out. Note that the process can be time consuming (it may involve fairly complex algorithms, depending on the nature of the data structures involved in freeing memory); moreover, it may interact with other processes running on the same system that have

---

[13] Note that, in contrast to many programming languages, algorithms do not stipulate that discarded memory be explicitly put back for later reuse. Since memory in the algorithm paradigm is unlimited, such an action would be unnecessary and perhaps even confusing.

[14] There are even some compilers (of Pascal) that ignore statements for deallocation of space. This is adding insult to injury — the programmer stipulates explicitly that the memory must be freed but the compiler blithely ignores these statements.

nothing to do with our program. Thus, even if our program executions are identical in instructions and input, the system configuration may differ from one run to the next, implying that garbage collection may not occur at the same times or with the same frequency.

Finally, dynamic memory allocation can happen even if the programmer thinks that no dynamic structures are created in the program. The problem is that *every* call to a recursive function involves a dynamic recursion stack. Thus, unless the program terminates abnormally, every program containing recursive function calls must deal with freeing memory. Since the deallocation of this memory is outside of the programmer's influence, freeing recursion stack memory must be done automatically. Since the size of the recursion stack is often unpredictable (consider search trees, for example, where we can bound from above the size of the stack, but the actual size depends on the specific tree), whether or not garbage collection in this context is carried out, and how often, may be unpredictable.

4.4 Infeasibility and Impossibility

The last topic we mention in our litany of woes is fundamentally different from the previous three, but usually a disappointment nevertheless. This is the case when the theory of algorithms tells us that a certain problem does not have a solution; the problem is unsolvable or undecidable. Alternatively, there may be a solution, but its time complexity is so large that it is unrealistic to expect a solution; the problem is intractable. This situation is quite similar to the physicist who is told that the integral she wishes to solve is indefinite (has no finite solution), even though the integral's solution should exist since the underlying problem has a solution. In the same vein, the programmer feels typically quite strongly that the problem she wishes to solve is a reasonable one, in fact one that arose in the context of an eminently sensible problem setting. We contend that in some cases the difficulty is not the problem itself, but a seemingly sensible generalization of the problem at hand. Reverting to the original problem or restricting it to the cases one is really interested in frequently allows one to circumvent the problems of undecidability and infeasibility.

A typical example is provided by compilers.[15] When designing a compiler for a programming language, one invariably starts with a formal description of that language. This formal definition is almost always based on a context-free grammar, a precise formalism for specifying language constructs and how they relate to each other within a valid program. In essence, a context-free grammar specifies all valid programs in this programming language. It

---

[15] Another example of an undecidable problem is provided by the question of whether a given program contains an infinite loop.

turns out that different context-free grammars can define the same language. If two grammars generate the same language, they are called equivalent. It is important to note that certain types of context-free grammars are more convenient for constructing a compiler (especially the parsing phase of the compiler) than others. Therefore, it is quite sensible to change the original context-free grammar into one more amenable for the purpose of parsing it; this new grammar must generate the exact same programming language.

Ordinarily, when going from one grammar to another, certain rules are applied that have the property that the resulting grammar is equivalent to the original one. However, one might wish to be able to verify separately that the two grammars do indeed generate the same language. Thus, instead of verifying the equivalence of transformation rules, one might come up with the idea of writing a program that accepts as input the two context-free grammars and determines whether they are equivalent. Since it appears to be easier to solve this problem in general, the designer of the program might decide to refrain from imposing restrictions on the two grammars. This is where things go badly wrong: It is known that such a program cannot exist. More specifically, the problem of determining whether two arbitrary context-free grammars are equivalent is undecidable. Undecidability means one can prove with mathematical rigor that no algorithm for the problem at hand can exist, now or ever. This is surprising in the context of our grammar problem, but the root cause is the undue generalization of the problem. Had we restricted our attention to grammars that were similar to the original (that is, were obtained in some transformational way from it), the problem would most likely have been solvable. It is the decision to consider two arbitrary context-free grammars as input that rendered the problem undecidable. In other words, in most cases it is possible to define interesting subcases of the given problem that do have solutions.

Another aspect of impossibility is extremely large time complexity.[16] While this is not as dire as undecidability (which says we cannot fully solve the problem under any circumstances), from a practical point of view, it can be equally devastating. Generally, one assumes that algorithms with a time complexity greater than $O(n^c)$ are infeasible, for c some fixed constant and n the size of the input set (such algorithms are said to have a *polynomial* time complexity). In most cases the constant c should be relatively small. Clearly, algorithms with complexities that are not polynomial are practical only for relatively small values of n. So what is a programmer to do when faced with the problem of implementing an algorithm with a prohibitively high time complexity?

In many cases the programmer focuses on the worst-case time complexity. While the worst-case complexity is an appropriate measure if one is inter-

---

[16] Extremely large space complexity would also be a concern, but as we pointed out earlier, it makes little sense to have an algorithm in which the time complexity is smaller than the space complexity. Therefore, an algorithm with an extremely large space complexity most likely has also an even larger time complexity. (It is true that the example of BinarySearch discussed in Section 6.4 contradicts this assertion, but in this case, the program is in error.)

ested in an upper bound, in practical situations the average complexity may be much more sensible (unless we are dealing with a hard real-time application, such as the control of a nuclear power reactor or air-traffic control). We have already seen that some algorithms have substantial gaps between the worst-case and the average complexity, for example finding the *k*th largest element in an unordered array (Section 3.2.9) and QuickSort (Section 3.2.5). One major difficulty is in determining what is *average* (we commented on this in Section 1.3). Nevertheless, it is well known that certain algorithms are *usually* quite fast, even though they have a miserable worst-case time complexity.

Probably the most celebrated algorithm with an astonishingly large gap between the worst-case and the average time complexity is the simplex algorithm for linear programming.[17] This algorithm is known to have an extremely bad worst-case time complexity: there exist input sets for which the algorithm requires *exponential* time. Yet for almost all practical problems it runs in *linear* time. Most interestingly, there are other algorithms for solving linear programming problems that have a polynomial time complexity, but their average time complexity tends to be slower than that of the simplex method. Therefore, the simplex method is still the most widely used algorithm for solving linear programming problems.

The upshot of this discussion is that the worst-case time complexity may be the wrong way of looking at an algorithm when implementing it as software. It may be far more reasonable to determine the practically significant cases to which the program is to be applied and then to determine what the average time complexity is for these cases.

4.5   Conclusion

In preparation for a systematic treatment of the major disappointments programmers are likely to encounter when translating algorithms into software, we outlined the more important sources of these disappointments. Even though we assume that the starting point of our discussion, the algorithm, is correct, we indicated several ways in which one might still end up with an incorrect program. We then zeroed in on performance, in particular, factors that can cause a major discrepancy between the complexity that the analysis of the algorithm supplied and the observed performance of the resulting program. Related to this is the issue of unpredictability, specifically

---

[17] In linear programming we are to minimize (or maximize) a quantity subject to certain constraints where both the quantity and the constraints must be linear functions of the n variables $x_1, ..., x_n$. For given constants a_{ij}, b_i, and c_i, minimize the linear function $c_1 x_1 + ... + c_n x_n$ subject to the linear constraints $a_{i1} x_1 + ... + a_{in} x_n \le b_i$ for all $i = 1, ..., m$. Many practically important problems can be formulated as linear programming problems. As a result, a vast body of knowledge as well as algorithms focus on these problems.

of performance, whereby seemingly identical program executions may display substantial performance differences. Finally, we addressed issues related to impossibility, either provable impossibility, also known as undecidability, or practical impossibility, namely, where the time complexity is large enough to be essentially prohibitive for practical consumption. All these problems will be revisited in subsequent chapters, where we present a systematic coverage of aspects of computing systems that underlie, and consequently explain, these and similar problems.

Bibliographical Notes

Collecting references for the material on which this chapter is based provides an excellent indication why software practitioners find it difficult to understand how algorithms fail to translate properly into software. There are many diverse topics that come to bear on this issue. Moreover, these topics tend to be taught in different courses and are covered by different textbooks, making it even more difficult for the interested software designer to understand all the ramifications for effective programming. Apart from the obvious, namely diverse programming languages and algorithm analysis, the areas implicated are numerical analysis, programming language design, compiler design, and operating systems. While it is not necessary to be on the forefront of research in each of these areas, it is important to have a reasonable understanding and working knowledge of all of them.

Exception handling is covered by the language manual of the programming language employed. Rounding errors, stability, and other aspects of numerical errors analysis and propagation are comprehensively covered in standard textbooks on numerical analysis and methods, for example Higham: *Accuracy and Stability of Numerical Algorithms*; see also the paper by Goldberg, entitled "What Every Computer Scientist Should Know about Floating-Point Arithmetic". Methods for passing parameters as well as memory mappings are traditionally covered in three quite different places: in the language manual of the programming language employed (but this tends to be cursory and only focused on that language), in comparative programming language books, and, perhaps most detailed, in standard compiler text books (for example Aho, Sethi, and Ullman: *Compilers: Principles, Techniques and Tools*), since it is the compiler that has to grapple with the implementation of the various mechanisms stipulated by a programming language. Virtual memory management is part of the coverage of operating systems. We refer to standard textbooks on this topic, for example, Silberschatz, Gavin, and Gagne: *Operating Systems Concepts*. The same applies to garbage collection, which is usually part of operating or runtime support systems. Undecidability and intractability are part of the general algorithm repertoire that is covered in textbooks on the design and analysis of algorithms, for example Kleinberg and Tardos: *Algorithm Design,* and textbooks on formal language theory, for example, Hopcroft and Ullman: *Introduction to Automata Theory.* Additional references will be given in the chapters covering these issues in more detail.

Exercises

Exercise 1

Determine which of the sorting algorithms covered in Chapter 3 are stable.

Exercise 2

Verify, using 16-, 32-, and 64-bit words, using your favorite computer (under some operating system) and your favorite programming language,[18] that the product of the floating point (real) numbers 1.0/3.0 and 3.0 is not equal to 1.0.

Exercise 3

Write a program, using your favorite computer (under some operating system supporting VMM) and your favorite programming language, that demonstrates that the timings of matrix addition differ substantially for large enough matrices, depending whether you use Version 1 or Version 2:

```
for i:=1 to n do            for j:=1 to n do
  for j:=1 to n do            for i:=1 to n do
    C[i,j]:=A[i,j]+B[i,j]       C[i,j]:=A[i,j]+B[i,j]
  Version 1                   Version 2
```

Choose a sequence of values for n, say 128, 256, 512, 1024, 2048, 4096, 8192, 16384, 32768, and 65536, and study the timings of both versions. (Be aware that some runs may take longer than you are willing, or able, to wait.) Keep in mind that the two versions should have the same timings, and doubling the value of n should result in a quadrupling of time spent to do the addition, assuming everything is done in core (which is of course not the case, since the last value corresponds to a memory requirement of almost 50 Gigabytes, assuming four bytes per word). Note that you must initialize your matrices **A** and **B**, but the time required for this should not be part of the measurements.

---

[18] Some programming languages, notably COBOL and PL/1, use an internal decimal representation of numbers; for them, the result would indeed be 1.0. However, most modern programming languages, such as C or Java, use an internal binary representation, in which case the result of the product will not be 1.0.

Exercise 4

Discuss in detail how the parameters must be passed so that the recursive functions for insertion and deletion in AVL trees are correct.

Exercise 5

Study the run-time environment of your favorite programming language on your favorite computing platform and determine how freed-up space is recaptured for subsequent use.

Exercise 6

Conduct the following experiment that should provide some information about the use of garbage collection on your computing platform. Implement insertion and deletion for AVL trees, but instead of having as the content I(N) of the node N a single integer *val*, let it consist of *val* (to govern the insertion into its appropriate location in the search tree) plus a large matrix of size M. Choose M as follows: If *val* = 0 mod 3, then $M = 2^{18}$; if *val* = 1 mod 3, then $M = 2^{17} + 2^5$; if *val* = 2 mod 3, then $M = 2^{16} + 2^7$ (these values should guarantee that fragmentation of the available memory will occur rapidly). Now randomly choose a large number, perhaps 1,000 or 10,000, of values between 0 and 299 for insertion and deletion, making sure that the tree never contains more than 50 nodes. (If your compiler is very clever, it may be necessary to assign values to some of the array elements to ensure that the compiler is unable to conclude that the array is not needed since it is never used.) Measure the time each of the insertions and deletions takes. Since your tree never has more than 50 nodes, its height cannot exceed 6 (since an AVL tree of height 7 must have at least 54 nodes); consequently, the complexity of the insertion and deletion operations is small. However, the repeated insertions and deletions, together with the size of the matrices in the nodes created, should result in extensive memory fragmentation, which in turn should engage garbage collection and, subsequently, memory compaction in a major way.

—

5

Implications of Nonuniform Memory for Software

About This Chapter

The memory model assumed for the complexity analysis of algorithms is highly unrealistic for software development. We outline the differences and discuss their implications for software. The primary villain is virtual memory management, which relies extensively on disks, but a secondary one is the ubiquitous use of caches in most modern computing systems. We then address techniques that help in avoiding bad performance of programs whose data structures cannot be accommodated in their entirety in the available memory. This requires an extensive understanding of the memory hierarchy in modern computers and the implications for the development of out-of-core programs.

In Part 1 we described the properties of the memory space assumed for the complexity analysis algorithms are subjected to. The key feature is its uniformity: All available memory is assumed to have the random access property (RAM). While this greatly simplifies the complexity analysis of algorithms, it is also wildly unrealistic; almost all modern computer systems violate this assumption, most of them grievously.[1] We first outline what the use of VMM implies for software and its behavior; we also sketch to what extent these lessons are applicable to caches as well. Then we address the question of how to deal with the issues raised by the nonuniformity of memory. We distinguish between solutions that require programmer effort and those that can be implemented automatically.

---

[1] The only exception is provided by older Cray supercomputers, which do not support any caches or virtual memory management (VMM). (Thus, in these systems programs requiring more space than provided by the system's main memory must be written as explicit out-of-core programs.) All other architectures provide for caches, even if VMM (which is strictly software-based) is not supported.

5.1   The Influence of Virtual Memory Management

Recall the horrific example from Section 4.2, a seemingly innocent matrix addition that nobody would give much thought were it not that it glaringly illustrates that the interplay between memory mapping, VMM, and the program's instructions can have enormous consequences. This is greatly aggravated by the general ignorance that most programmers have about memory mappings and related systems aspects. This ignorance may be entirely acceptable for in-core programs (programs that use strictly main memory for all storage needs, including all intermediate storage, and that access external memory, such as disks, only for the initial input of the data and output of the final result), because for in-core programs the memory-mapping function has no significant performance implications. If all data are in main memory, any direct access to any data element takes time independent of its location because of the random access property (RAP) of main memory. Consequently, it makes no difference in what way the data structures are mapped into the main memory (as long as that mapping preserves the RAP). However, this ignorance can be fatal as soon as the program ceases to be in-core, instead using external memory (usually magnetic disks) in conjunction with either VMM or a direct out-of-core programming approach.

It is instructive to examine the differences between VMM and overt out-of-core programming. In out-of-core programming the programmer must specify which blocks of data are transferred between disk and main memory and exactly at what point during program execution. This results in considerable additional effort for the programmer; it also is a potent source of errors. For these reasons, most programmers avoid out-of-core programming at all costs. Nevertheless, it should also be clear that out-of-core programming affords the programmer a significant amount of control over the actions of the program. In contrast, VMM creates a virtual memory space that is dramatically larger than the main memory; for most practical purposes it is unlimited.[2] As a result, the programmer can proceed as if this virtual memory space were the actual one. Thus, the programmer need not concern herself with the explicit manipulation of (units of) space; instead, the instructions of the algorithms can be translated into code, without having to manipulate blocks of data that must be moved between main memory and disk. While this approach is clearly convenient (who wants to worry about the transfer of blocks of data?), the programmer loses a good deal of control over the behavior of the program.[3]

To understand the serious implications of these processes, we need a better understanding of the underlying architectural aspects of the various types of memory and in particular of the access characteristics of the types of

---

[2] In physical terms, it is essentially limited by the amount of (free) space on the disks available to the system.

memory involved. Traditionally, the memory hierarchy of a computer system is as follows:

Registers – Cache – Main memory – External memory

Most programmers consider registers as places of action — the only components that perform instructions.[4] However, they are also storage[5] — the fastest storage available. It is beneficial to structure computations so that values stay in registers as long as they are needed. Caches are somewhat slower than registers, but faster than main memory. Therefore, values that will be needed in subsequent computations but that cannot be kept in registers should be stored in a cache, since access to these values is faster than if they are in main memory. If a value cannot be kept in the cache, it moves further down in the memory hierarchy, namely into main memory. The last element in this progression is external memory, usually magnetic disks, which are much slower than all the other storage structures.

It is crucial that programmers realize how much data transfer occurs implicitly in this computation model. In contrast, algorithms are typically not concerned with the effort required to retrieve or store a data item. Thus, while an algorithm may simply stipulate that a data item occurs in an operation, a program will have to retrieve this data item from whatever storage it resides on. This may involve several steps, all of which are implicit, that is, the programmer is not aware of them. Moreover, while the algorithm specifies one data item, many types of implicit retrieval do not read or write a single item, but an entire group in which that item resides (regardless of whether those other items of that group are used or not). Specifically, data are read from disks in blocks and are written to caches in (cache) lines.

While technology of storage devices is a moving target, it is nevertheless very useful to have a rough idea of the access characteristics of these components. For our purposes, two are paramount: the size of the memory and the time required to access a data item. While one may quibble about specific numbers, it is the relationship between the numbers that is of interest here.

---

[3] In VMM the space required by a program, the logical address space, is divided into pages. Each data item has a logical address. When an item is used in the program, VMM determines whether it resides physically in main memory. If it does, execution proceeds; otherwise, its logical address is used to find the page containing the item, which is then located on, and read from, disk. Since VMM is allocated a fixed amount of memory, the so-called active memory set consisting of a fixed number of pages, reading a page ordinarily implies that another page in the active memory set must be displaced (unless the entire memory set is not yet full, something that would usually occur only at the beginning of execution). Which page is displaced is determined by the replacement strategy, usually a variant of LRU (least recently used; the page that has not been used for the longest time is displaced). If the displaced page is dirty (has been modified or written), it must be written back to disk.

[4] This means that actions (operations) can only occur if a data item resides in a register.

[5] If registers did not play the role of storage, computers would need far fewer of them.

Let us first look at size, in words.[6] The size (which is the number) of registers is on the order of 10, the size of caches is on the order of 10^3, the size of main memory is on the order of 10^8 or 10^9, and the size of magnetic disks is well in excess of 10^{10}. The gap between cache and register is about two orders of magnitude, but that between main memory and cache is five or six, and that between main memory and disk is perhaps three.

Related to the sizes of the components is the unit of access. The basic unit of data that can be transferred from disk to main memory is a block or page, whose size is on the order of 10^3; the basic unit of data from main memory to cache is a cache line, of a size on the order of 10^2; the basic unit of data from cache to register is a single word. To illustrate this, suppose we want to carry out an operation involving a specific data element x, and suppose it is determined that this data element resides on magnetic disk. The following steps must typically be carried out: Locate the block that contains x and transfer it into main memory, likely displacing another data block there. Then determine the cache line in main memory that now contains x and transfer that line to the cache, likely displacing another data line there. Finally, locate the data item x and move it to the appropriate register. In all but the last transfer, a significant amount of data must be manipulated that has nothing to do with x.

Let us now consider the time required for each of these transfers. Again, the important factor is more the relationship between the numbers than their absolute values. Roughly speaking, transferring a word from cache to register takes on the order of 1 nsec, and transferring a cache line from main memory to cache may take on the order of 10 nsec, but transferring a block or page from disk to main memory takes on the order of 10 msec, or 10,000,000 nsec.[7] Here is the root of all evil: It takes about six orders of magnitude longer to access a data item if it resides on disk than if it resides in the cache.

We can summarize the situation as follows:

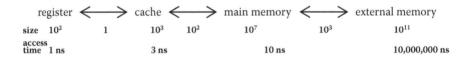

	register		cache		main memory		external memory
size	10^2	1	10^3	10^2	10^7	10^3	10^{11}
access time	1 ns		3 ns		10 ns		10,000,000 ns

---

[6] While historically there have been changes in the word length (it was 16 bits 20 years ago, then it became 32 bits, and it is now moving to 64 bits), we will ignore them in this comparison, since a change in word length will affect all components equally.

[7] The process of reading a block off a magnetic disk is somewhat complicated. There is the seek time of the read/write head — finding the track in which the requested block is located and moving the head to that track. This cannot be speeded up arbitrarily because of vibrations. Then the head must read almost one entire track (in the worst case) to determine the beginning of the block on the track; in the next rotation, that track is read. Thus, in the worst case, two rotations are required to read a block once the head has been moved to the correct track.

This gap of six orders of magnitude is astounding. It is also unlikely to be reduced; if anything, it will grow. The reason is quite simple: While registers, caches, and main memory are electronic (solid-state) devices, disk drives are mechanical. Since electronic devices can be speeded up by making them smaller, this means solid-state storage will continue to reduce its access times. Magnetic disk drives cannot be speeded up significantly;[8] in fact their access speeds have shrunk by less than one order of magnitude over the past 20 years. Consequently, the outlook is that the gap between access speeds between disk to main memory and between main memory and cache will get wider, from the current six orders of magnitude to seven or more.[9]

This has dramatic consequences for access times, depending on where a data item resides. The location of a data item is the overriding factor when determining the time required to carry out an operation. We may reasonably assume that an operation takes on the order of 10 nsec. Thus, if the operands of the operation reside in the cache or in main memory, the time to retrieve the operands and then to carry out the operation is still on the order of 10 nsec. If the operands reside on disk, the overall time is dominated by the time required to retrieve them; instead of 10 nsec, it now is a million times more.

Here is where it is vitally important to be able to control data movement. While it may be a very painful experience to write (and debug!) an out-of-core program, it allows one to exercise complete control over the determination of which block of data to retrieve from disk and at what time. In contrast, VMM hides these highly unpleasant details from the programmer, but at the cost of taking away the ability of determining, or even knowing, which data are transferred when.

When one analyzes the problem more carefully, it turns out that it is not so much the question what is transferred that is crucial, but what is being replaced. We noted that absent unlimited main memory, when we bring in a new block or page or line, we must find space for that unit of memory. This typically involves displacing values that occupy the space we want to use. This is where things can go very wrong. If we displace values that are needed later, these values will have to be brought back in, requiring the displacement of other values. This is particularly dire when we need one (or a few) values of a block or page, but given the process of transferring blocks, the entire page will have to be brought in. This was precisely the situation of the example in Section 4.2 if the memory mapping function

---

[8] There are just two ways of reducing the access speed of magnetic disk drives: increasing the rotation speed of the spinning platters and refining the granularity of the magnetic recordings in the platters. The rotation cannot be increased much further since eventually the centripetal forces will tear the platter apart. Making the granularity of the magnetic recordings finer implies getting the read/write head closer to the platter surface, which is also not feasible because the distances are already very small. Essentially the technology plateaued about two decades ago, as far as access speed is concerned, and no further improvements are likely, owing to the mechanical limitations of the device.

[9] A direct consequence is that more programs will change from being compute-bound to being input/output (I/O)-bound.

was column-major. We managed to use one array element out of each page of size 2048, requiring this page to be brought back 2047 times. Since we did this for every page, the resulting performance became truly execrable. The situation changes completely if the memory-mapping function is row-major. In that case we use all the elements of a page before the page is displaced, so it never has to be brought back again.

Practically, this is the worst-case scenario, as far as performance is concerned. Since in one situation (row-major memory mapping) all elements of a page are used and no page must be brought back again, and in the other situation (column-major mapping) every page must be brought back as many times as that page has elements, it follows that the performance hit here is 2048. In other words, column-major requires 2048 times more page retrievals than row-major. Since the retrieval of a page takes six orders of magnitude longer than an operation involving two operands, we can ignore the time taken by the operations; the retrieval times dominate by far. For the following program fragment,

```
for j:=1 to n do
  for i:=1 to n do
    C[i,j] := A[i,j] + B[i,j],
```

under the same assumptions, the situation is exactly reversed: Row-major memory mapping is horribly inefficient, while column-major memory mapping is optimal.

We pointed out earlier that different programming languages follow different conventions about memory-mapping functions; specifically, Fortran compilers invariably use column-major, while all other languages tend to use row-major. Thus, for a non-Fortran language, one should use the original code:

```
for i:=1 to n do
  for j:=1 to n do
    C[i,j] := A[i,j] + B[i,j],
```

while in Fortran, the code with the *i*-loop and the *j*-loop interchanged should be used:

```
for j:=1 to n do
  for i:=1 to n do
    C[i,j] := A[i,j] + B[i,j].
```

Of course, it should be clear that both code fragments produce exactly the same result. It is the performances that will differ drastically if VMM is involved.

Since the size of a block or page is usually on the order of 1000, it follows that the greatest gain we can obtain (if we are lucky) is also on the order of 1000.[10] In this argument we assume synchronous I/O; in other words, the program must wait for the page to be retrieved before it can continue executing. This is a fairly simple computation model; more sophisticated models may attempt to predict which page is needed in the future and initiate its retrieval while other computations continue. This requires that I/O be done in parallel with computations. This type of speculative page retrieval is complicated, and it is made difficult by the fact that about 1 million operations can be carried out in the time it takes to retrieve one page from disk. To do this automatically (which is what a sophisticated VMM would have to do) is exceedingly challenging.[11] This is significantly aggravated by the fact that VMM is part of the operating system and as such knows nothing about the program being executed. It is much more likely that a highly competent out-of-core programmer is capable of anticipating sufficiently in advance of the computations which page to retrieve next. (*Sufficiently* here means about a million operations earlier.) Unfortunately, this skill is very rare. Most programmers prefer to rely on the VMM, with occasionally disastrous (performance) results. An intermediate approach is turning the task of scheduling the I/O of a program over to the compiler. We will return to this idea in Section 5.4.

5.2   The Case of Caches

As indicated in the discussion of the memory hierarchy, the interplay between main memory and cache is similar to that between disk and main memory. The atomic unit of access is a group of data items (line, block), not a single word, and access times are faster, the higher we are in the memory hierarchy. Thus, most of what we commented on in the previous section also holds for caches in relation to main memory. The one fundamental difference is that the performance difference between main memory and cache is much

---

[10] One may think that the factor should be a million, since it is a million times slower to retrieve an item from disk than from main memory. This argument would only be applicable if one compared an in-core with an out-of-core program. Generally, this makes little sense, since one would always use an in-core program if enough main memory were available — nobody wants to do out-of-core programming. Here, we are comparing two out-of-core programs (i.e., we are assuming that not enough main memory is available in either case); the only difference is the type of memory-mapping function employed. In this case the size of the page or block is essentially the upper bound on the factor of difference in time requirements.

[11] Ideally, we would want to initiate the retrieval of a page or block one million operations before the first element of that page is needed. Thus, we must be able to look one million operations ahead to know what pages are required to be in main memory when a specific operation occurs. Since this speculative approach may go wrong (a different page may be needed from the one we retrieved), it should be clear that this is a very nontrivial task.

smaller than that between disk and main memory. Also, in practice one would never assume that a cache is sufficiently large to run an entire program without having to use main memory (except to load the cache at the beginning and to dump the results into main memory at the conclusion of the program); thus, there is no analogue to an in-core program for caches.

We observed that for an out-of-core program, choosing an appropriate memory-mapping function might improve the performance by a factor equal to the size of the block or page. This factor is typically on the order of 1000. What is the corresponding factor for caches? Since the access times to main memory and to cache differ typically by a factor of less than 10, and since the sizes of page and cache line also differ by about a factor of 10, we can conclude that the most efficient utilization of a cache may improve the performance of the resulting program by a factor that cannot be larger than 10. This implies that the I/O transfer between disk and main memory is far more important for the performance of a program than the I/O transfer between main memory and cache.[12]

5.3   Testing and Profiling

While testing and profiling are not directly related to our objectives in this chapter, these two concepts should at least be mentioned in passing. Our approach is to use the computational complexity of algorithms as a tool for determining the (likely) performance of a program. Thus, we do not execute the program. Both testing and profiling require the execution of a program, usually one that has been armed with appropriate probes. Once a programmer has produced a program, that program must be tested extensively, both to ascertain its correctness and to determine its performance. While this is obvious, it does not conform to our objective of transitioning from algorithm analysis to predicting software performance. Therefore, we do not intend to discuss aspects of program testing.

Profiling is quite similar. It is concerned with finding bottlenecks in programs and with isolating hot spots and discovering excessive paging and cache misses. Knowing about the bottlenecks in a program is important since otherwise a programmer may spend an inordinate amount of time on insignificant code (insignificant from the performance point of view). Determining whether thrashing or cache misses occurred is done after the fact — after the first (or second or third) version of a program has been produced and its performance was found wanting. Since these activities, albeit crucial for

---

[12] It is intriguing that in spite of the observation that far greater gains can be obtained from looking carefully at disks and virtual memory management than at caches, there is a much greater body of literature pertaining to optimizing the transfers between main memory and cache than the transfers between disk and main memory.

software production, are not directly related to the objectives of this book, we will not discuss them in any further detail.

5.4   What to Do about It

The most important aspect of this chapter is to make the programmer understand that there is a problem in using the memory available in modern computing systems. This problem is complex, since it involves three parties: the program itself, the memory hierarchy of the target computer, and the system software, in particular the compiler (which defines the memory-mapping function) and the VMM. To a large extent, once a programmer understands these players and their interactions, unexpected performance deterioration should no longer be completely mystifying. However, it is not sufficient to understand why things go wrong — we have to have ways of making them go right.

Two approaches can be employed: manual and automatic. The manual approach requires a good deal of work and insight from the programmer and is based on typical out-of-core programming techniques. The automatic approach is less demanding of the programmer but is not generally available. We will describe both in this section.

As we mentioned, different programming languages use different memory-mapping functions. It is crucial for the performance of an out-of-core program that the programmer be aware of the type of mapping. With the compilers currently available, this is not something the programmer can change or influence (short of changing to a different programming language). Thus, once a programming language is chosen, the programmer is locked into a specific memory-mapping function.

What is under the control of the programmer is the program. Central to what follows is that there are often several equivalent ways of programming the same operation. For example, to implement matrix addition, either of the two program fragments in Section 5.1 will do. The two versions produce the same result and if they were in-core programs, they would both have the same performance.[13] It is important to realize that these equivalent versions may have very different performances when they are executed as out-of-core programs. The task is then to ensure that the most efficient of these

---

[13] We are focusing on the transfers between disk and main memory and ignoring the influence of the cache. Thus, if there is no cache (Cray systems), there is no difference in performance. If there is a cache, then the way in which the cache lines interact with the access patterns defined by the program instructions will have some influence on the performance. However, since the performance is affected much less by cache interactions than by disk interactions, this aspect can often be ignored. Additionally, more available tools are designed to minimize cache misses than page misses.

versions be selected. Below we will comment on how this selection can be made.

Frequently, one assumes that one starts with an in-core program (as suggested by the algorithm) and obtains from it an out-of-core program. Unfortunately, in some situations an efficient out-of-core program does not follow systematically from a good in-core program. Instead, we may have to take a substantially different programming approach to achieve out-of-core efficiency. This can complicate the design of a program considerably. As an illustration, consider the following problem: Suppose we are given a sequence of data items, each of which modifies a large $[n,n]$ matrix $\mathbf{M}$.[14] Assume that each data item is a triple $[i,j,x]$, where i and j are row and column indices, $1 \leq i,j \leq n$, and x is a real value, with the interpretation being that the value x is to be added to the value $\mathbf{M}[i,j]$. Initially, $\mathbf{M}$ is assumed to be 0. Let us furthermore assume that $\mathbf{M}$ is too large, by a factor of 10, to fit into main memory. Finally, we assume that the input is a random data sequence (i.e., one where a data item is equally likely to modify any of the entries of the matrix). An acceptable *algorithm* would be as follows:

```
while more input do
  { read a triple [i,j,x];
    M[i,j] := M[i,j] + x
  }
```

As a result, the complexity of this algorithm is $O(m)$, where m is the number of data items. We assume that $m >> n^2$; that is, there are far more data items than elements in the matrix $\mathbf{M}$. Translating this algorithm into an *in-core* program preserves the time complexity of $O(m)$; with $\mathbf{M}$ residing in main memory, no data transfers are required between disk and main memory. (Again, we ignore the influence of the cache and concentrate exclusively on the lower end of the memory hierarchy.) However, the situation changes unpleasantly for an out-of-core program: After an initial period during which the available main memory is filled up with pages, we will encounter change requests (that is, increment $\mathbf{M}[i,j]$ by x) that require elements of $\mathbf{M}$ that are not currently in main memory and whose transfer into main memory displaces other blocks. Thus, after the initial ramping up, the likelihood of having $\mathbf{M}[i,j]$ in main memory is 1 in 10, since only 1/10 of $\mathbf{M}$ fits into main memory; 9 in 10 change requests will cause a new block to be transferred into main memory, thereby displacing one already there, which then has to be transferred (written) to disk. Moreover, all displaced pages are dirty and must therefore be written back to disk. Under our stated assumption of randomness of the data sequence, we have about $9m/10$ page transfers (ignoring the ramping up). These

---

[14] This is a fairly abstracted computation model that occurs frequently in practice. For example, many seismic data processing algorithms are of this type.

dramatically dominate the time requirement of this naïve program, based on the algorithm (and the in-core program).

What is a better out-of-core program? Here is an approach that is clearly not based on the in-core version: Divide $\mathbf{M}$ into 10 portions, $\mathbf{M}_1$, $\mathbf{M}_2$, ..., $\mathbf{M}_{10}$, defined in a way that allows easy testing of whether an index $[i,j]$ falls into a specific portion. For example assuming n is divisible by 10, we might define $\mathbf{M}_t = \mathbf{M}[(t-1)n/10 + 1 : tn/10, 1 : n]$, $t = 1$, ..., 10; that is, $\mathbf{M}_1$ consists of the first $n/10$ rows, $\mathbf{M}_2$ of the next $n/10$ rows, and so on. First we go through the sequence of data items and either make the change if it pertains to the portion of $\mathbf{M}$ that is currently in memory, say $\mathbf{M}_1$, or create a new subsequence $\mathbf{S}_t$ consisting of all those data items that pertain to the matrix portion $\mathbf{M}_t$, for $2 \ t \ 10$. Once we have read all the elements in the original sequence, we have completed all changes to $\mathbf{M}_1$ and we have also created nine subsequences, each of which pertains to one portion of $\mathbf{M}$ (those not yet considered), which are then processed after loading that portion into main memory.[15] The out-of-core algorithm is as follows:

```
allocate M₁ in the available main memory and initialize it to 0;
set the sequence Sₜ to empty, for all t=2,...,10;
while more input do
    {read a triple [i,j,x];
     if [i,j] is in M₁ then M[i,j] := M[i,j] + x
                      else { determine t such that [i,j] is in Mₜ;
                             append [i,j,x] to the sequence Sₜ
                           }
    }
for t:=2 to 10 do
    { write Mₜ₋₁ to disk;
      allocate Mₜ in the available main memory and initialize it to 0;
      while more input in Sₜ do
          { read a triple [i,j,x] from Sₜ;
            M[i,j] := M[i,j] + x
          }
    }
```

How does this *algorithm* differ from the corresponding *program*? We have to initialize the sequences $\mathbf{S}_t$ to be empty, and the manipulation of these subsequences must be specified more carefully. There are nine blocks in main memory, one each for each of the nine incipient subsequences. Once a block

---

[15] A thoughtful reader may observe that the original algorithm was essentially on-line; the modification for out-of-core is clearly off-line. This is unavoidable, if one wants an efficient out-of-core version.

is full, it is written to disk. Thus, we need nine more blocks in main memory than what the current portion of **M** consumes.[16]

We now determine the time requirements of this out-of-core version. We will ignore the initialization of the matrix portions as well as the transfers involved in writing the resulting portions of **M** back to disk, since this has to be done even for an in-core version. Thus, we count only the transfers required because of the out-of-core situation; that is, we count only *implicit* transfers. We ignore explicit transfers, which would be the initial retrieval of **M** from disk and the final writing of **M** to disk. In this (off-line) version we have no implicit transfers stemming from (any of the portions of) **M**; we do, however, have implicit transfers stemming from the subsequences.[17] We created nine subsequences, S_2 through S_{10}. On average each is of size $m/10$. This means the creation of the subsequences involves the following amount of block transfers. Let us assume that each block is of size B; then each subsequence consists of $m/(10B)$ blocks. Each of the nine subsequences must be written to disk and then retrieved from disk so that the data items in it can be processed. For each subsequence this requires $m/(5B)$ implicit block transfers. Thus, the total number of implicit block transfers (transfers that are not the initial or final ones) involved in this process is $9m/(5B)$. Contrasting this with the total number of additional block transfers involved in the naïve out-of-core version of about $9m/10$, the new version is more efficient in additional block transfers by a factor of $B/2$. If B is 1000, the new version is about 500 times more efficient, since the block transfer times significantly dominate the actual computations.[18]

It is important to understand that the new version is not one a programmer would devise for an in-core program. Although we formulated it in terms

---

[16] If this assumption is not acceptable, the size of the portions of **M** could be decreased and their number increased, as well as the number of subsequences. Since generally the size of a block is substantially smaller than the total amount of memory available, this assumption is reasonable. An alternative approach would be to create a single new subsequence of all change requests not applicable to the portion of **M** currently in main memory. This reduces the required number of blocks for the subsequence from 9 to 1 (since there is now only one subsequence of rejected change requests, instead of the nine before). However, it also implies that this new subsequence must now be read in its entirety for the processing of the next portion M_2 of **M**, yielding all changes to M_2, plus a new subsequence consisting of all change requests not pertaining to M_1 or M_2. This subsequence is of size $8m/10$. Proceeding in this way yields the same results, albeit requiring fewer additional blocks (1 rather than 9) but also requiring more time since now the requests for changes to M_{10} will be selected out 9 times, whereas in the previous version they were selected out once. In this way, we can trade space for time.

[17] In the naïve (in-core based) program, all of our implicit transfers stem from portions of **M** being read from, or written back to, disk.

[18] The modification of this technique that requires only one subsequence gives rise to a somewhat larger number of implicit block transfers. For the first subsequence we need $9m/(10B)$ blocks that must be written to, and then read again from, disk. This means $18m/(10B)$ implicit block transfers. The next iteration yields a subsequence that needs $8m/(10B)$ blocks, or $16m/(10B)$ implicit transfers. The third iteration involves $14m/(10B)$ implicit transfers, until the 10th and last iteration, which needs $2m/(10B)$. Summing this up, we get a total of $9m/B$ implicit block transfers, or five times more than the version with nine subsequences of size $m/(10B)$ each. This approach is significantly less attractive, even though it is still 100 times better than the naïve one.

of 10 portions, this value 10 could be a parameter, adjusted according to the ratio of available main memory and size of the matrix **M**. The key insight is that it must be the matrix **M**, not the sequence of data items, that determines the processing even though this seems to be the natural way to think about the problem. This reversal of the natural processing order is a frequent aspect of efficient out-of-core programs.

An important feature of many efficient out-of-core programming programs is that they are not directly derivable from an in-core version (as this example just demonstrated). However, numerous programs can be derived. We have already seen an example in matrix addition, where the two versions are transformable into each other. To understand this process of program transformations, we have to make a brief excursion into dependence analysis, which forms the formal basis for program transformations.

The overriding goal of program optimization is to reduce the average execution time of a program. To this end, a program is subjected to a rigorous analysis of the dependences between its instructions. The objective of this dependence analysis is to determine the *absence* of dependences.

An instruction S_1 depends on another instruction S_2 if the latter uses a result computed by the former. Not having any dependence between the two instructions means they can be executed in any order; in particular, they could be rearranged without affecting the semantics of the program. Modern optimizing compilers carry out extensive (and expensive) dependence analyses. They also have a catalog of program transformations that are semantically valid, provided there are no dependences between the instructions involved in the transformations. For example, the program transformation that interchanges the two loops in the matrix addition programs is called loop interchange; this transformation is semantically valid (correct, producing the same results) if there are no dependences between the instructions involved.[19] Analyzing the instructions in these two program fragments, one realizes quickly that each iteration computes a different element of the result matrix, independent of any of the other elements of the result matrix. Thus, there are no dependences and the loop interchange is valid.

In addition to loop interchange, loop distribution is a useful program transformation to keep in mind. While it goes beyond the scope of this book to explain this transformation in detail, an example will help in understanding how its application may impact the running time of a program. The general idea is stated easily: When confronted with a complicated loop, we want to replace it with a sequence of simpler loops. This will result in a significant reduction of implicit block transfers if each simpler loop requires substantially fewer implicit transfers (because all the required blocks fit into main memory) than the complicated loop (because not all the required blocks do). Consider the following program fragment:

---

[19] This requirement can be greatly relaxed. We refer to the extensive literature on dependence analysis and program transformations.

```
for i:=1 to n do
  { A[i] := B[i-1] + i;
    C[i] := A[i] + D[i-1];
    B[i] := A[i] - i;
    D[i] := A[i-1] + i;
    E[i] := D[i] + F[i-1];
    F[i] := D[i] - F[i-1]
  }
```

There are several dependences among the statements in the loop; for example, the assignments to **B** (third statement in the loop body) change the values that are used in the assignments to **A** (first statement). Similarly, the assignments to **A** (first) affect the values used in the assignments to **B** (third). The other dependences in this loop involve the first and second statements (the changes to **A** affect the assignments to **C**), the second and fourth statements, the fourth, fifth, and sixth statements, and finally the sixth and fifth statements. The upshot of this dependence analysis is that by applying loop distribution, this single, complicated loop can be replaced by the following four simpler loops:

```
for i:=1 to n do
  { A[i] := B[i-1] + i;
    B[i] := A[i] - i;
  }
for i:=1 to n do
  { C[i] := A[i] + D[i-1];
    D[i] := A[i-1] + i;
  }
for i:=1 to n do
  { F[i] := D[i] - F[i-1]
  }
for i:=1 to n do
  { E[i] := D[i] + F[i-1],
  }
```

Note that these four loops must be in exactly this order; any other order would result in different results (that is, it would be semantically invalid).[20] Moreover, the two loops with two statements each cannot be further distributed (i.e., cannot be replaced by two loops of one statement each). How can this reduce the number of implicit block transfers?

---

[20] This is because in contrast to our previous stipulation that there be no dependences, here there are some dependences, but they are preserved by the stated order of the loops.

Observe that the original loop required that portions of each of the six arrays, **A** through **F**, had to be in main memory if excessive thrashing (paging in and out of only very partially processed blocks) is to be avoided. Assuming that many blocks are required to accommodate an array, it follows that in the worst case we need one block for **A** (to use on the right of assignments and to write on the left of assignments), two blocks for **B** (since both **B**[i] and **B**[$i - 1$] occur and may be in two different blocks), one block for **C**, two for **D**, one for **E**, and two for **F**. This yields a total of nine blocks that must be in memory at the same time if we want to avoid writing partially used blocks back to disk and then reading those blocks again from disk. Carrying out this analysis for each of the four loops individually results in the following:

1. The first loop requires one block from **A** and two from **B**.
2. The second loop requires two blocks from **A** and **D** and one from **C**.
3. The third loop requires two blocks from **F** and one from **D**.
4. The fourth loop requires one block from **E** and **D** and also only one block from **F** (since **F**[$i - 1$] occurs, but not **F**[i]).

This might lead one to conclude that five blocks are sufficient. While this is true, it does require more careful analysis and argumentation, as well as a further restructuring of the code.

The first problem is that it is not correct to simply take the maximum of the block requirements of the four loops involved. The difficulty is illustrated by the use of **F**[$i - 1$] in the fourth loop. That this could create problems is evident once one examines the global use of blocks, that is, the interplay between the different loops. To see this, observe that the second loop requires from the first loop the values **A**[i] and **A**[$i - 1$]. Thus the blocks for **A**[i] and **A**[$i - 1$] must be imported from the first loop to the second to enable that loop to compute **C**[i] and **D**[i] (one block each). While the **C** values are not needed further, the **D** values are, namely in the third and fourth loops. Thus, the block for **D**[i] has to be passed along to the third and then to the fourth loop before it can be discarded. This requires us to redo the computation so that each loop is broken up into several loops of an iteration count equal to the size of the block.

Let M be the size of the block and assume for simplicity that M divides n: $M = n/m$, for some positive integer m. We now do the first M iterations of the four loops, then we do the next M iterations, until we do the last group of M iterations of the four loops. This becomes:

```
for k:=1 to m do
  { m1 := (k-1)*M + 1; m2 := k*M;
    for i:= m1 to m2 do
       { A[i] := B[i-1] + i;
         B[i] := A[i] - i;
       }
    for i:=m1 to m2 do
       { C[i] := A[i] + D[i-1];
         D[i] := A[i-1] + i;
       }
    for i:=m1 to m2 do
       { F[i] := D[i] - F[i-1]
       }
    for i:=m1 to m2 do
       { E[i] := D[i] + F[i-1].
       }
  }
```

Now it should be clear how blocks are transferred from one loop to the next. Reviewing this flow, it is apparent that five blocks are indeed sufficient. However, if the fourth loop had required five blocks, this argument would have to be modified. Here is why: Suppose the statement in the body of the fourth loop were

```
E[i] := A[i] + B[i] + D[i] + F[i-1].
```

Clearly, one block of **A**, **B**, **D**, **E**, and **F** is needed if this is executed in isolation. Two observations are in order: First, the blocks for **A** and **B** must be passed through the third loop, which in general might increase the block requirements (although not in this case). Second, the element of **F** required in the fourth loop is $F[i-1]$, not $F[i]$, and this implies that (in the worst case) we would need to keep two blocks for **F** — the old one that contains $F[i-1]$ and the new, second one that contains $F[i]$ (which is not needed for the computation of the current $E[i]$ but will be needed in the next iteration). This would increase the number of blocks required for the (modified) fourth loop from five to six.

While this example started out rather simple, it rapidly became quite complicated. Nevertheless, we can see that fewer blocks are required for the loop-distributed version (sequence of four loops) than for the original loop. If enough space exists in main memory for the loop-distributed version, but not for the original one, the savings resulting from the avoidance of memory thrashing can be significant.

If one is unsure of the effect of loop distribution, a reasonable alternative to carrying out a usually quite involved analysis is to implement both versions and execute them, counting the implicit transfers affected by each. Then one chooses the code that requires fewer such transfers. Alternatively, it is possible to carry out an automatic analysis of block transfers at compile time.

In summary, no implicit block transfers are needed in the loop-distributed version of our code if five blocks can be accommodated in main memory. It is important to understand that small changes in memory can result in dramatic changes in performance; in other words, the relationship is definitely not linear — quantum jumps may occur. In this example, the availability of only eight pages will produce extensive thrashing with the original version (which needs nine pages), but the loop-distributed version exhibits no thrashing at all, even though the reduction in memory is small.

This still leaves us with the problem of deciding whether applying a program transformation pays, and if so, how to carry it out effectively. Neither of these two steps is trivial.

To determine whether a program transformation results in savings, the transformation must be applied, the implicit block transfer analysis must be carried out, and the version that requires fewer implicit block transfers should be selected. Experience indicates that loop interchanges are most likely to affect the number of implicit block transfers, with loop distribution coming in a distant second.

Unfortunately, we are still hobbled by the memory-mapping function. Neither of the two standard memory-mapping functions (row-major and column-major) is particularly attractive when it comes to matrix multiplication.[21] The problem is that matrix multiplication accesses one matrix in terms of rows and the other in terms of columns. Consequently, choosing either of the two standard mappings will work badly for one of the two matrices involved. This is not a new problem, nor is it open; research dating back to the 1960s indicates that tiling is a much better approach. This would entail subdividing the two-dimensional (2D) structure (the matrix) into smaller 2D structures (submatrices of smaller sizes). To illustrate, we can represent a matrix of size $[n,n]$ by its four submatrices of size $[n/2,n/2]$. For our three matrices **A**, **B**, and **C**, we have

$$A = \begin{pmatrix} A_{11} & A_{12} \\ A_{21} & A_{22} \end{pmatrix} \quad B = \begin{pmatrix} B_{11} & B_{12} \\ B_{21} & B_{22} \end{pmatrix} \quad C = \begin{pmatrix} C_{11} & C_{12} \\ C_{21} & C_{22} \end{pmatrix}.$$

Consequently, the matrix multiplication **C** := **A** * **B** can be restated as

---

[21] We use matrix multiplication as a representative example. There are other commonly used operations, but matrix multiplication is by far the most important operation that performs badly regardless of which of the two standard memory-mapping functions one chooses.

$$C_{11} := A_{11} * B_{11} + A_{12} * B_{21}$$

$$C_{12} := A_{11} * B_{12} + A_{12} * B_{22}$$

$$C_{21} := A_{21} * B_{11} + A_{22} * B_{21}$$

$$C_{22} := A_{21} * B_{12} + A_{22} * B_{22}$$

If each of the submatrices fits into a block, the computation can be carried out as indicated below; if submatrices are larger than blocks, the approach may have to be iterated.

Assuming 1 submatrix is 1 block, each matrix requires 4 blocks, for a total of 12. Each of the four statements involves one **C**-block and two blocks each from **A** and **B**, for a total of five. Thus, each submatrix statement requires five blocks. The interstatement flow of blocks is also important. If one were to execute the four statements in the given order, we would have to retain B_{11} and B_{21} through the second statement since both are required in the third statement. This would necessitate that we keep four **B**-blocks in main memory during execution of the second statement; a similar argument applies to the third statement with respect to the **B**-blocks B_{12} and B_{22}. Consequently, this execution order requires us to keep seven blocks in main memory. However, by reordering the computations so that we do the first statement first, then the second, then the fourth, and finally the third, one can verify that we need to keep no more than six blocks in main memory.

This type of tiling has been known for a long time; moreover, it has been known that it is much more efficient in terms of implicit block transfers for matrix multiplication. However, modern compilers do not use it. This leaves one with two, equally unpalatable, options: Accept the inefficiency of modern compilers caused by their refusal to implement vastly superior memory-mapping functions or manage the entire memory space as a 1D memory space. This means one does one's own memory-mapping functions so that the compiler deals exclusively with 1D arrays (which are mapped into main memory identically, whether with row-major or column-major mapping). The first alternative is potentially inefficient to an astonishing degree (as our examples indicate). The second is prohibitively complicated to program (the programmer must take over a major functionality of the compiler) and leads to truly awful (that is, unreadable) programs (since everything is now a 1D array).

The refusal of compiler writers to implement nonstandard memory-mapping functions can only be explained by their lack of appreciation of how serious an effect the memory-mapping function can have on the performance of a program. It is not a particularly difficult task to carry out. In fact, it is entirely conceivable that a good compiler automatically determines the access patterns for a particular array (usually a 2D matrix) and selects the best memory-mapping function according to that determination. Indeed, we will go further: A good optimizing compiler should be capable of applying program transformations automatically, determining at compile time which version is better in terms of implicit block transfers, and selecting the best for the object code produced by the compiler. In this way, the programmer is not burdened with determining a better version, does not have to implement that better version, and does not have to verify the correctness of the substitute version. Instead, she can concentrate on programming tasks that require human intelligence.

We argue that the tasks of applying program transformations systematically, of determining which of two given program fragments requires more implicit block transfers, and determining the best of a (relatively small number of) memory-mapping functions can be done by the compiler, automatically (that is, without user intervention) and at compile time. The ultimate goal is compiler-driven I/O analysis and program transformation. While it is clearly beyond the scope of this book, compiler-driven I/O management is entirely based on techniques that have been used successfully in optimizing compilers for many years, in particular dependence analysis (used for decades in vectorizing and parallelizing compilers) and program transformation. While the goals of vectorizing compilers are different, the techniques are the same.

Finally, it is possible under some rather mild assumptions to take a program and determine automatically at compile time how many blocks will be transferred between disk and main memory, assuming knowledge of basic systems information, such as available main memory, block or page size, replacement strategy, and access times to disk and main memory. This would remove a great deal of difficulty in obtaining reasonably efficient programs. By *reasonably efficient* we mean the running time of the program should be in a clear and understandable relationship with the time complexity that the complexity analysis provided for the algorithm that the program implements.

The current state of compilers is not conducive to efficient memory utilization, even though the techniques that would enable such an approach to minimizing implicit transfers have been available for many years.[22] As a result, programmers must attempt to carry out some of these steps directly. For example, loop interchanges and loop distributions can be done by the programmer, independent of whatever steps the compiler takes. Mapping issues are harder. The programmer can either accept the inefficiencies or program her own memory mapping. Both alternatives are unpalatable, for different reasons. Ultimately, the decision rests on the importance of performance. If it is imperative that the program execute as efficiently as possible, the programmer may have to accept that the resulting program is

---

[22] Any efficient vectorizing compiler carries out dependence analyses and applies program transformations to an extent that goes well beyond what would be required for our purposes. The only portion not yet routinely implemented in vectorizing/optimizing compilers is the automatic determination of the number of implicit transfers.

substantially unreadable, because all arrays (or at least the important ones) are now one-dimensional.

Bibliographical Notes

Standard computer architecture textbooks cover the memory hierarchy and its attributes and characteristics. It is important to keep in mind that different architectural components have different speeds of development; for example, processor speed has historically (during the past three decades) increased faster than the speeds of memory accesses, be they cache or main memory, which in turn have significantly overtaken the speeds with which access to data on external memory, specifically magnetic disks and tapes, occurs. These performance gaps are widening, as reflected in recent technological developments. VMM is a standard part of operating systems and is covered in all modern operating systems textbooks. Operating systems have been the subject of texts for almost five decades. One of the earliest is Rosen (ed.): *Programming Systems and Languages*. The book by Coffman and Denning, *Operating Systems Theory*, reflects an early attempt to establish the theoretical foundations of operating systems. Silberschatz, Gavin, and Gagne: *Operating Systems Concepts* is widely used to teach operating systems; other textbooks are Stallings, *Operating Systems: Design and Principles*; Bic and Shaw: *Operating Systems*; and Tanenbaum: *Operating Systems: Design and Implementation*. Books specifically covering the Unix operating system are Leffler, McKusick, Karels, and Quaterman: *The Design and Implementation of the 4.3BSD Unix Operating System*; and Bach: *The Design of the Unix Operating System*.

Independent of operating and run-time support systems are compilers that implement memory mappings and do code optimization. Code optimization, in particular dependence analysis and code transformations, is covered in textbooks on compilers, especially optimizing compilers and compilers directed at vector and parallel computing. Much of the background material for Section 5.4 can be found in these textbooks, for example in Aho, Sethi, and Ullman: *Compilers: Principles, Techniques and Tools*; Muchnik: *Advanced Compiler Design and Implementation*; and Zima and Chapman, *Supercompilers for Parallel and Vector Computers*. The specific emphasis on I/O management, intended to use code transformations to minimize implicit block transfers, is introduced in Chapter 7 of Leiss: *Parallel and Vector Computing*. The compile time analysis of block transfers is described in Zhang and Leiss: *Compile Time Data Transfer Analysis*.

Exercises

Exercise 1

Consider the code fragments below, to be executed under a virtual memory management system with pure least recently used (LRU) replacement policy. Assume that the arrays involved are of type $[1:n,1:n]$, with n being 512, 1024, 2048, and 4192, and each array element requiring one word of four bytes. Assume that the page size is 512 words and that the active memory set size is 300 pages. Determine the exact number of page transfers, both from disk to main memory and from main memory to disk (only if dirty), assuming that the arrays are mapped into the main memory space using (1) row-major and (2) column-major.

Code fragment a:

```
for i:=1 to n do
  for j:=1 to n do
    A[i,j] := B[j,i]*A[i,j] + C[i,j]
```

Code fragment b:

```
for i:=1 to n do
  for j:=1 to n do
    A[i,j] := B[2*i,j]
```

Code fragment c:

```
for i:=1 to n do
  for j:=1 to n do
    { for k:=1 to n do
      C[i,j] := C[i,j] + A[i,k]*B[k,j];
      D[i,j+1] := D[i,j] + C[i,j]
    }
```

Code fragment d:

```
for i:=1 to n do
  for j:=1 to n do
    A[i,j] := B[j,i]*A[i,j] + C[j,i]
```

Code fragment e:

```
for i:=1 to n do
  for j:=1 to n do
    for k:=1 to n do
      C[i,j] := C[i,j] + A[k,i]*B[k,j];
```

Code fragment f:

```
for i:=1 to n do
  for j:=1 to n do
    A[i,j] := C[j,i]
```

Exercise 2

For which of the code fragments in Exercise 1 would replacing the standard memory-mapping functions by tiling improve the performance (reduce the number of required block transfers). Give the explicit algorithm for these cases.[23]

Exercise 3

Design a program that illustrates the influence of the cache on execution. Specifically, for a computer platform that uses a cache, determine the cache's size and its access characteristics (size of cache line, access times, etc.). Then write a synthetic program that uses a relatively small amount of data for extensive computations. In more detail, if the size of the cache is M, have your program load a data set of size C into the cache and carry out a number of operations (involving this data set) that is several orders larger than C. Determine the timings for $C = 0.8 \cdot M$, $0.9 \cdot M$, $0.95 \cdot M$, $0.99 \cdot M$, $1.0 \cdot M$, $1.01 \cdot M$, and $1.05 \cdot M$. Pay attention to the replacement policy of the cache lines and structure your computations so you can be certain that thrashing occurs for $C > M$.

Exercise 4

Design a program that illustrates the influence of VMM on execution. Specifically, for a computer platform that uses VMM, determine the size of the active memory set and the access characteristics of the components involved in the VMM (size of page, access times, etc.). Then write a synthetic program that uses a relatively small amount of data for extensive computations. In more detail, if the size of the active memory set is M, have your program

---

[23] This exercise considers the various code fragments in isolation. In a complete program, it would be necessary to consider all usages of a particular array to determine the overall most beneficial mapping. Also note that different mapping strategies may be required for different arrays.

load a data set of size C into the cache and carry out a number of operations (involving this data set) that is several orders larger than C. Determine the timings for $C = 0.8 \cdot M$, $0.9 \cdot M$, $0.95 \cdot M$, $0.99 \cdot M$, $1.0 \cdot M$, $1.01 \cdot M$, $1.5 \cdot M$, $2 \cdot M$, $5 \cdot M$, $10 \cdot M$, and $100 \cdot M$. Pay attention to the replacement policy of the VMM and structure your computations so you can be certain that thrashing occurs for $C > M$.

6

Implications of Compiler and Systems Issues for Software

About This Chapter

Numerous aspects of software depend on compiler and systems aspects. In addition to the already mentioned memory mappings that are in a way arbitrary because they are not inherently part of the language design and could be changed, there are fundamental issues of programming environments and programming languages that have significant implications for the performance of software. The most important of these are recursion and its consequences for space complexity, the allocation of dynamic data structures and its consequences for time complexity, the consequences of and implications for optimization, and the consequences of providing certain language constructs as part of the programming language. All of these have in common that the resulting performance is unexpected, unpredictable, or inexplicable to the software developer.

6.1   Introduction

Software is written in a specific programming language, compiled by a specific compiler, and executed under a specific run-time support system.[1] All of these have implications for the functioning of the software. Typically, these implications are noticed by the programmer only when the behavior of the faithfully implemented algorithm does not conform to the expectations that the computational complexity analysis of that algorithm raised. Some of the explanations for this unexpected behavior are based on language aspects alone (parameter passing and recursion, for example), but many

---

[1] Hardware is ultimately involved, but this is of little interest in this chapter and is therefore not emphasized.

straddle language constructs and compilers (for example, the treatment of dynamic data structures and the complications caused by optimizing compilers). We first look at recursion and dynamic data structures; these influence the space complexity of the code in a fairly obvious way but may also impact the time complexity of a program in a much less obvious and often unpredictable way.

6.2   Recursion and Space Complexity

Recursion is an elegant tool that allows us to demonstrate solutions of complex problems.[2] Recursion is, however, not always as efficient as one might expect. Apart from the already touched upon problems of the clear abuse of recursion (e.g., computing the Fibonacci numbers recursively — with an exponential time complexity, even though a halfway decent iterative implementation would take no more than linear time), recursion also has implications for the space complexity that are easy to ignore. While any rigorous space complexity analysis will account for the memory requirements resulting from recursion, in particular, the recursion stack, there are more subtle implications for programs.

While it is convenient to start with a recursive formulation of an algorithm, and in some cases virtually unavoidable (see the Towers of Hanoi problem or AVL trees), when implementing an algorithm, programmers tend to avoid recursion for various reasons. Some programming languages simply do not support recursion. Many programmers are reluctant to use recursion, either because they do not understand it sufficiently well (for example, many find out the hard way that failure to specify the basis case correctly can lead to catastrophic failures) or because the performance of the resulting software is frequently worse than they expected.

If the recursion at hand is tail recursion (see Chapter 3), its elimination is highly desirable, since recursion will unavoidably incur a space penalty for the allocation of the recursion stack, while the technique that allows us to replace tail recursion by an iterative process requires no recursion stack and no other data structure that would need additional space. Thus, replacing tail recursion by iteration materially improves the space complexity of the resulting program. Moreover, since the implementation of recursion in a programming environment is a fairly complicated process (even if the instance at hand may be simple, compilers tend to treat all types of recursion identically, which means the most complicated situation is adapted to simpler ones), the time complexity of the iterative version is usually also better.

---

[2] To wit, the solution of the Towers of Hanoi problem (Section 3.1) cannot be understood without recursion. Insertion and deletion in AVL trees (Section 3.2) are only slightly less unintelligible without recursion.

If the recursion at hand is not tail recursion, the situation is much more complicated. While recursion can always be eliminated, this process involves the explicit administration of the information that would automatically be administered by the run-time support system in the recursion stack.[3] While one may avoid allocating space for some of the items that are part of the recursion stack, this saving tends to be small. Thus, if the recursion cannot be replaced by iteration without additional data structures, it may be advisable to stay with the recursive implementation. An added advantage is the increased readability and therefore maintainability of the software.

One significant aspect of recursion is the variability of the size of the recursion stack. Typically, it is not possible to predict the exact size that the stack can attain; in most cases, we can only derive an upper bound. For example, in QuickSort, a fundamentally recursive algorithm (although iterative versions exist, their space complexity is essentially the same as that of the recursive version), the upper bound for the worst-case space complexity is $O(n)$ when sorting n numbers. This is because in the worst situation for QuickSort, the number of activation records on the recursion stack can be $O(n)$. One may point out that the worst case occurs exceedingly rarely; indeed, since the average case requires an amount of space proportional to the height of the tree structure that describes the recursive calls and since this height is $O(\log_2(n))$ on average, one might be seduced into believing that $O(\log_2(n))$ space is sufficient on average.

The problem with this argument is the following: Suppose we allocate a certain amount of memory for the use of QuickSort and assume this amount is well above the requirements for the average case of QuickSort. What will happen if one of those exceedingly rare, worse than average cases occurs? If the memory is fixed (that is, the size of the allocated memory cannot be exceeded), the program simply crashes. This is not what one expects when looking primarily at the time complexity. One might perhaps expect that the program will take much longer than predicted but that it will nevertheless terminate correctly. If the program crashes for lack of memory, this expectation is sadly wrong. However, if exceeding the allocated space results in the invocation of virtual memory management (VMM), the run time of the program, already very bad since we are considering a case with bad time complexity, may become dramatically worse because of the additional time required to do page transfers from and to disk.

It should now be clear that recursion can have major implications for the overall behavior of a program. To emphasize this point, let us reexamine the conventional wisdom about QuickSort. It is generally accepted that Quick-Sort is faster than any other sorting program on average. Thus, the notion persists that QuickSort should be used for applications that are not time critical. However, even if we concentrate on average case behavior, it is

---

[3] At a minimum, copies of all parameters, copies of all local variables, and the reentry point (place in the program where execution is to resume when the recursive call returns) are stored in a separate activation record for each recursive call. This is true even if some or most of these data items are not necessary in a specific instance.

TABLE 6.1

Complexities of QuickSort, MergeSort, and HeapSort

Method	Space Complexity Prudent	Time Complexity	
		Average	Worst Case
QuickSort	$O(n)$	$O(n \cdot \log_2(n))$	$O(n^2)$
MergeSort	$O(n)$	$O(n \cdot \log_2(n))$	$O(n \cdot \log_2(n))$
HeapSort	$O(1)$	$O(n \cdot \log_2(n))$	$O(n \cdot \log_2(n))$

probably unacceptable that the program crashes occasionally.[4] Therefore, it is highly advisable to allocate an amount of memory for the recursion stack that corresponds to the *worst-case* situation. We must prudently conclude, then, that QuickSort has a space complexity of $O(n)$. This is no better than that of MergeSort, which has a comparable time complexity as QuickSort on average and a much better worst-case time complexity. It is also much worse than HeapSort. We summarize the various complexities of these three sorting algorithms in Table 6.1.

The upshot is that from a practical point of view, it is very difficult to see why anyone would want to use QuickSort to sort arbitrary sets of numbers. QuickSort requires as much space as MergeSort (proportionally to n and absolutely actually more since the recursion stack requires more space per recursive call than one array element) and is slower for both average (slightly) and worst case (significantly), while HeapSort requires significantly less space than QuickSort and is significantly faster in the worst case than QuickSort and only marginally slower on average.

In general, it is probably a bad idea to look at *average* space complexity when it comes to recursion, since failure to comply with the average may result in the program's crash.[5] In situations where average complexities are of interest (that is, no real-time, time-critical applications), it is far more sensible to assume the worst-case space complexity. If we are wrong with our average-case assumption for time, the program may take significantly longer than expected, but at least it will still terminate correctly. If we assume average space complexity, the program may instead crash, which is an unacceptable outcome, even if one were willing to accept that the program occasionally takes much longer than was predicted by the average time complexity of the underlying algorithm.

---

[4] Program crashes may have consequences that go beyond the termination of the program; they may affect the proper functioning of other processes as well. Thus, the argument that a very rare crash of a program can be handled by a programmer manually is not a good one. It is extremely bad programming practice to accept occasional crashes that could easily be avoided.

[5] This assertion holds for space complexity in general, not just in conjunction with recursion. No program should be allocated less space than it needs in the worst case, since the alternative is that it may crash.

6.3   Dynamic Structures and Garbage Collection

Dynamic data structures are data structures whose size can vary during the execution of a program or from one run of the program to the next. Because their size is not known at compile time, processes must be set up that allow the allocation of dynamic data structures during run time. Numerous data structures are considered dynamic data structures, among them trees, linked lists, queues, and stacks. In some cases instances of these structures are represented by a fixed-size array, but then they are no longer true dynamic data structures. These simulated structures will fail to function properly once their maximum size (as hard-coded into the array representation) is exceeded. A key aspect of true dynamic data structures is the absence of the test of the type

   if data structure full **then** reject insert operation.

In other words, a dynamic data structure can never be full. It is unbounded in size, at least when used in an algorithm.

The unboundedness of dynamic data structures is a reasonable assumption for algorithms, since in this worldview, memory is assumed to be unlimited. It is, however, a very tenuous assumption for software, since memory is not unlimited in any practical computing system. The way around this problem is to allocate a pool or heap of memory (usually of fixed size) to be used to accommodate requests for space generated during run time. To make this paradigm work well, it is desirable that concomitant with requests for the allocation of space, instructions for freeing or deallocating space be issued by the program and processed by the run-time support system. This is one way to reuse dynamically allocated memory that is no longer needed by the program. The burden of determining which memory locations are no longer needed lies with the programmer in this approach.

In another way of freeing space the run-time support system determines autonomously that certain memory locations can no longer be referenced by the program. If a memory location can no longer be referenced by a program, it is useless and can be recycled. If memory is needed, space considered available in this process can then be collected and allocated to satisfy requests. In this case the programmer is not burdened with the task of issuing explicit deallocation instructions. This appears to be a very attractive approach until one examines its implications more carefully. (In this sense, it is similar to VMM.)

Let us first consider allocation requests. Whenever a unit of memory is needed in a program, the program issues a request for memory. This may involve the creation of a new node of a tree or a stack, or it may mean allocating an array of a size that has just been read in as input. These two cases are different, simply because the new node tends to be a very small unit of memory while the dynamic array is most likely much larger. It turns out that the size of an allocation request is important, since it also implies the size of the memory that is to be freed when a concomitant deallocation instruction is issued. It is not so much the size, but the variation in size that has important implications for the gathering of freed-up space. Specifically, if all allocation requests have the same size (for example, in Lisp programs), it is relatively simple to devise highly efficient strategies for collecting unused space.[6] If, however, the allocation requests are very different in size, it becomes much more difficult to allocate memory efficiently.[7]

For our purposes, it suffices to keep in mind that space can only be allocated to a process (program) if it is available. For the space to be available, it is necessary that the run-time support system determine the availability of the space (of the appropriate kind; in particular, space allocated for single entities should be contiguous[8]) and then assign this memory space to the process. Note that for algorithms, this process is unproblematic since there is an unlimited amount of space available. This unlimitedness of space makes it unnecessary to reuse space. Thus, it should be obvious that allocation requests in algorithms are negligible in their effect on the algorithm's time complexity — they are always $O(1)$.[9]

For programs, one generally assumes that space allocation also takes a constant amount of time, since it is assumed that the size of the allocation request is known at the time of issuance and the process of assigning memory consists of marking a chunk of the appropriate size as in use. Assuming a (contiguous) chunk of memory is known by its starting and end addresses, it is easy to test whether the size of a particular chunk is sufficient for satisfying the request. Strictly speaking, the time complexity may be greater than $O(1)$ because of the question of finding an appropriate chunk (depending on the specific algorithm used for this purpose; numerous techniques are employed for choosing the most appropriate chunk when allocating allocation requests of varying sizes, from best fit, to worst fit, to various buddy systems), and that would ordinarily depend on the number of chunks available (except in the case of uniform-sized requests, called cells, à la Lisp, where the run-time support system maintains a linked list of free cells and

---

[6] Simply maintain a linked list of cells (allocation units of identical size) that are available. Initially, the list contains the entire space (all cells) available. Any request for a cell is satisfied by supplying the next available cell and removing it from the list. Any deallocation request simply places the freed cell at the end of the linked list of available cells. In this way, allocation and deallocation can be done in time $O(1)$.

[7] This is related to the fact that allocation requests are usually processed so that the entire space request is allocated *contiguously* in memory. If the pool of available memory is fragmented, it is possible that no contiguous chunk of memory of a required size is available, even though the sum of all free memory chunks far exceeds the request. In this case, it will be necessary to carry out a memory processing step in which memory fragments are collected and compacted so that a large contiguous chunk of memory is created. The complexity of this compaction process is of great concern for us.

[8] In particular, for dynamic arrays, it *must* be contiguous, since otherwise none of the standard memory-mapping functions (which preserve the random access property) are applicable.

[9] Note, however, that the initialization of an element need not be $O(1)$; only the actual allocation of the memory takes $O(1)$ time. More specifically, if a node in a linear list consists of a pointer and a 2D matrix of size n^2, the allocation of this space of size $n^2 + O(1)$ can be done in time $O(1)$, but any initialization of the matrix would take at least an additional $O(n^2)$ time.

allocates cells from this linked list upon request by a program instruction in constant time). Nevertheless, the time required to carry out an allocation is usually fairly negligible — provided there is a readily available chunk of memory to satisfy that request. This is precisely the problem.

Note that as described, the process of allocating a chunk of memory does not include any compaction operation; this would be required if there was no single chunk of memory of a size sufficient to accommodate the request, but there are numerous smaller free chunks the sum of whose sizes exceeds the size of the request. Memory compaction techniques may take a significant amount of time. Worse, this amount of time may be incurred at completely unpredictable times. It is even possible that running the same program twice with substantially identical data sets may result in very different running times, strictly because of the time taken by memory compaction.

Memory compaction has to be done when memory fragmentation impedes the satisfaction of a request whose size does not exceed the available memory. A memory compaction algorithm typically must examine the available chunks of memory, because a sequence of allocations and deallocations of memory requests of varying sizes will often result in memory fragmentation. This means that even though we started out with one large chunk of (contiguous) memory, after allocating and subsequently freeing portions of memory, we may end up rather quickly with relatively small chunks of free memory. To illustrate this, assume we have memory M[1:1000] available and consider the following sequence of memory requests $R_i(s_i)$ and deallocation requests D_i, where R_i is request number i, which is of size s_i, and D_i frees the memory allocated when processing request R_i:

$$R_1(200), R_2(400), R_3(200), R_4(200), D_2, D_4, R_5(500).$$

The first four requests present no problem; we may allocate [1:200], [201:600], [601:800], and [801:1000], respectively, to these requests. After executing the two deallocation operations, only the locations [1:200] and [601:800] remain occupied; all other locations are free. However, it is impossible to satisfy the fifth request, because there is no contiguous chunk of size 500, even though there are altogether 600 free locations. Up until now, it should be evident that both allocation and freeing operations can be carried out efficiently.[10] However, realizing that the request $R_5(500)$ cannot be satisfied, we have to compact the remaining chunks to

---

[10] This requires the use of a suitable data structure that allows access to a specific, previously allocated chunk. Also, an algorithm must be employed for the determination of the most appropriate chunk from which to satisfy a request. For example, if the fifth request were not of size 500, but 100, we would have two possibilities: allocate out of the chunk [201:600] or allocate out of the chunk [801:1000]. If the best fit strategy is employed, the smallest possible chunk would be selected, that is, the chunk [801:1000] in this case. If the worst-fit strategy is employed, the request would be satisfied out of the largest chunk, [201:600]. While worst fit seems to be counterintuitive (why use a larger chunk than necessary?), it turns out that best fit results in worse fragmentation since what is left after satisfying a request from the smallest possible chunk is a much smaller chunk (which is likely to be useless for all subsequent requests) than if one satisfies a request from the largest chunk (where the remnant is more likely to satisfy a subsequent request).

consolidate them into a large chunk. This requires shifting one or more chunks of memory to different locations. In our (very simple) example, we can either shift the memory for R_1 to [801:1000] or we can shift the memory for R_3 to [201:400]. Only after this operation is carried out can the fifth request $R_5(500)$ be satisfied. The problem is that this shifting operation takes an amount of time that is linear in the sum of the sizes of the chunks to be shifted; this can be proportional to the size of the memory pool. Moreover, it is not at all transparent to the programmer when such a compaction operation is invoked by the run-time support system. Thus, its occurrence appears to be entirely unpredictable, resulting in situations where a feasible request for an allocation of a certain size is carried out instantaneously and a later, equally feasible request of the same size seemingly halts execution of the program for an inexplicably long time. (We say a request is feasible if the amount of free memory exceeds the size of the request.) Understanding the role of memory compaction will at least help in understanding why this may happen.

We now indicate how substantially identical runs may result in different compaction behavior. Programs on modern computing systems do not execute in isolation; numerous other processes operate at the same time. Variations in the behavior of these processes may have subtle impacts on the availability of memory to our program, which in turn can cause major repercussions for its compaction algorithm. To illustrate this, assume in our example that the amount of memory was M[1:1100] instead of M[1:1000]. In this case the fifth request would not necessitate a compaction operation. However, if an external process causes the amount of available memory to shrink to M[1:1000], compaction must be carried out.[11] Most programmers do not know what the size of the pool of memory is. In some systems, this is not a fixed quantity. Even if the pool size is fixed and cannot be affected by other processes, a permutation of requests for allocation and deallocation may cause significant differences in run time. Assume that the sequence of requests of allocation and deallocation in our example was reordered as follows:

$$R_1(200), R_3(200), R_2(400), R_4(200), D_2, D_4, R_5(500).$$

It follows that after the two deallocation operations, only the locations 1:400 are occupied; therefore, the request $R_5(500)$ can be satisfied without compaction. Even though both sequences contain the same allocation and deallocation requests, their permutation may cause differing compaction operations.

Note that allocation requests may occur explicitly or implicitly. For example, the expansion of the recursion stack during execution of a recursive function is always implicit, but the allocation of a node in a linear list or a binary tree is usually explicit. Deallocation requests can also occur explicitly or implicitly. In the case of the recursion stack, deallocation would be always

---

[11] Note that the program may at no time need more than 1000 units of memory. Therefore, the reduction in the memory pool from 1100 to 1000 units may appear entirely reasonable, but this ignores the interplay between allocation and deallocation requests.

implicit. However, for the node of a list or a tree, we can free the memory explicitly using an instruction provided for this purpose by the programming language, or the run-time support system may implicitly determine that a particular node can no longer be accessed in the program. For example, when deleting a node in a linear list, we may merely change pointers so that there is no longer any way to access that node. Run-time support systems have methods of determining that such a situation has occurred and that there is no other way of accessing that node (for example, because we explicitly had a pointer pointing to the node); in this case the memory assigned to that node is available and can therefore be freed.

Explicit deallocation tends to be carried out when the corresponding instruction is executed. Implicit deallocation usually occurs only when necessary, that is, when a request can no longer be satisfied using the currently available free space. In implicit deallocation, memory is free only after the deallocation has been carried out. Just because it is possible to determine that a certain space could be freed (and therefore reused) does not mean it is free. As long as no deallocation is done, that space is still considered occupied. In implicit deallocation, operations for freeing up memory are effectively batched together, and the deallocation of these several operations is carried out as one step. Implicit deallocation tends to be more complicated and time-consuming, so it typically is carried out only when necessary. Since it is more complicated, its impact on execution time can be fairly dramatic when it occurs. Again, this event tends to be completely unpredictable from the programmer's point of view.

Some run-time support systems cleverly manage to combine the worst of both worlds: Although the programmer issues explicit deallocation instructions, the run-time support system only collects memory when needed.[12] While this may be convenient since in this way only one type of deallocation algorithm must be carried out (note that in many programming languages, both implicit [think recursion stack] and explicit [think dynamic structures] deallocation is required), it does mislead the programmer into thinking that deallocation of space occurs whenever an explicit deallocation instruction is issued.

The upshot of this section is that the programmer should know what type of memory deallocation is done in a specific compiling and run-time support system; this may include various types of memory compaction. While this knowledge does not guarantee that no disappointments happen, at least these disappointments will no longer be inexplicable. In many cases, know-

---

[12] There have even been compilers that ignore deallocation instructions altogether; in effect, they acted as if the memory model were that of algorithms — no limits on available memory. Thus, even though the programming language provides instructions for freeing up memory and a program may execute such instructions, the compiler acts as if no such instructions exist. This approach can work, either because enough memory exists for a specific program (especially if the programs targeted by this compiler are "toy" programs, with unrealistically low memory requirements) or when coupled with VMM. However, for many applications the run-time behavior may become even more inexplicable than when explicit deallocations are carried out.

ing the enemy makes it easier to defeat it, although in the end the programmer is still at the mercy of systems not under her control.

6.4   Parameter-Passing Mechanisms

Every (conventional) programming language provides the facility of specifying functions or procedures or subroutines; these are subprograms with parameters. The purpose of the parameters is to make it possible for the operation embodied in the function to be applied to varying data. For example, when coding matrix multiplication, we want to be able to apply the subprogram to different matrices of different sizes. This is traditionally achieved through the use of parameters. It is useful to think of parameters as data structures that are explicitly designated for import and export.[13]

The use of parameters is tied intimately to the way in which parameters are passed. The three fundamentally different ways are call by value, call by reference, and call by name. Other ways of passing parameters are variants or combinations of these. How parameters are passed depends on the programming language; parameter passing is defined as part of the language definition, and most programming languages do not support all three methods.

The three methods differ fundamentally in the way in which the parameters of a function call are tied to the formal parameters that are placeholders in the formulation of the function. Since this connection between actual and formal parameters can be very important for the run-time behavior of a program, we will briefly describe the three methods.

Call by value is generally considered the simplest of the three. It assumes that the actual parameter has a value and that the formal parameter corresponds to a memory location. Assuming these assumptions are satisfied, the actual parameter is evaluated and the resulting value is copied into the memory location(s) corresponding to the formal parameter. If an assumption is violated, call by value cannot be carried out (or results in an error, either at compile time or run time). The execution of a successful function call then proceeds as if the formal parameters were local variables of the function, except that they had been assigned initial values before the instructions in the body of the function were executed. As with all local variables, the formal parameters of a

---

[13] Global parameters are sometimes used to circumvent the notion of restricting import and export strictly to parameters. The use of global variables tends to result in programs that are difficult to debug and maintain. Unfortunately, today's widely used programming languages do not force programmers to import and export explicitly, that is, through parameters. The strict prohibition of global variables would significantly reduce the debugging effort required and improve the maintainability of software.

function are no longer accessible once execution of the body of the function has ended and control is returned to the calling program.[14] An important aspect of call by value is that the space required for the formal parameters is to be considered additional space; therefore, it increases the space complexity of the resulting program. Since copying (of the values of the actual parameters to the locations of the formal parameters) is an operation that takes time, this also increases the time complexity.

Call by reference assumes that each actual parameter corresponds to a memory location. The corresponding formal parameter is then associated with this memory location for the duration of the execution of the function call. Thus, the use of a formal parameter in an instruction in the body of the function results in the use of the memory location that was assigned to the corresponding actual parameter. Since the memory space allocated to the actual parameters is also used by the formal parameters, call by reference tends to require less space.[15]

Call by name is essentially the invocation of a macro. It allows passing functions as parameters.[16] Since it is supported by very few programming languages and since it is rarely used even in those that do support it, we will not discuss it further.

Ordinarily, call by value is considered the safest way of passing parameters, followed by call by reference, and (a distant third) call by name. This is in part because passing by value cannot affect anything in the calling program, except for the results that are reported back from the function. In contrast, the other ways can modify values in the calling program, since memory locations of the calling program (actual parameters) are manipulated by the function.

Typically, when designing an algorithm for a specific problem, one tends to ignore the need for a precise specification of the way in which this algorithm is tied into the overall program. For example, we may design an algorithm for the multiplication of two matrices or for the binary search of a sorted array. In doing so, the interface between the resulting algorithm, now encapsulated as a function, and the algorithm from which this function is called is usually of little concern. This changes as soon as this algorithm

---

[14] Any space no longer accessible can be returned to the pool of available dynamic memory. This means that when invoking a function twice, there is no guarantee that the same space is allocated again.

[15] Typically, one ignores the time required to establish the correspondence. This is reasonable since the number of parameters is negligible (compared with the space required by the data structures of a complex program). The issue for space is even less serious since no additional space is required (except when it comes to recursion, where the connection between actual and formal parameters must be recorded. To see the necessity for this, consider the Tower of Hanoi problem discussed in Chapter 3).

[16] For example, it makes it possible to have a function Integral(f,a,b) that determines the definite integral of a given function f(x) between two points a and b in a way that permits the function f(x) to be a parameter.

is implemented as a program in a specific programming language. The way in which the function interacts with the calling program is crucial, as the following two examples indicate.

Consider the standard matrix multiplication algorithm, consisting of three nested loops, which assigns the product of the two $[1:n,1:n]$ matrices **A** and **B** to the matrix **C** of the same type:

```
for i:=1 to n do
   for j:=1 to n do
      {  C[i,j]:=0;
         for k:=1 to n do
            C[i,j] := C[i,j] + A[i,k]*B[k,j]
      }
```

While this algorithm may not be the most efficient (see our discussion of a more efficient matrix multiplication algorithm in Chapter 3), it at least has the advantage of being correct. When encapsulating this algorithm into a function, for example, MatMult, the three matrices **A**, **B**, and **C** (as well as n) must be parameters:

```
function MatMult(A,B,C,n)
   {  for i:=1 to n do
      for j:=1 to n do
         {  C[i,j]:=0;
            for k:=1 to n do C[i,j] := C[i,j] +
               A[i,k]*B[k,j]
         }
   }
```

Now we have to address the question of in what way these four parameters are to be passed. It is not difficult to see that n can be passed by value since the value, not the memory location, is what is relevant. How about the three matrices? Clearly, call by value does not work, since it would not allow the reporting back of the result (the matrix **C**) to the calling program. Recall that upon completed execution of the body, the local variables (including the formal parameters) are no longer accessible.[17] Moreover, copying a $[1:n,1:n]$ matrix requires time proportional to n^2. Thus, we may conclude that call by reference is appropriate for the three matrices.

Now consider the following entirely legitimate function call (essentially squaring the matrix **X** and assigning the result again to **X**), where **X** is a $[1:n,1:n]$ matrix:

```
function MatMult(X,X,X,n)
```

---

[17] Most programming languages do not allow the result of a function to be anything but an object of a simple type. Thus, the result of our function MatMult cannot be an array in these languages.

Unfortunately, if we pass our three array parameters by reference, our code is *wrong*. To see this, consider the following matrix **X**:

$$X = \begin{pmatrix} 1 & 2 \\ 3 & 4 \end{pmatrix}, \text{ the square of X (X*X) is } \begin{pmatrix} 7 & 10 \\ 15 & 22 \end{pmatrix},$$

$$\text{but MatMult(X, X, X, n) yields } \begin{pmatrix} 6 & 0 \\ 0 & 0 \end{pmatrix}.$$

Consequently, this approach of passing parameters does not work either. It turns out that the only correct way of passing parameters to MatMult is to pass **A** and **B** (and n) by value and **C** by reference. Only in this way does the original algorithm yield a correct implementation of matrix multiplication. This has important consequences for the time and space complexities of MatMult. Clearly, since **A** and **B** are passed by value, we must allocate additional space for these two matrices; this requires $2n^2$ locations. Note that **C** requires no additional space, since in call by reference the memory locations of the actual parameter are used for the formal parameters. Moreover, the act of copying the actual parameters corresponding to the formal parameters **A** and **B** requires time proportional to the number of elements that are copied, that is, $2n^2$. While the time complexity of the algorithm [$O(n^3)$] dominates the time complexity of copying, the space complexity is increased substantially, from $O(1)$ to $2n^2 + O(1)$.[18]

The second example is binary search. Assume we are given a sorted array **A** of size $1:n$ and a value x; BinSearch is to return an index i between 1 and n such that $x = A[i]$, or else 0 if x is not present in **A**. Here is the code:

---

[18] One can show that there is a superior way of doing this type of matrix multiplication:

```
function MatMult'(A,B,C,n)
  { declare a local [1:n,1:n] matrix D;
    for i:=1 to n do
      for j:=1 to n do
      { D[i,j]:=0;
        for k:=1 to n do D[i,j] := D[i,j] + A[i,k]*B[k,j]
      };
    for i:=1 to n do
      for j:=1 to n do
      { C[i,j]:= D[i,j]}
  }
```

It follows that we can now pass all three array parameters by reference (the situation for n can be safely ignored since n is a single memory location; while both call by value and call by reference would work, one tends to go with the simpler approach, that is, call by value). In this way we save the $2n^2$ memory locations for **A** and **B**, since these two matrices are passed by reference, which does not require additional space, at the cost of allocating a local matrix **D** that requires n^2 memory locations. Thus, the total saving of the new version MatMult' (over MatMult, each with the stated ways of passing its parameters) is n^2 memory locations and time proportional to n^2.

```
function BinSearch(x,A,lo,hi)
  { allocate a local integer variable p;
    while lo ≤ hi do
      { p:=⌈(lo+hi)/2⌉;
        if x=A[p] then return(p)
                      else if x<A[p] then hi:=p-1
                                     else lo:=p+1
      };
    return(0)
  }¹⁹
```

Again, the question arises of how to pass the four parameters when calling the function BinSearch(x,**A**,1,n). One can easily verify that the formal parameters x, lo, and hi can be passed by value, since neither time nor space complexity are greatly affected by this. The situation changes dramatically when it comes to the array **A**. It is true that we could pass **A** by value — the resulting function would certainly be correct. However, in this case the space complexity is n, and the time complexity is $O(n)$, plus the time complexity of the algorithm for binary search. Binary search (the algorithm) requires time $O(\log_2(n))$; thus, the time complexity of the code is $O(n + \log_2(n))$ or $O(n)$. Consequently, the code (with the array **A** being passed by value) has a time complexity that is exponentially greater than that of the algorithm. This is truly awful — and clearly indicates that call by value is highly inappropriate. If we pass **A** by reference, there is no copying involved; as a result, the space complexity is $O(1)$ and the time complexity is exactly that of the algorithm, namely $O(\log_2(n))$.

We conclude that the treatment of parameters can have major implications on the behavior, and indeed on the correctness, of a program. This is an aspect of code that is generally not considered carefully by those designing algorithms. However, as these two simple examples indicate, this issue can make or break an implementation.

6.5 Memory Mappings

We discussed memory mappings in the previous chapter. Here we merely reiterate that memory mappings tend to be outside of the programmer's control (they are a compiler aspect), unless the programmer wants to convert explicitly all multidimensional arrays into one-dimensional ones. This is

---

¹⁹ It would be slightly more efficient to allocate a local variable y and assign to it the value of A[p]; then y would take the place of both occurrences of **A**[p] in the two *if* statements. This is because an array reference (to **A**[p]), although $O(1)$, is more expensive than a simple memory reference (to y).

generally considered a horrible idea, since readability and maintainability of a program would be enormously affected by this decision.

6.6 The Influence of Language Properties

Several aspects of programming languages can negatively affect the behavior of a program. We will discuss three here: initialization of variables, packed data structures, and the problems caused by programming languages forcing a programmer to provide far more detail than is necessary to carry out a given operation. In a class by its own is the unfortunate tendency of programming languages (and their compilers) to forgo the test of whether the indices to structures are within their proper ranges.

6.6.1 Initialization

Algorithms tend to be somewhat cavalier in the way they deal with the initialization of variables. In many cases the assumption is that the reader of the algorithm is sufficiently intelligent to understand what is meant. This approach does not work with programs. Programs (or compilers) are emphatically not prepared to read the mind of the programmer. As a result, one has to pay much more attention to the question of initialization.

There are three ways of dealing with this question. For the most part, they are part of the language specification. Absent a statement describing this issue in the language definition, the question is left to the compiler to resolve.[20] These three approaches are undefined variables, predefined variables, and unspecified (or random) variables.

> **Undefined variables:** This refers to requiring that every variable must be explicitly assigned a value before the variable can be used (in an expression, or as a parameter passed by value). Failure to do so will result in an error.[21] These variables are called undefined.[22] Many programmers are less than happy with this, mainly because they have become accustomed to a different approach. However, this is

---

[20] This is generally quite undesirable, since it means different compilers for the same programming language may make differing assumptions. This has serious implications for the portability of programs written in that language, since the results of the same program may differ from one compiler to another.

[21] This error is usually a run-time error, since it is undecidable in general to determine whether there is a way to reach an undefined variable

[22] This refers to the lack of a value for that variable. In contrast, variables that are not declared at the beginning of the program are called undeclared. Again, different programming languages adopt different approaches. Many programming languages permit implicit declaration of simple variables but require explicit declaration of complex structures, such as arrays. While important for software design, this issue is less important for us.

by far the most secure way of dealing with the initialization of variables. On the one hand, we would argue that a programmer should not expect a variable to have a value unless an (explicit) instruction was executed that assigned that value to the variable.[23] This clearly indicates that programmers should write code to initialize variables if they expect these variables to have values. On the other hand, preassigning values to variables may be inefficient, as we will see.[24] The only disadvantage of this method is that the representation of a variable must permit the determination of whether a value has ever been explicitly assigned to it. This may require some additional space (either in the symbol table or in the memory used for the structure).

Predefined variables: This refers to the compiler assigning a specific, predefined value (typically 0) to all variables. While this may be convenient and is usually safe, it may also introduce inefficiencies. For example, if an array is initialized, the time complexity of this operation is proportional to the number of its elements. If this initialization turns out to be unnecessary (because the program explicitly assigns values to the array), the time required by the initialization is wasted. In general, it is impossible to determine whether there is a path through the program execution to the use of the array that avoids every explicit assignment of values to the array; this is the only case when this initialization would be of use. Therefore, it is unclear whether this approach will ever be useful. More importantly, it deprives the programmer of a useful tool for detecting logical errors (see the discussion in the previous paragraph, including the footnotes).

Unspecified variables: No values are preassigned to variables, but the variables are not considered undefined either. Instead, the content of the memory location corresponding to a given variable is interpreted according to the type of that variable and used whenever the variable appears in a place that requires a value (for example, in an expression or in call by value). This is supremely unsafe since it is entirely unpredictable what this value is during a specific execution.

---

[23] This may be a very useful way of detecting logical errors. If a variable has not been explicitly assigned a value, this is likely the result of an oversight in the program implementation. Such an error is usually a semantics error; nevertheless, this type of error can be detected by the compiler or the run-time support system. (As a general rule, semantics errors cannot be detected by compilers.) It is generally an excellent idea to employ methods that allow the detection of semantics errors by syntactical means, since the detection of true semantics errors (which are based on what the programmer did program instead of what she wanted to program) amounts to mind reading.

[24] Or at least not any more efficient than having undefined variables (which are effectively predefined as *undefined*). In practice, the assignment of *undefined* can be carried out uniformly for all memory locations involved in the program when space is allocated to a program (at the very beginning of execution). Thus, this assignment may be more efficient than the setting to 0 of the space of an individual array, discussed in the next paragraph.

In this scenario that value can (and usually will) be different from one execution of the program to the next. It is clearly the most efficient way, since effectively no initialization occurs. Also, it will be of no concern if the programmer explicitly defines the values of all variables. However, if the programmer omits, perhaps because of a programming error, to assign a value to a variable, this error will not be detected easily. This is highly undesirable since it can be a source of extremely subtle errors that could be easily avoided.[25]

The choice between these three approaches is part of the programming language definition. It is therefore outside of the programmer's influence. Nevertheless, programmers should at least be aware of the advantages and disadvantages of the three methods. They may have a choice of programming language, and the treatment of variable initialization could be one factor in deciding which language to use.

6.6.2 Packed Data Structures

Some programming languages recognize that certain data types do not require an entire word or byte for their representation. A typical example is the boolean or logical type, whose representation requires only one bit. As a result, these programming languages may offer the capability of *packing* data structures. In this approach an array of 1024 boolean variables would use only 128 bytes, instead of 1024 bytes. The difference becomes even more pronounced if the basic unit of memory access is the word (four bytes), in which case packing the array would require 32 words, instead of 1024. This savings in memory comes at a price — access to an individual element of the array becomes more complicated. In our packed array, access to any element requires that we first determine in which byte or word the value of the array element resides. Then this byte or word must be decoded (since it encodes numerous array elements). Only then can we access the desired element. For assignments, a similar process must be carried out.

It follows that in using packed structures, one trades time for space. (Note that this generally makes sense only for arrays, since other structures tend to be relatively small; only arrays have the property that a small instruction can specify a huge data structure.) In our example of the boolean array, it should be clear that the encoding and decoding process takes time that would not have to be expended if the array were not packed. At the same time, a packed array tends to use less space. One may conclude from this that packed structures should not be used if there is enough space available in the main memory, because then one would have to determine how much time the I/O management for the *packed* structure requires, how

---

[25] The only thing positive that can be said about this type of initialization is that it wastes no time, since no operation must be carried out. This is a terrible justification of an indisputably unsafe practice.

much time the I/O management for the *unpacked* structure requires, and whether the difference justifies the additional time required for encoding and decoding. If using packed structures allows one to avoid the use of VMM (or out-of-core programming), it is always better to pack. If even the packed structure is too large to be accommodated in main memory, a more careful analysis of the program behavior is necessary to resolve this issue.

Unfortunately, some compilers ignore packing instructions; in other words, the programming language provides instructions that specify packed structures, but the compiler acts as if they were null statements. It is useful to know what one's compiler does if one wishes to avoid surprises. If the compiler ignores packing instructions and we are in the situation where packing would avoid VMM, it may be advantageous from a run-time point of view to carry out the packing instruction explicitly. However, this is almost as bad as doing one's own memory mapping. It results in awful code that is difficult to debug and terrible to maintain. This is true even if one encapsulates these mechanisms in (properly documented) functions.

6.6.3   Overspecification of Execution Order

The vast majority of programming languages require a programmer to formulate aspects of an operation that are neither necessary nor useful. A simple example is the addition of two matrices. In an algorithm one might simply state that the two matrices are added. In most programming languages, this obvious operation ends up as two nested loops. This is necessitated by the absence of appropriate language constructs. This excessive specificity can be very harmful; one could reasonably argue that specifying matrix addition generically, that is, without giving any implementation details, places the burden of choosing an acceptable way of computing this operation on the compiler. As we have seen, coding two nested loops can go horribly wrong if the arrays are too large to fit into main memory and the loops clash with the memory-mapping function. The truth is that any order of traversing the elements of the three matrices involved will do, as long as each location $[i,j]$ is visited exactly once.

Programming languages frequently force the programmer to specify details that may impede efficient execution. This is in marked contrast to algorithms, where details usually are glossed over, in many cases deliberately, frequently assisting in a more efficient approach to execution. For example, if matrix addition were simply stated as such, the compiler could select the most efficient order of visiting the individual matrix elements. Instead, the stipulation of a specific execution order (which is now to be followed) may result in excruciatingly slow programs. This is a direct consequence of the programming language's failure to allow the specification of a generic "for all array elements" operation. While this example is simple enough to be immediately obvious, other instances may be subtler. Nevertheless, it is important to be aware that language constructs (or the lack thereof) can be sources of inefficiencies for a program written in that language. This can be particularly important when combined with the actions of a good optimizing compiler.

6.6.4   Avoiding Range Checks

Many programming languages, in an extremely ill-advised pursuit of efficiency, forgo explicit tests that determine whether the index into a structure, usually an array, is within the appropriate range for that index. Because of problems discussed in the next chapter, sometimes even correct algorithms give rise to incorrect indices. Such problems are notoriously difficult to identify, since absent any meaningful range checks, no error is indicated when this occurs; instead, wrong values are used in calculations or, worse, values are assigned to memory locations that correspond to entirely different variables or structures. This is an egregious instance where a serious semantic error could be detected during run time, but many programming languages value a superficial efficiency (avoiding the test of whether the index is within its proper range) higher than the programmer's time and effort, which must be expended on debugging once the program misbehaves. The avoidance of range checks might be blamed on a desire for program optimization, but the difference is that optimization can be turned off if the programmer wishes. In contrast, a compiler that does not implement range checks (perhaps because the language specification does not stipulate it) will fail to do so whether it applies optimization or not.

6.7   The Influence of Optimization

Techniques employed by optimizing compilers can result in unexpected behavior of a program in several ways. One is the interplay of an optimization step with a specific code. The other is the lazy evaluation of expressions.

6.7.1   Interference with Specific Statements

The more details a program specifies, the less an optimizing compiler can do with it to improve its performance, because optimizing compilers tend to be extremely conservative. Therefore, if it appears that the programmer really wanted a particular formulation, optimizing compilers tend to leave it alone. If it is clear that the programmer expressed a general operation, it is up to the compiler to optimize that operation according to the *target platform*. This is an important notion. While not every platform is amenable to certain optimizations, this should not be the programmer's concern; the compiler should ensure that the best possible (or at least a very good) version be executed. For example, if a programmer were able state that she wanted to multiply the matrices **A** and **B** of size [1:n,1:n] and store the result in **C**, it would be up to the optimizing compiler to select the best possible approach. If n is small, the standard three nested loops might be appropriate, but if n is large, a more efficient algorithm might be employed (see Chapter 3). Furthermore, if the matrices do not fit into main memory, an appropriate memory mapping might be selected by the compiler to minimize the transfer of blocks between main memory and disk.

While most programming languages do not provide the ability of specifying operations very loosely, this example indicates that the programmer should not attempt to be too clever. Trying to program to a specific platform is generally highly undesirable. It sacrifices the portability of a program written in a higher-level language (as opposed to assembly language or machine code) and it may render a highly tuned program less efficient since it interferes with optimization. Programmers should firmly keep in mind that today's optimization compilers tend to produce code that is much more efficient than most hand-tuned code — provided one lets the optimizing compiler do what it is supposed to do. The less detail the programmer stipulates in the code, the more likely it is that the optimizing compiler will attain its goal of producing efficient code. Finally, highly tuned programs tend to be unmaintainable since a relatively simple idea in them is transmogrified into something that frequently looks quite bizarre.

Programmers should also be aware of the importance of software portability in this context. This is very pointedly illustrated by the following observation: Hardware tends to be obsolete in 5 to 10 years, often even faster; software, however, is much longer-lived. As a result, much of the software executing on today's systems was written long before these hardware platforms existed. Since software portability is reduced by a tendency to fine-tune programs, this temptation should be firmly resisted.

A good rule of thumb is to formulate an operation in as simple a form as possible and leave the optimization of the simple idea to the optimizing compiler.

6.7.2 Lazy Evaluation

A particular instance of optimization that can generate surprises for programmers is the lazy evaluation of expressions. The general principle is that the evaluation of an expression proceeds inside out, starting with the simplest subexpression and composing from these values more complicated subexpressions until the final value of the entire expression is determined. Lazy evaluation is based on the observation that knowledge of the value of a certain subexpression may permit knowledge of the final value, without the evaluation of other subexpressions. For example, knowing that one factor of a product has the value 0 permits one to conclude that final value of the product is also 0, without evaluating the second factor.

Lazy evaluation is particularly important for boolean expressions. For example, the **and** of two expressions is **false** if one of the two is **false**; similarly, the **or** of two expressions is **true** is one of the two is **true**. In both cases it is not necessary to evaluate the other expression.

Lazy evaluation of expressions tends to be unnoticed if there are no side effects — instances where the evaluation of an expression not only provides a value but carries out other operations as well. For example, consider the product of two values. If these two values are function calls that execute print statements in addition to returning a value, whether or not each of the functions is executed is quite important. If a function is evaluated, it carries out the print statements, but if it is not, then it does not print. Thus, a programmer may expect certain actions to occur because the expression is evaluated, without realizing that in lazy evaluation, not every component of an expression is evaluated.

A particular side effect could be the indication that a particular variable does not have a value. This would be the case if the language recognizes that that variable is undefined (see the discussion in Section 6.6). One can easily see that lazy evaluation can defeat the purpose of this (safe) approach to initializing variables. A programmer may infer that all variables are defined since the entire expression was evaluated, but in lazy evaluation obtaining a value for an expression does not mean that every variable in that expression had been inspected. Thus, it is entirely possible to execute all statements of a loop 100 times successfully, only to be told in the 101st iteration that a particular variable in one of the statements is undefined.

Lazy evaluation can be easily defeated by the programmer by breaking up expressions. For example, instead of testing whether

```
(F(j)>10.0) or (F(j+1)<0.0)
```

is **true**, we could write the two assignments

```
b1:=(F(j)>10.0); b1:=(F(j+1)<0.0)
```

and then test whether

```
b1 or b2
```

is **true**. In this way, both function calls are executed since they are needed to assign values to the two boolean variables b1 and b2.

6.8 Parallel Processes

In modern computing systems, many processes occur in parallel. Thus, a programmer may not be aware of processes that occur at the same time as the execution of his or her program; this in turn may influence the behavior of that program. These processes may be related to the program being executed (as in the case of asynchronous I/O, whereby the disk controller may execute while the program proceeds with its own instructions) or they may be entirely unrelated to the program executing. In both cases the programmer has virtually no influence on these processes.[26]

In most cases parallel processes are used to improve the performance of a program. While some overhead is incurred, it is usually not significant enough to be noticeable. However, asynchronous I/O may improve the runtime behavior of a program measurably by allowing the retrieval of data and the execution of instructions to proceed in parallel. Ordinarily, this is controlled by the compiler and the run-time support system of the target platform on which the software is executed. The only way in which this may result in disappointments would be if one were to migrate from a platform supporting asynchronous I/O to one that does not. That such a migration negatively affects the run-time performance of the code is unavoidable.[27]

An altogether different situation occurs if we are dealing with an overtly parallel program. In this case, the program itself would explicitly create parallel processes whose coordinated execution results in the solution of the overall problem. Determining the time complexity of parallel programs tends to be significantly harder. Parallel programs are outside of the realm of this book, so we refer readers interested in this topic to the literature.

6.9   What to Do about It

Several lessons can be distilled from the observations in this chapter. We mention the more salient points.

An important lesson concerns space complexity. While it may be of interest to know the average space complexity of an algorithm, for programs the average space requirement is not a very useful concept. Instead, the programmer should concentrate on the worst-case space complexity. A program that crashes because of insufficient space is not very useful, even if this occurs

---

[26] The second type of processes, unrelated to the program, can be excluded by running the program in an environment where no other processes may execute. This is an expensive proposition that is rarely available in practical situations. Thus, we will not consider it any further.

[27] Supporting asynchronous I/O typically means a more sophisticated computing platform. Such a migration would therefore regress from an advanced platform to a more primitive one. Such a migration would be highly unusual and should be avoided if at all possible.

only rarely. This has also implications for the selection of algorithms to implement.

Programmers should pay particular attention to dynamic data structures and the memory management issues they engender. Allocation and deallocation of memory are important for the run-time behavior of software. This includes hidden operations, especially those generated by the use of recursion.

Of particular interest is the question of garbage collection. While memory compaction is clearly outside of the control of the programmer in most contexts, awareness of this and related issues will at least remove the element of surprise when the behavior of a program appears unpredictable. It may also allow the programmer to avoid some hidden land mines, especially those related to the use of recursion.

A similar observation holds for parameters. The programmer may not have much choice once the programming language is selected, but she should at least be knowledgeable about the various ways of passing parameters and their implications for time and space complexities. Moreover, an incorrect use of parameter passing mechanisms may result in erroneous code.

Most of the remaining issues enumerated and explained in this chapter are even less tangible. Initialization of variables is a language property, as is the absence of range checks and the treatment of packed arrays. Lazy evaluation may or may not be stipulated in the language definition; absent any statement in the definition, it becomes a compiler issue (with the obvious negative implications for software portability).

Optimization issues, however, are quite tangible. The programmer should always keep the program as simple as possible, resisting the temptation to fine-tune it to a particular target platform and thereby enabling a good optimizing compiler to hold up its end of the bargain.

Bibliographical Notes

Most of the background material for this chapter can be found in standard textbooks covering programming languages and compilers, for example, Aho, Sethi, and Ullman: *Compilers: Principles, Techniques and Tools*; Aho and Ullman: *The Theory of Parsing, Translation, and Compiling*; Muchnik: *Advanced Compiler Design and Implementation*; and Zima and Chapman: *Supercompilers for Parallel and Vector Computers*. Garbage collection is also discussed in conjunction with operating and run-time support systems. This also holds for the parallel processes briefly mentioned in Section 6.8. We refer to Silberschatz, Gavin, and Gagne: *Operating Systems Concepts* and other texts mentioned in this chapter. An interesting discussion (almost amounting to a mea culpa) can be found in "Good Ideas, through the Looking Glass", written by Niklaus Wirth, author of Pascal and several other programming languages, in which he provides his view of a number of language constructs and their usefulness (or lack thereof). This echoes some of the criticisms listed in this chapter.

Exercises

Exercise 1

Consider the following function:

```
CheckSums(A,B,C)
```

where **A** is a two-dimensional (2D) array of size [1:n, 1:n] and **B** and **C** are vectors of size [1:n], n being a positive integer. The body of CheckSums implements the following computations:

$$B[i] = A[i,1] - A[i,2] + A[i,3] - .... A[i,n]$$

$$C[i] = A[1,i] - A[2,i] + A[3,i] - .... A[n,i].$$

a. Give the complete function CheckSums (**A,B,C**), including the code of the function body and the method of passing the three parameters.

b. Determine the time and space complexity of your function (space complexity is the amount of memory space required by the function, in addition to the space for the actual parameters).

Warning: Your function must work correctly for calls such as

```
CheckSums(D[1:n,1:n], D[1:n,1], D[1,1:n])!
```

where **D**[1:n,1] is the first column of the 2D array **D** and **D**[1,1:n] is the first row.

Exercise 2

In Section 3.2 we discussed search trees and their height-balanced version, AVL trees.

a. Determine the minimal prudent space requirements for insertion and deletion for general search trees and for height-balanced search trees. Keep in mind that the use of recursion may not be the most appropriate approach.

b. Examine how the parameters must be passed for the functions for insertion and deletion with minimal prudent space requirements, both for general and for height-balanced search trees.

Exercise 3

Examine how the compiler for your favorite programming language handles space allocation and deallocation in conjunction with recursive calls. You may be able to obtain information from the compiler's documentation, but you can also glean a good deal of information by conducting an experiment, for example as follows:

a. Create a recursive function RF(n) (it must not be tail recursive — otherwise a clever compiler might substitute iteration), where the parameter n indicates the depth of the recursion stack. (To keep RF efficient, it should have only one recursive call in its body.) Make sure the local variables of RF require sufficient space so that repeated executions of RF(n) do not only result in allocation requests, but also require releasing the memory upon return. Then call RF(n) repeatedly, say 100 times, for several values of n, say 10, 100, 1,000, 10,000, and 100,000. Carefully instrument your program so you can measure the time each recursive call takes. If garbage collection occurs, it will introduce timing discrepancies that are not explainable by the program's instructions alone. These discrepancies will indicate when and where garbage collection functions were invoked during the program's execution.

b. A refinement of (a) would be to obscure the recursion as follows: Instead of RF calling itself, RF might call a function RG (which is very similar in structure to RF, but the size of the local variables should be slightly different). This function RG then calls RF. These recursive functions RF and RG are also called coroutines. (There are only two coroutines in this case, but in general the chain of function calls connecting RF back to itself can be arbitrarily long: RF0 calls RF1, which calls RF2, which calls RF3, etc., until finally RFn calls RF0.)

7

Implicit Assumptions

About This Chapter

In algorithms there are obvious assumptions that are tacitly presumed to be satisfied. However, a program must be able to handle exceptional situations that violate these tacit assumptions. Programs must also test for assumptions that are fundamental for the correct functioning of the approach. What may be quite obvious for the algorithm designer is nevertheless to be verified in a program.

Implicit assumptions occur frequently in algorithm design; they are less common and far less acceptable in software. This tension between reasonable assumptions and unreasonable attention to detail is an important aspect of the difference between algorithms and software. We examine exceptions as well as more fundamental issues related to this topic.

7.1   Handling Exceptional Situations

Algorithms presume that the reader has some intelligence. Therefore, they tend to be formulated without covering every possibility or aspect. In contrast, programs must be written so that even unexpected input and results do not cause them to crash. This implies that programs do not have the luxury of concentrating on the important aspects of a problem's solution — all aspects must be covered comprehensively. Modern programming languages recognize this need and provide facilities for handling exceptions, but these facilities must be used by the programmer or they will not improve the programs. Another aspect an algorithm may ignore but a program must not is the initialization of function calls, especially recursive ones. Algorithms may be able to get away with assuming reasonable starting conditions, but programs must test for them. Moreover, if the assumptions are not satisfied, some specific action must be taken so that the program does not crash![1] Finally, problems related to incorrect

---

[1] This assessment may be tempered by considerations related to the question of whether the program is a batch program or interactive. We will take up this issue later.

input tend to be ignored in algorithms; programs, however, must ensure that the input is in the format required by the program.

7.1.1 Exception Handling

The need for exception handling can arise in various ways. A typical exception is division by zero. The occurrence of a division by zero may be the consequence of several events. It may be the result of incorrect input, the result of a sloppy algorithm[2], or the result of a rounding error. We will argue below that testing whether the input satisfies the requisite conditions is necessary for code, even though it may not be considered in an algorithm. We will deal with problems caused by the finite representation of numbers in programs in the next chapter. Here, we want to emphasize that exception handling is crucial for the correct functioning of programs. This implies in particular that code must be provided that specifies the action to be taken when an exception is thrown. Before one can do this, it is necessary that the programmer analyze where things can go wrong — where exceptions may occur.

This brings us to a serious weakness of general exception handling: Not every exception of a specific type should be treated in the same way. For example, consider division by zero. If one were to deal with this generally, the exception-handling mechanism could consist only of a generic notification of this event. It usually does not allow us to deal with it in a specific way. For example, we may want to determine the average salary of a group of employees. The algorithm may not make any provisions for the case where that group, defined in some way, contains no employees, resulting in a careless division by zero if no test was carried out for this special case. Generic exception handling would merely notify us of a division by zero; it does not allow us to ignore the empty group and the effects this may have on the overall computation. To be able to do this requires a careful analysis of all implicit assumptions together with a careful design of code for each of the possible violations of them.[3]

---

[2] While we do assume that the algorithm we start out with is correct, its designer may not have paid sufficient attention to all details to be directly translatable into code. For example, we may use BinarySearch to determine an index ind of an item in a sorted array. The value of ind may then be used to access information related to that item. This works only if the item is present in the array; otherwise ind has a value that signals that the item is not present, for example 0, and use of this value to access information related to this (nonexisting) item results in an error. In other words, the algorithm formulates a solution assuming the item is present and ignores the alternative. A program must specify explicitly what to do if the alternative is encountered.

[3] Not all programming languages provide facilities for general exception handling. These comments suggest that this lack is not nearly as serious as one might assume. Many exceptions must be handled in specific ways, geared to the concrete instance where they arise, and this cannot be done through generic exception handling. By and large, generic exception handling allows continued execution, that is, the program does not crash, but it does not allow actions to be taken that make sense in a specific situation. This means generic exception handling is essentially syntactic, not semantic, error handling. Semantic error handling requires an understanding of the meaning of the program and can therefore be carried out only by the programmer.

7.1.2 Initializing Function Calls

The initialization of function calls, especially recursive ones, is another trouble spot that differentiates algorithms from programs. As with exceptions, the problem arises from values that were computed or determined elsewhere but may now cause our function to misbehave. For general functions, the problem is often that the values of the actual parameters do not make sense for reasons that are too obvious to belabor in the formulation of the algorithm. Unfortunately, once we transition to a program, these nonsensical situations must be dealt with explicitly since otherwise the program may either produce incorrect results or crash. In the special case of recursive functions, we also have the problem of ensuring that every possible call will eventually end up in a basis case, thereby terminating the recursive calls.

Values that do not make sense (and are therefore not considered in the formulation of the algorithm) might be 0 for the number n of elements in a group, for example in the computation of the average salary. If this value is not positive, problems may arise (for example, division by 0). For an algorithm, this may be obvious and tacitly understood; for a program, the test $n \geq 1$ should be explicitly carried out, with additional code provided when the test is not satisfied. A similar situation occurs if we want to program matrix multiplication of two $[1{:}n,1{:}n]$ matrices. It would not occur to anyone formulating the algorithm to test explicitly for $n \geq 1$, yet not doing so might result in code that crashes if this condition happens not to be satisfied. A last example is related to the range checks mentioned in the previous chapter. If a function has a parameter that accesses an array element, it is highly desirable that this index be within the proper range. If the programming language does not test for this as a matter of course, it is probably advisable that the programmer carry out this test explicitly. Again, an algorithm may not bother with this, but a program should. It is important to realize that both the test and the additional code specifying what is to be done when the test fails are not optional, but are mandatory for good software.

It is not merely sufficient to test for these implicit assumptions. To ensure proper functioning of our programs we must also provide code that addresses the consequences of such a test not being satisfied. By and large, it is unsafe to assume that input to functions will always be as expected. Surprises may occur because of a variety of issues, from incorrect user input to rounding errors and other exceptions.

For recursive functions, we must additionally ensure that every recursive call terminates. This requires that for any legal input combination (and these parameters must have been tested), eventually a basis case is reached, terminating the recursion. Again, there is a subtle gap between algorithm and program. This should be particularly of concern if the variable that governs the recursion is not an integer. For example, consider the following recursive skeleton:

```
F(x)
  if x=0.0 do { basis case }
  else { statements; F(x-0.1); statements }
```

The idea is that we apply recursion, reducing the argument by 1/10, so if the actual parameter is an integer, the algorithm will terminate. As we pointed out above, this is playing with fire since at a minimum, we must test whether this assumption (that the actual parameter is an integer) is satisfied. However, even if this assumption holds, it is unlikely that a direct implementation of this algorithm will terminate. The problem lies in the representation of floating point numbers and the test for equality, which are taken up in the next chapter. Here, we merely want to state unequivocally that proper functioning of recursion requires that for all inputs, a basis case must be reached. This assumption is violated in this example program, as it would be in similar examples based on floating point numbers, even though the original algorithm does satisfy it.

Finally, users may simply provide incorrect input, possibly through carelessness or because of transmission errors or an incompatibility of the input device with the receiving unit. Programs will differ depending on whether they are batch programs or interactive ones. For batch programs, an incorrect input usually means the program must terminate execution. There is no way to correct the erroneous input supplied. An interactive program would ordinarily be expected to prompt the user for input; thus, if the input does not conform to the specifications, another prompt may be in order. Even in this case the program may have to stop executing if the user insists on supplying erroneous input (for example, if there is an incompatibility).

It is not always possible to determine that an input is wrong; this would amount to being able to predict what the input should be. Instead, a program can only test whether a certain general format is complied with. Thus, if a pair of integers specifying a date within a year is required, certain combinations are obviously incorrect, for example "50 50". It is less obvious whether "31 12" is incorrect. It would be if the month comes first (American-style dates), but if the day comes first (European-style dates), it is correct. Finally, there is no way to tell whether "9 10" is correct (maybe it should be "10 9"), but it conforms to the expectations of a date and should therefore be accepted.[4] Another difficulty arises if an integer input is required but the user inputs a real value or a character string. In such a case, it may be quite cumbersome to produce code that rejects input whose type is not valid. This kind of input error will probably have to be assessed case by case. For example, when being prompted for a percentage value, a user may input "15" while another user may input "0.15". What is clear is that programs must pay far more attention to these questions than any algorithm ever would (or should).

---

[4] Input such as "2 29" is also problematic, since (assuming American-style format) it is only valid in leap years. Thus, without knowledge of the year, it is impossible to decide whether this is a valid input.

7.2 Testing for Fundamental Requirements

The previous section focused on relatively low-level assumptions. Occasionally, assumptions occur at a much higher level. They may nevertheless be eminently reasonable, so algorithm designers ignore them (beyond perhaps stating that the assumption must hold). In contrast to the low-level test mentioned before, such tests may have significant implications for the complexity of a program.

We will illustrate the underlying difficulty with two examples: the implementation of matrix multiplication discussed in Section 6.4 and binary search. In both cases certain assumptions are crucial for the correct behavior of the functions, but testing for these assumptions can be a significant burden to the extent that the approach that relies on the assumption may have to be discarded in favor of one that does not make this assumption.

In Section 6.4 we discussed parameter passing for the function MatMult (A,B,C,n) (see the code there). We observed that this function produces wrong results if the three arrays are passed by reference. Let us analyze this a bit more carefully. It is not difficult to see that the function is correct with call by reference, provided the three arrays A, B, and C do not have any memory locations in common.[5] This assumption was violated when we computed the square of the matrix X in place, $X := X^2$, since all three matrices refer to the same locations. Note that far more complicated situations may arise; for example we may call MatMult$(X,Y,Z,1000)$, where the three matrices X, Y, and Z are fined as follows: Let U be a matrix of type $[1:100000,1:100000]$ and define:

$$X[1:1000,1:1000] := U[M+1:M+3000:3, M+2:M+2001:2]$$

$$Y[1:1000,1:1000] := U[20000-M:20000-M-4999:-5, 10000-M:10000-M-2999:-3]$$

$$Z[1:1000,1:1000] := U[501:7500:7, 301:7300:7],$$

where $a{:}b{:}c$ denotes the a sequence of integers $m := a, a + c, a + 2c, a + 3c$, and so on, up to and including the number $a + kc$, with the largest integer value for k such that $a + kc$ is no larger than b for positive c and no smaller than b for negative c. For example, 5:29:7 denotes the sequence $[5,12,19,26]$, and 111:39:-17 denotes $[111,94,77,60,43]$. Then $U[a{:}b{:}c,d{:}e{:}f]$ denotes the subarray of U that consists of all elements $U[i,j]$, where i occurs in the sequence $a{:}b{:}c$ and j occurs in the sequence $d{:}e{:}f$.[6] For example, the specification

---

[5] It is sufficient to assume that the third matrix, C (which accumulates the result), has no overlap with the matrices A and B. Since under this assumption neither A nor B are modified during the execution of the code of MatMult (it is only the matrix C whose values are written; A and B are merely read), the resulting matrix for the product will be correct.

[6] Note that this way of specifying matrices is possible in some programming languages, most importantly the newer standards of Fortran.

M[1:4,1:5] := **U**[5:29:7, 111:39:–17] identifies 20 elements of the array **U** with the 20 elements of the matrix **M** in the following way:

M[1,1]=U[5,111], M[1,2]=U[5,94], M[1,3]=U[5,77], M[1,4]=U[5,60], M[1,5]=U[5,43],

M[2,1]=U[12,111], M[2,2]=U[12,94], M[2,3]=U[12,77], M[2,4]=U[12,60], M[2,5]=U[12,43],

M[3,1]=U[19,111], M[3,2]=U[19,94], M[3,3]=U[19,77], M[3,4]=U[19,60], M[3,5]=U[19,43],

M[4,1]=U[26,111], M[4,2]=U[26,94], M[4,3]=U[26,77], M[4,4]=U[26,60], M[4,5]=U[26,43].

It should now be obvious that testing for the overlap condition is anything but trivial. If one allows arbitrary sequences of indices to define subarrays, then it turns out that determining whether a given [1:n,1:n] matrix **A** has any element in common with another matrix **B** of the same type [1:n,1:n] requires time proportional to n^4. For each of the n^2 elements of **A**, we have to determine whether it refers to a memory location referenced by **B**. Since determining whether one element of **A** is an element of **B** requires time $O(n^2)$ because this **A**-element could be any of the n^2 **B**-elements, doing this n^2 times (for each of the elements in **A**) requires $O(n^4)$ time.[7] The consequence is that testing for a condition that guarantees us that a marginally more efficient approach works properly requires dramatically more time than the savings one could possibly obtain. Moreover, one should realize that this test would have to be carried out every time MatMult with call by reference is to be called, even though in the vast majority of all cases, the test for overlap would fail (thereby permitting the use of the more efficient scheme). Finally, if the test succeeds (that is, overlap is detected), alternative code would have

---

[7] Note that it is not easy to determine whether two references (variables) refer to the same memory location. This is related to the fact that we have to manipulate logical memory locations, not values (logical, since the corresponding absolute memory locations may change owing to paging in and out, relocatable code, etc.). Under some mild assumptions, the following approach works: Given two references x and y, determine the value x' of the memory location referenced by x and the value y' of the memory location of y. Then change the contents of the memory location of x to something different from x'. Determine the value referenced by y now. If this value is different from y', then x and y refer to the same memory location; otherwise they do not. In either case, we must change the contents of x back to x', since this test should be *nondestructive* (the values should not be affected). We must make some assumptions for this to work: We must be able to determine a value that is different from x' (note that in general, x and y may not be of the same type, so their corresponding values need not be the same) and we must be able to assign the value x' to the memory location referenced by x. If x' is undefined (in the scenario where the programming language supports undefined variables), it is impossible to restore the contents from within the program (since in programs with undefined variables, it is impossible to explicitly set a variable to be undefined). In fact it is usually impossible to find out that x' is undefined without aborting program execution.

to be provided to deal with this situation. In general, it makes much more sense to use call by value for **A** and **B** and call by reference for **C** if one wants to use MatMult (or better yet, to use MatMult' with call by reference for all three matrices [see footnote 18 in Chapter 6]). However, this conclusion can be arrived at only after one has done the analysis that demonstrates that this overlap test will never pay for itself.

Our second example involves binary search. It is well known that this highly efficient technique is applicable only if the underlying array is sorted. The question arises therefore whether it is mandatory that this condition be verified before calling the function BinarySearch. While one may be tempted to answer affirmatively, the consequences are unpleasant: Any test of whether a given vector of type [1:n] is sorted requires time proportional to n.[8] Recall that binary search takes time proportional to $\log_2(n)$. Thus, testing for the fundamental condition without which the method fails miserably is exponentially more expensive than the operation itself. One might be tempted to view this example as no different from the matrix multiplication example. However this is not so.

The assumption in MatMult was rather esoteric. Moreover, there is an alternative formulation of the technique (with a minor increase in complexity) that does not depend on the assumption. In BinarySearch the assumption of sortedness is fundamental and indispensable. There is no alternative formulation of binary search that would work without the assumption.[9] Dropping the stipulation that the vector be sorted is a total change in the computing paradigm. Without this assumption, we are no longer dealing with binary search but with sequential search, which is a different algorithm altogether. Therefore, it is probably acceptable to dispense with this test. This is partly driven by complexity considerations. If the test could be carried out in constant time, we might advise to do it. However, since it takes exponentially more time than the operation itself, common sense suggests that we suppress testing for the assumption that the array is sorted. In contrast, MatMult can be formulated so that the overlap test can be completely dispensed with.

These two examples indicate that we will be frequently confronted with assumptions that are crucial for the correct functioning of our programs, but it is not entirely clear whether it is advisable to verify whether they are satisfied. The answer usually depends on the context of the problem. The

---

[8] Note that we do not sort; we merely test whether the vector is sorted. Here is how to test whether the array **A**[1:n] is sorted in ascending order (for descending order, change the comparison):

```
for i:=2 to n do if not(A[i-1] ≤A [i])
then {output("array not sorted"); exit}
```

This requires at most $n - 1$ comparisons and cannot be improved, since for the conclusion that the array is sorted, $n - 1$ comparisons are required.

[9] It is disingenuous to view linear search as an alternative formulation of binary search even though it would obviously work.

case of MatMult with call by reference is probably a surprise to most programmers; analysis of the test indicated that it made no sense to do it since there exists a perfectly serviceable alternative code that does not depend on any overlap condition. However, BinarySearch works by definition only if the vector is sorted; therefore it makes sense to forgo testing for this condition. In general, similar analyses should be carried out to decide on a case-by-case basis whether high-level implicit assumptions of the algorithm should be explicitly verified. Ordinarily, complexity considerations will play a role in these decisions.

7.3   What to Do about It

Exception handling is absolutely mandatory when designing and implementing programs. It is highly advisable that the programmer ensure that all possible cases be covered and that code exist that takes the appropriate actions for each case. At a higher conceptual level, the question of whether to test for implicit assumptions made in algorithms may not be as clear-cut. It is probably prudent to be pragmatic. If there are ways of carrying out the test efficiently (at a minimum, this would mean the complexity of the test does not exceed that of the operation), it should be considered. If there are inexpensive ways of obviating the need for a test, this would be another good alternative. (If both are applicable, choose the one that is more efficient; all things being equal again, choose the simplest approach.) However, if the assumption is fundamental, as is the sortedness of the vector for binary search or the squareness of the matrices for matrix inversion, it may be permissible to forgo the test (even though in the latter example, the test would be relatively easy, but it is inconceivable that someone would want to invert a matrix that is not square).

Bibliographical Notes

Exception handling for a specific programming language is covered in that language's manual. General discussions can be found in textbooks on programming language principles and compilers. See for example Aho, Sethi, and Ullman: *Compilers: Principles, Techniques and Tools*. Assumptions underlying an algorithm might be considered as part of the development of that algorithm, but if the assumptions are too obvious, the algorithm designer may not view them as interesting or relevant.

Exercises

Exercise 1

Assumptions pertain frequently to the size of a structure. For example, the fast Fourier transform (FFT) on n values typically assumes that n be a power of 2. Examine the influence of this assumption for the complexity of the resulting algorithms and consequently the programs. Assume that n is the measure of input and that $f(n)$ is the time complexity of a given algorithm that works only if a certain assumption about n is satisfied. Typically, if n does not satisfy the assumption, the next larger value of n that does satisfy it is chosen (and the structure representing the data associated with the problem is padded, so this is applicable). For each of the eight standard complexity classes (see Chapter 1), determine the worst-case increase of the complexity (worst case would be that the value of n is larger by 1 than the last value satisfying the assumption), provided the assumption is that:

    a. n is even.

    b. n is a perfect square ($n = m^2$ for some integer m).

    c. n is a perfect cube ($n = m^3$ for some integer m).

    d. n is equal to m^k for some positive integer k.

    e. n is a power of 2.

Exercise 2

Formulate a test of whether a given binary tree is height balanced. Determine the time and space complexities of your test. Note that you may not use height information contained in the node (it may not exist or may be incorrect).

Hint: For a tree with n nodes, the worst-case time complexity should be $O(n)$, and the worst case space complexity should be no greater than $O(\log_2(n))$ — more specifically, space should be less than $1.45 \cdot \log_2(n) \cdot O(1)$, where the $O(1)$ constant reflects the space required for each recursive invocation of the test.

Exercise 3

Formulate a test of whether a given undirected graph is connected. Determine the time and space complexities of your test, assuming the graph is given:

    a. by its incidence matrix.

    b. by its adjacency lists.

8

Implications of the Finiteness of the Representation of Numbers

---

About This Chapter

Algorithms assume that numbers are not afflicted with any limitation of representation. Programs, however, must operate within a very different universe. All numbers in computer systems are represented in a way that invariably implies limitations on what can be represented internally. These limitations have important implications for programming, from the question of which numbers actually exist inside a program to the problem of testing for equality, the issues related to mathematical properties, and curious behaviors related to convergence.

The finiteness of the number representation in programs has several important implications. They are mainly related to floating point numbers, but even fixed point numbers occasionally display quirky behavior. We first revisit the distinction between bit and word complexity in the context of software development and point out that many numbers that we expect to be representable are not. Then we examine the implications for several issues related to arithmetic, in particular, the question of how to test for equality. Related to this problem is the validity (or lack thereof) of various mathematical properties, identities that we take for granted in algorithms but that provide numerous surprises in programs. Related to this is the convergence of a sum of a sequence of numbers that mathematically diverges.

8.1 Bit and Word Complexity Revisited

Every item in a program necessarily has a finite representation. In almost all instances, this representation is not just finite, but bounded. For the most part, bit complexity does not arise naturally in software; programs may specify how many bytes are to be used to represent an item, but once this decision is made, the number of bits used for this item remains fixed. An unbounded representation inherently requires dynamic memory allocation techniques and is used only in exceptional circumstances.[1] For most practical purposes, complexity in programs is word complexity. The only question is how many bits that word has.

Once a fixed-length representation (i.e., a word) is chosen, several limitations follow immediately. For one, only a finite number of different values can be represented using a fixed number of bits, certainly no more than 2^m if we have m bits. This implies that we will have to contend with issues such as overflow, underflow, and rounding errors. Before we address these, we must point out another aspect of software that differentiates it from algorithms.

Everybody is aware that certain real values do not have a finite representation, for example the square root of 2, $\sqrt{2}$. Most people also know that certain rational numbers do not have a finite decimal representation, for example $1/3$.[2] However, very few programmers are aware that numbers with a perfectly good finite representation, for example 0.3 or 1.3, do not have a finite representation in ordinary programs. This is because the internal representation of numbers in ordinary programs is binary, and many decimal numbers with a finite representation do not have a finite binary representation. To state it more pointedly, when we write the constant 1.3 in a program, this is, strictly speaking, not a number; it is an identifier that refers to a value that is close to the (decimal) value 1.3, but is never exactly 1.3. Even more confusing is that the value of this identifier 1.3 can change. Its value depends on the number of bits of the word used to represent this identifier. Since program portability does not address the question of the word length of a processor, the same program when run on different platforms (with different processors) may yield different values for the identifier 1.3. In other words, what seems to be the constant 1.3 is not a constant and does not have the value 1.3.[3]

---

[1] In some instances extremely long representations of numbers are considered. Prominent examples are software packages that support operations on arbitrarily long integers. The need for arithmetic on extremely long integers arises, for example, in public-key cryptography; in particular, the RSA encryption method is based on prime numbers with several hundred digits and employs operations on integers of such lengths for the encryption and decryption of messages.

[2] One might argue that $1/3$ is a *finite* representation, but it is not a *decimal* representation. We know from mathematics that any rational number can be represented in the form a/b, where a and b are integers. However, ordinary programs do not use this representation of rational numbers (although some software packages do); moreover, no such finite representation exists for real numbers that are not rational.

[3] We will not enter into a discussion of processor arithmetic. This is a complicated topic and well beyond the scope of this book. For our purposes, it suffices to know that many processors implement some standard, usually the IEEE standard. However, many processors also deviate in some instances from the standard they ostensibly implement. While in most cases the differences are negligible, it behooves programmers to be at least aware of the underlying problematic.

It is obvious that in this, algorithms differ significantly from software. Nobody expends any time worrying about the representation of numbers in an algorithm; we essentially assume that all ordinary mathematical aspects of numbers are satisfied. This implies that there is no over- or underflow, there are no rounding errors, and every number we can write down exists exactly as we wrote it. This holds even truer for the difference between decimal and binary representation.

The finiteness of the representation of numbers, coupled with the fact that the internal representation is binary, has a number of surprising consequences. In particular, testing for equality is suddenly a complicated matter and many mathematical identities no longer hold.

Some data items' entire range of values can be represented exactly.[4] This is usually the case whenever the range is finite. Prominent representatives of this type of values are boolean items; also in this category are strings.[5] It is not difficult to verify that any item whose entire range is finite (and presumably not too large) presents no significant representational problems. Consequently, any operations applied to such items will yield again exactly representable values as long as they yield values of that type.[6] Consequently, there are no differences between algorithms and software for items whose range is finite, so no problems owing to their representation can arise when algorithms are implemented in software.

Many programmers believe erroneously that problems owing to the finiteness of the number representation are irrelevant to their applications, indeed that these difficulties are only of concern when doing heavy-duty numerical analysis. However, representational issues arise in many contexts that have nothing to do with numerical analysis. A simple illustration comes from banking. Consider a program that calculates interest on bank balances. The interest is calculated monthly on the average balance during that month. Here are two instances where number representation is important: for the calculation of the average daily balance in an account and for the application of the interest rate to that average balance. It is important in this application

---

[4] Clearly, integers and real numbers do not satisfy this. For reals, $1/3$ is an example; for integers, the integer following the largest representable integer is an example.

[5] The case of strings is perhaps not entirely obvious since strings could be of unbounded length (in contrast to the type character, which can be viewed as a string of length 1). However, given a string (however it may be represented), we can first determine its length, and for this length there is a finite number of different strings (assuming the strings are over a finite alphabet). Why does this argument not carry over to floating point numbers? Because by general agreement, two strings of the same length that differ anywhere are considered different, while two floating point numbers, if they differ by a very small quantity, may be considered equal (see the discussion of testing for equality in Section 8.2). Moreover, in many cases a floating point number is a finite representation of a real number that would require an infinite exact representation; therefore, a better approximation would have more bits or digits, and the length could be increased arbitrarily without ever providing an exact representation.

[6] We assume that an operation applied to items of a certain type yields again an item of that type. This is somewhat tenuous when it comes to integers and division — the integers are not closed under division, but the reals are. However, the integers are closed under addition, subtraction, and multiplication (as are the reals).

that all values be in terms of dollars and cents; in other words, there are no fractional cents. Thus, there should be exactly two decimal digits after the decimal point. If the balances are represented as floating point numbers, once the average is computed, the final result must be converted into dollars and cents. Note that the average is unlikely to be in this format. It is even more unlikely for the interest calculation; again, the result must be explicitly converted into the requisite format. It should be clear that care must be exercised, since for large balances, the interest computation may not be correct if the number of bits employed to represent the result is too small. While any differences are probably only on the order of a few cents, the bank is nevertheless unlikely to be forgiving about such errors.

Another instance where ordinary programs may encounter unexpected problems that are ultimately due to the finiteness of the number representation relates to something seemingly trivial, namely testing whether two values are equal.

8.2   Testing for Equality

In an algorithm testing for equality is trivial and requires no further discussion. In a program, however, testing for equality can be quite complicated because two values that mathematically are identical may be different because they were computed in different ways that resulted in differences owing to their finite representation. A fairly straightforward example is the test of whether the square of the square root of 2 is equal to 2:

$$(\sqrt{2})^2 =? \ 2,$$

which is virtually guaranteed to fail in all programming languages.[7] A more confusing example is the following test:

$$1.3 * 10 =? \ 13,$$

which again would usually fail for the following reason. Recall that 1.3 does not have a finite binary representation; as a result, its product with the number 10 is not exactly equal to 13. This is true even if we were more careful with the question of type. In both examples, we are mixing reals and integers.

---

[7] We could be more deferential to type concordance and ask whether $(\sqrt{2.0})^2 = ? \ 2.0$ is true; the test would likely fail, nevertheless.

For algorithms, this is generally ignored; for programs, it is often frowned upon.[8] So, even if we tested

$$1.3 * 10.0 =? 13.0,$$

the result would be false.

The problem alluded to in these examples does not arise with integers or with any type where the entire range can be represented (booleans, characters, strings).[9] Consequently, testing for equality for these types of items is not problematic.

Given the difficulty in obtaining the correct answer when testing for equality of two real values, how can we finesse this problem? We look at two different aspects of a test for equality, namely a test where we increment or decrement a value until some other value is reached and a general test of whether two values are equal.

The first type of testing for equality is a modified enumeration, where the step size is not an integer. This is frequently unsafe and should be avoided if at all possible. Thus, the test for equality arises in the context of reaching a termination condition. Since it is imperative to obtain termination, we could simply replace the test for equality with a test of equal to or less (greater) than. For example, recall the skeleton of a recursive function discussed in Section 7.1:

```
F(x)
    if x=0.0 do { basis case }
    else { statements; F(x-0.1); statements }
```

---

[8] Some programming languages insist that only operands of like type may be combined. In this case operands would have to be converted explicitly to the more general type, in this case from integer to real. Failure to convert would result in an error.

One might question why conversion has to be from integer to real. If one were to convert from real to integer, the above test would hold. There are two arguments against this assertion. First, one always wants to go from a more restricted situation to a less restricted one; since the integers can be viewed as a subset of the reals (at least mathematically; the internal representation of the fixed point number 13 is very different from that of the floating point number 13.0), this would indicate conversion from integer to real (which would always preserve the value involved, in contrast to going the other direction). Second, even if one were to convert a real to an integer, this would not guarantee that one would obtain 13 when applying this conversion to 1.3*10. It would depend on the way in which a real is converted into an integer. There are at least three different standard ways of doing this: rounding down ($\lfloor x \rfloor$ is the largest integer such that $\lfloor x \rfloor \leq x$), rounding up ($\lceil x \rceil$ is the smallest integer such that $x \leq \lceil x \rceil$), and rounding ([x] is the unique integer satisfying $x - 0.5 < [x] \leq x + 0.5$). (To see that these three techniques are all different consider the values 3.9 and –3.9: $\lfloor 3.9 \rfloor = 3, \lfloor -3.9 \rfloor = -4, \lceil 3.9 \rceil = 4, \lceil -3.9 \rceil = -3, [3.9] = 4,$ and $[-3.9] = -4$.) Consequently, if the actual representation of 1.3*10 is smaller than 13, $\lfloor 1.3*10 \rfloor$ would yield 12, not 13. Similarly, if the actual representation of 1.3*10 is larger than 13, $\lceil 1.3*10 \rceil$ would yield 14, not 13.

[9] This problem does not arise with integers either, even though they do not have a finite range, because it fundamentally derives from underflow. Integers do not suffer from underflow — only overflow. Overflow, however, is not an issue in testing for equality, since we are considering only the test of whether two values are equal, and either both values are overflow or none is. How these two values are obtained is a separate issue, which is taken up in the next section.

If this function is called with a positive integer as an actual parameter (ignoring again the mixing of integer and real types), say F(2), it is unlikely to terminate because the test for equality $x = 0.0$ most likely will fail since 0.1, the decrement, does not have a finite binary floating point representation. Thus, the basis case will never be encountered. Were we to replace the test $x = 0.0$ with $x \leq 0.0$, we would at least be guaranteed that the recursion terminates, but it is not clear that the result would be what we expect.

Why might the result not be correct? This depends on the actual value of the number 0.1. Since we have already established that that value cannot be exactly 0.1, it is either larger or smaller (admittedly by very little, but this very small quantity nevertheless trips us up). The obvious intent of the original algorithm is to invoke recursion 10 times for each unit; thus F(2) should give rise to 20 recursive calls, namely F(1.9), F(1.8), ..., F(0.2), F(0.1), and finally F(0.0), which then invokes the basis case. However, if the actually represented value of 0.1 is smaller than the real value 0.1, then the actually represented values of the intermediate quantities (1.9, 1.8, ..., 0.2, 0.1, and 0.0) will all be larger than the values of their *identifiers*.[10] As a result, it will not be this last value that invokes the basis case (since it is objectively larger than 0.0), but the next value computed in this sequence, which is something quite close to –0.1. This is why the test for equality was such a bad idea, since in the original formulation, the basis case ($x = 0.0$) would never be reached.[11]

This brings up the second aspect of a test of equality, namely when we really want to know whether the two items are equal. Clearly, if the values are of a type whose entire range can be represented exactly, no problems exist. However, if the values are floating point type, it is surprisingly difficult to decide whether they are equal.

The obvious approach is to define a margin, say ε, and to decree that the value x is considered equal to the value y if x and y differ by no more than ε:

$$|x-y| \leq \varepsilon.$$

The problem is how to determine ε. On the one hand, ε should be small enough to avoid considering two values as equal that should really be considered different; on the other hand, ε should be large enough that all values one might consider equal are in fact equal. The problem is that there may not be a single fixed value of ε that would work in all instances. In

---

[10] This is not absolutely guaranteed, although it is extremely likely. We are assuming monotonicity here; that is subtracting something smaller than 0.1 from 2 yields something larger than 1.9, and then subtracting something smaller than 0.1 from this value yields something larger than 1.8, and so on. To obtain a definitive answer of whether this is true depends on the specific implementation of arithmetic in the processor. (The reason it could not be true is related to the way in which the representation is determined, especially the rounding that occurs when one goes from one order of magnitude to another. Note that since the internal representation is binary, 1.99999 is an order of magnitude larger than 0.99999.)

[11] We note that it is good programming practice to avoid testing for equality and replacing it by $\leq$ or $\geq$ if the values involved are considered safe, for instance integers.

many cases the size of ε depends on the context. Thus, the decision of how large to make ε generally lies with the programmer who is called upon to implement an algorithm in software.[12]

It should be clear that the difficulties with testing for equality carry over to other comparison operators, such as ≤ and ≥ (when applied to floating point numbers). However, tests for < and > are ordinarily safe.

8.3 Mathematical Properties

Mathematical identities are frequently invoked; most people are familiar at least with commutativity, associativity, and distributivity of common numbers (integers, reals, and booleans). Unfortunately, because of the finiteness of the representation of the values involved in the expressions, these mathematical identities and other properties do not necessarily hold.

Mathematical identities fail to hold for two reasons: because of rounding errors (also referred to as underflow) or because of overflow. Rounding errors arise with floating point numbers. The most common situation is that a very large value is combined with a very small value, swamping the smaller one. These rounding errors are common and usually do not attract much attention, but they do call into question the overall notion of mathematical identities. Overflow conditions are unlikely (but not impossible) for floating point numbers; they occur more often with fixed point numbers.

Table 8.1 shows the most common mathematical identities together with an indication of whether or not each holds for floating point and fixed point numbers. The parenthetical notes indicate why the identity does not hold. Here max indicates an integer that is the largest representable integer (a value that depends on the word length). The quantity ε_{min} denotes the largest floating point number such that

$$1.0 + \varepsilon_{min} = 1.0.$$

Because of the finiteness of the number representation, this value always exists. Finally, very large (very small) refers to a value that is close to the maximum (minimum) of the values representable as floating point numbers, given a certain number of bits for the mantissa and for the exponent, the idea being that the sum and the product of two such very large numbers is

---

[12] If the order of magnitude of the values to be compared is known, the quantity ε_{min} to be discussed in Section 8.3 may be employed. More specifically, if x and y are of the order of 1, then we might use for ε a small multiple of ε_{min}, for example $2*\varepsilon_{min}$. If x and y are larger, say on the order of 1000, we could use $2000*\varepsilon_{min}$; if they are smaller, say on the order of 0.01, we could use $0.02*\varepsilon_{min}$. Even if the size of the values to be compared is not known when the program is written, we can still use those sizes to compute an appropriate value for ε.

TABLE 8.1

Mathematical Identities

Identity	Fixed Point	Floating Point
Commutativity		
$a + b = b + a$	Holds	Holds
$a*b = b*a$	Holds	Holds
Associativity		
$(a + b) + c = a + (b + c)$	Does not hold (a,b max, $b + c = 0$)	Does not hold ($a = 1, b = c = \varepsilon_{min}$)
$(a*b)*c = a*(b*c)$	Does not hold (a,b max, $c = 0$)	Does not hold (a,b very large, c very small)
Distributivity		
$(a + b)*c = a*c + b*c$	Does not hold (a,c max, $a + b = 0$)	Does not hold (a,b very large, c very small)

no longer representable, while the product of a very large and a very small number would yield 1.

A few words are in order about the overflow conditions for fixed point numbers. We take the position that overflow is overflow; in other words, if any subexpression of an expression results in an overflow, then the entire expression is afflicted with overflow. Therefore, if a and b are max, $a + b$ results in an overflow, and the fact that c is a very large negative number does not erase the overflow condition of the expression $(a + b) + c$. However, since $b + c$ is 0, the addition of a and $b + c$ results in max, which is not an overflow condition. Therefore, the two sides of the identity are different: One yields overflow and the other yields a perfectly good integer value. If $a + b$ (or $a*b$) results in overflow, so will $b + a$ (or $b*a$); thus, the two sides are equal.

Given that the basic mathematical identities do not necessarily hold, it should not be surprising that more complicated identities generally do not hold either. For example, we know from arithmetic that $a^2 - b^2 = (a + b)*(a - b)$, but this identity does not hold generally (for example, if a and b are both large numbers so that a^2 is not representable but $a + b$ is, for both fixed and floating point numbers).

The upshot is that programmers should not assume that common mathematical identities hold in programs. While they do hold in most cases for fixed point numbers (whenever all intermediate results on both sides are valid integers), the situation for floating point numbers is a bit more tenuous. If the sizes of the numbers involved differ substantially, the identities tend not to hold, although usually the differences are not too great. Note, however, that small errors can accumulate and propagate, so one should not be overly sanguine about the insignificance of these errors, as the next section indicates. However, boolean expressions are always exact, so any identities involving boolean values and operators hold unconditionally.

8.4 Convergence

Consider summing up a sequence of numbers. One would ordinarily assume that it makes no difference in what order one sums. One would be correct if this were done in an algorithm (that is, mathematically), but one would be very wrong if one held the same expectation for a program. The poster child of this phenomenon is the sequence 1, 1/2, 1/3, 1/4, 1/5,..., whose sum is well known (at least to mathematicians) to diverge. In other words, for any constant M there exists an integer n such that the sum of the first n terms of this sequence exceeds M. Yet if we program this summation, for example, as

```
sum :=0.0; for i:=1 to N do sum := sum + 1.0/i,
```

we will discover that there exists a value of N such that the sum S_N of the first N terms is equal to the sum S_{N+k} of the first $N + k$ terms for any $k > 0$. This type of convergence is a special instance of the failure of associativity to hold. The explanation is quite simple: Adding the term $1.0/(N + 1)$ to the sum S_N of the first N terms presents us with a situation very much like 1.0 + ε_{min} = 1.0, except that both S_N and the term $1.0/(N + 1)$ must be normalized by S_N to yield 1.0 and ε_{min}. In other words, we have to solve

$$\varepsilon_{min} * S_N > 1.0/(N + 1)$$

for N. This yields a value s for N such that $S_s = S_{s+1}$. This value s can easily be obtained as follows; it depends on the word length used for the representation of sum:

```
sum :=0.0; i:=1.0;
while sum < sum +1.0/i do
    { sum:=sum + 1.0/i; i:=i+1.0 };
s:=i
```

Let us now sum up from the back; here we assume we know the value of s from before:

```
sum :=0.0; for i:=s to 1 by -1 do sum := sum + 1.0/i
```

Let us denote the result of this summation (as a function of s) by T_s. The first surprise is that $T_s \neq S_s$; in other words, summing up backwards yields a different result than summing up from the beginning. The second surprise is that $T_s < T_{s+1}$. When summing up from the back, we can add many more terms that affect the total than when summing up from the front!

The reason for this surprising result is that first summing up the smaller terms allows them to amount to a quantity that is not as easily overwhelmed by the larger values toward the front. Starting at the front first adds up all the larger terms, so by the time we get to the smaller terms, they are wiped out à la 1.0 + ε_{min} = 1.0.

One might get the impression that the difference between summing up sequences of simple numbers either forward or backward is just a parlor game that has no significance to general programming. This is by no means valid, even though this type of sum is usually not encountered when designing software. However, it does serve as a rather drastic warning about the assumptions that programmers make. These assumptions are generally rooted in their understanding of mathematics, and more specifically, arithmetic. Unfortunately, what holds unconditionally in mathematics, with its disregard of representational issues, does not necessarily hold for software, where the finiteness of the number representation can play surprisingly nasty tricks on the unsuspecting programmer.

8.5 What to Do about It

Programmers tend to dismiss issues related to the representation of numbers as relevant only to number crunching. This is not entirely incorrect. For example, bit complexity tends to be irrelevant for almost all practical programs; programmers will use whatever words are provided in a particular language. While heavy-duty numerical error analysis is clearly not needed for software outside of numerical analysis, every programmer should be aware of some of the differences between what mathematics teaches about numbers and what happens to numbers in programs. The fact that certain values cannot be exactly represented can have some impact on software that is far removed from number crunching. The same goes for mathematical identities that mysteriously cease to be valid in software. Finally, testing for equality is often not well understood when it involves floating point numbers. All of these problems can render software unreliable, if not outright wrong. While there are limits to a programmer's ability to control the errors caused by the finiteness of the number representation, the awareness of these problems may be very helpful in avoiding them. Certainly, using a test for equality as a termination condition, for iteration or for recursion, is generally not a good idea when floating point numbers are used; these tests should be replaced by safer ones. If testing for equality is directly required, it should be carried out using a margin of error that depends on the context of the test (magnitude of the numbers involved).

Bibliographical Notes

Error analysis and error propagation for floating point numbers is comprehensively covered in standard numerical methods textbooks. Wilkinson's books dating back to the early 1960s are classics: *Rounding Errors in Algebraic Processes* and *The Algebraic Eigenvalue Problem*. Other texts are Golub and Van Loan: *Matrix Computations* and Higham: *Accuracy and Stability of Numerical Algorithms*. Focused on specific computer platforms are Startz: *8087/80287/80387 for the IBM PC and Compatibles* and Asserrhine, Chesneaux, and Lamotte: *Estimation of Round-Off Errors on Several Computers Architectures*. Papers discussing the importance of error analysis for general computing are Moler: "Double-Rounding and Implications for Numeric Computations"; Goldberg: "Computer Arithmetic"; and, in particular, Goldberg: "What Every Computer Scientist Should Know about Floating-Point Arithmetic". The internal representation and its consequences for programs are also treated in textbooks on programming language concepts and compilers, for example, Aho, Sethi, and Ullman: *Compilers: Principles, Techniques and Tools*.

Exercises

Exercise 1

Using different word lengths (2 bytes, 4 bytes, and 8 bytes), determine experimentally the value of ε_{min} for your computing platform.

Exercise 2

Using different word lengths (2 bytes, 4 bytes, and 8 bytes), determine experimentally the smallest value of s such that $S_s = S_{s+1}$, where $S_j = 1.0 + 1.0/2.0 + 1.0/3.0 + \ldots 1.0/j$. Also determine experimentally the smallest value of t such that $T_t = T_{t+1}$, where $T_j = 1.0/j + 1.0/(j-1.0) + \ldots 1.0/2.0 + 1.0$.

Exercise 3

a. Using different word lengths (2 bytes, 4 bytes, and 8 bytes), find fixed point numbers a, b, and c such that their associativity (distributivity) does not hold.

b. Using different word lengths (2 bytes, 4 bytes, and 8 bytes), find floating point numbers a, b, and c such that their associativity (distributivity) does not hold.

Exercise 4

In view of the problems with representing rational numbers a/b, where b is not a power of 2, one may consider representing an arbitrary rational number

a/b as the pair $[a,b]$ consisting of the two integers a and b, with b assumed to be positive. In order to obtain uniqueness of this representation, one assumes that a and b are relatively prime; if they are not, for example $a = ka'$ and $b = k \cdot b'$ with $k \geq 2$ an integer, then $a/b = a'/b'$, with a' and b' requiring fewer bits for their representation. This is a relatively simple approach that can easily be implemented. Note that the rational numbers are closed under the four basic arithmetic operations.

  a. Formulate and implement methods for the addition, subtraction, multiplication, and division of the pairs $[a,b]$ and $[c,d]$.

There is however a problem with this approach which affords absolute precision; in order to understand this problem, we must go to bit complexity.

  b. Assume that the length of the integers a, b, c, and d is l. Show that the length of the integers f and g, where $[f,g]$ represents the sum, difference, product, or factor of a/b and c/d, may be $2l$. Generalizing this, show that a sequence of m basic arithmetic operations may require integers of length ml to represent the final rational number, for any $m > 1$. Hint: Assume that a, b, c, and d are all prime numbers.

9

Asymptotic Complexities and the Selection of Algorithms

About This Chapter

Asymptotics are the heart of the complexity analysis of algorithms, but their usefulness for software development is limited since by their very nature they ignore constant factors. When constant factors are taken into consideration, some overall bad algorithms may be competitive over a certain range of input size. If this range happens to include all practical cases, the bad algorithm may turn out to be superior to an asymptotically much better one. How to determine this and how to apply this to practical situations is the goal of this chapter.

9.1 Introduction

The complexity analysis of an algorithm aims at categorizing algorithms into a few clearly defined complexity classes. For most practical applications, these classes are polynomial, meaning that the complexity (time or space) is bounded by a polynomial p(n) of the measure of the input employed (usually size of input):

$$p(n) = a_s n^s + a_{s-1} n^{s-1} + \dots + a_2 n^2 + a_1 n + a_0, \text{ for s a positive integer.}$$

This polynomial is then equivalent to n^s. Thus,

$$p(n) = O(n^s) \text{ and } p(n) \neq O(n^{s-1}).$$

Complexities are thus compared using the highest-order term only, ignoring the constant attached to that term as well as all lower-order terms. As we discussed in Chapter 1, we are primarily interested in eight complexity classes, defined by their highest-order terms φ_i, $i = 1, ..., 8$, where $\varphi_1(n) = 1$, $\varphi_2(n) = \log_2(n)$, $\varphi_3(n) = \sqrt[2]{n}$, $\varphi_4(n) = n$, $\varphi_5(n) = n{\cdot}\log_2(n)$, $\varphi_6(n) = n^2$, $\varphi_7(n) = n^3$, and $\varphi_8(n) = 2^n$.[1] Considering only the highest-order term is justified if one is primarily interested in what happens for very large values of n, since for those the lower-order terms become increasingly irrelevant; their contribution is completely obliterated by that of the highest-order term. The dismissal of the constant factor of the highest-order term reflects the desire to keep things simple; if two polynomials have the same degree, it is convenient for comparison purposes to consider them equivalent. This allows us to construct a nice, orderly hierarchy of complexities. However, for software, things are not quite that nice and orderly.

To obtain a methodology that is practically useful for measuring the performance of a program, obtaining the algorithm's complexity functions is only the first step. We must also pay considerable attention to the constants that were hidden during the complexity analysis. Additionally, programs have certain time and space requirements that are usually ignored when algorithms are being analyzed. Furthermore, when deciding which of two algorithms or programs is better (in some sense), we must look at crossover points in the complexity functions.

9.2 The Importance of Hidden Constants

We have already argued that for software, it is highly unusual to have bit complexity as a valid concept. Virtually everything of practical importance is based on word complexity. This holds for both time and space complexity.

Assume now that we have obtained f(n) as the complexity of an algorithm, for n some measure of the input. If this is the space complexity of the algorithm, then the memory requirements of a program implementing that algorithm are essentially $f(n) + C_{sp}$, where the constant C_{sp} accounts for the space required for the program, for the symbol tables, and for other information associated with the program. This constant C_{sp} is independent of the measure n of the input to the program. Thus, the space complexity of the program is closely related to that of the underlying algorithm, provided space is measured in words.[2] We reiterate that space requirements should always be based on worst-case analyses (see Section 6.2); average space complexity has a limited usefulness for software.

[1] As pointed out, there are infinitely many complexity classes between (and beyond) these eight. For example, $\sqrt[2]{n}{\cdot}n$ is strictly between $\varphi_5(n)$ and $\varphi_6(n)$, that is, $\sqrt[2]{n}{\cdot}n = O(\varphi_6(n))$, $\varphi_6(n) \neq O(\sqrt[2]{n}{\cdot}n)$, $\varphi_5(n) = O(\sqrt[2]{n}{\cdot}n)$, and $\sqrt[2]{n}{\cdot}n \neq O(\varphi_5(n))$. However, for most practical purposes, these eight are generally considered sufficient to categorize complexity functions.
[2] If bit complexity is used for the algorithm, the actual space requirement of the program depends on the way these bits are represented. There is a good deal of variability, from using an entire word for each bit to using packed structures.

The relationship between the complexity of the algorithm and that of the corresponding program is not quite as clean when it comes to time. Recall that the time complexity of an algorithm is the statement count for the algorithm, in essence, each statement accounts for one unit of time. A program's time requirements are not quite that easily captured. By and large, we end up with $c_1 \cdot f(n) + c_2$, where the constant c_1 measures the duration[3] of an *average* statement and the constant c_2 reflects the amount of time required to load the program and initialize the processes associated with it. Each of the two constants hides a good deal of work.

The difficulty with the constant c_1 is the assumption that we know what an average statement is. We can make some educated guesses or we can determine a range for this constant. The most systematic approach is to base the value of c_1 on some limited test runs of the program at hand. In practice, c_1 will also depend on the target platform (thus, it is related not just to the architecture, but also to the instruction set and the ability of the compiler to exploit efficiently the instruction set). Generally, a reasonably acceptable value for c_1 is acquired experimentally. Nevertheless, the precise value of this constant depends on the program to be executed. Realistically we can only hope for a reasonably small range.[4]

The constant c_2 is a measure of the fixed cost of program execution. In other words, even if virtually no statements are executed, the amount of time c_2 must always be expended. A typical situation where this might occur is a wrong user input that causes the program to abort. It is important to understand that c_2 is definitely not 0. In fact, its value can be quite substantial. However, it is a time penalty that will always be incurred, so it may appear to be insignificant. While this is certainly not true for most programs, it does have the advantage that there are never any surprises; we always must take at least c_2 time, even if nothing happens.

In the next section we will discuss crossover points. These are particularly important when comparing two algorithms, and then the corresponding programs, according to some complexity measure. Here we explore a slightly different issue. Assume we have two programs with the same asymptotic (time) complexity $\varphi_i(n)$. The decision of which program to use will first hinge on the constant factors for each program. However, let us assume that both have comparable factors. We may encounter the following situation. One algorithm assumes that n is a power of 2; the complexity analysis is based on that assumption and if n happens not to be a power of 2, the algorithm simply assumes that we pad the input so that the assumption is again satisfied. The other algorithm works for any value of n. In this case, it may

---

[3] We are deliberately vague about the unit. One approach might be to use actual time, for example in nanoseconds. Another approach would be to assume that the unit involved is a synthetic one that allows us to maintain the simple idea of a unit statement. In this case, we would still be looking at some type of statement count, except that we now take into consideration the actual duration of this average statement.

[4] In practice, one hopes that the execution time of a program is within a range of one half of the predicted quantity and double that quantity.

be crucial to know whether the input is generally a power of 2 or not, for if this is not the case, the required padding, up to the next power of 2, may almost double the input size. The worst case is if $n = 2^s + 1$ for some positive s, where we would have to increase n to 2^{s+1}. However, if the complexity is proportional to n^c for some constant c, doubling the input size increases the complexity by a factor 2^c. This can make the algorithm requiring padding highly noncompetitive. Of course, if n is always a power of 2, this argument does not apply. Thus, it is important to examine underlying assumptions, even when two algorithms are considered to have the same time complexity.

Another aspect of considerable practical importance is that frequently, there exists a simple but not very efficient algorithm for a specific problem, as well as a more complicated but faster one. Since the complicated algorithm aims at large problems (large n), one customarily invokes the simpler algorithm if n is small.[5] This is particularly relevant if the complicated method is recursive. As long as n is large, we call the complicated algorithm that recursively calls itself for increasingly smaller values of n until n is smaller than a certain threshold, in which case the simpler algorithm is invoked. Thus, the simple algorithm serves as the basis case of the recursive method. A typical example is the matrix multiplication algorithm discussed in Section 3.2.2, in which we reduce the multiplication of two $[n,n]$ matrices to 7 multiplications and 15 additions of $[n/2,n/2]$ matrices. Each of these seven multiplications is then treated in the same way, recursively, until we reach a point where the size of the resulting matrices is smaller than a given value. Once this value is reached, the recursion terminates. For all multiplications involving matrices whose size is smaller than this threshold, the traditional approach consisting of three nested loops is invoked. In this particular situation, the simple $O(n^3)$ time algorithm is usually invoked if n is around 30, since below this value the more complicated approach does not result in further time savings (for reasonably efficient implementations of both algorithms).

For this matrix multiplication example, the threshold is realistically small. There is a large range of values for which the more complicated approach can be applied in practice. In general, the magnitude of this threshold is very important; for if the threshold is very large, the more complicated approach may have only theoretical significance, since for all practically important values, the less efficient method is used.

---

[5] From a computational complexity point of view, anything that is done for $n < N_0$, with N_0 a fixed constant, requires only constant time, $O(1)$. This is true no matter how much work is involved, because even the most time-consuming algorithm will not require more than a constant amount of work for a constant value of n. Thus, if n is bounded from above by N_0, no more than a constant amount of work is required. This somewhat counterintuitive reasoning is correct, simply because computational complexity is only interested in the asymptotic behavior of the function of n, but never in a specific instance; however, it generally has no practical significance, since the work in absolute terms must still be carried out.

9.3 Crossover Points

Our starting point for this section is the following: We have two algorithms A_1 and A_2, with complexity functions $f_1(n)$ and $f_2(n)$, where n is a measure of the input.[6] The two complexity functions for the algorithms give rise to complexity functions for the programs P_1 and P_2 that are based on the algorithms; let them be $g_1(n)$ and $g_2(n)$, such that

$$g_i(n) = c_i f_i(n) + d_i,$$

where c_i and d_i are constants (independent of n), for $i = 1,2$. We are to decide which program is more efficient.

First we must delineate our area of interest. We focus on time complexity. While space complexity is a valid concern as well, it is quite possible that P_1 is faster but requires more space, while P_2 is slower and requires less space. Most of what we discuss for time will have analogues for space, but ultimately, it is the programmer who must decide whether time or space is more important. We will only rarely be so lucky that one program is uniformly better, that is, faster and requiring less space.

Second, the approach we describe below is applicable to both average and worst-case time complexity, so we will usually not belabor which of the two we address. However, one should keep in mind that algorithms may compare differently depending on whether we look at average or at worst-case complexity. Again, it is the programmer who has to determine what matters most.

In keeping with the argumentation we advanced earlier, we will assume word complexity. As we have stated, in most instances bit complexity makes little sense for programs.

A last caveat is in order: The constants c_i and d_i for $i = 1,2$ are usually approximations (educated guesses), since the true values of the factors that allow us to go from $f_i(n)$ to $g_i(n)$ would only be known after execution, and even then, strictly speaking, these values would only be valid for that particular execution run. A similar cautionary note applies also to the functions $f_1(n)$ and $f_2(n)$.

How do we determine which program is more efficient (that is, which program should be used)? For algorithms, the answer is relatively simple. Choose the algorithm whose complexity function grows asymptotically slower, that is, choose A_1 if $f_1 = O(f_2)$ but $f_2 \neq O(f_1)$, and consider either of the two algorithms acceptable if $f_1 \equiv f_2$. For programs, this simple approach does not work. We must take into consideration the constants c_i and d_i ($i = 1,2$) to arrive at an answer. However, even if we can show that $g_1(n) \leq g_2(n)$ for all

---

[6] Once we have a way of deciding which of two candidates is better, this process can be iterated, so that we may select the best of a group of more than two.

$n \geq n_0$, this may still not be sufficient to answer the question.[7] The reason lies in the range of interest for our program.

Asymptotical behavior only concerns the situation for very large values of n. The range of values for n that we are interested in when executing our program may be quite different. Consider the following example. Suppose we want to determine the kth-largest element of an unsorted sequence of n numbers, presented in an unsorted array, and assume we want to determine whether to use a program P_1 based on the modified Select algorithm described in Section 3.2.9 (algorithm A_1) or whether to sort the array first in descending order using HeapSort[8] and then to return the kth entry in that sorted array (algorithm A_2 and program P_2). For algorithms, this is a silly question. The modified Select algorithm has linear time complexity, while sorting requires time proportional to $n \cdot \log_2(n)$; thus, it is obvious that the modified Select algorithm is superior.

For programs, this is not at all so obvious. First, we must look at the constant factors involved in the time complexity functions. The first algorithm, A_1, has a very large constant factor; it is easily verified that the time complexity of A_1 is at least $240 \cdot n$.[9] The second algorithm, A_2, has a rather small constant. HeapSort's time complexity is no more than $4 \cdot n \cdot \log_2(n)$. Thus, merely on the basis of a more careful analysis of the algorithms' time complexities, we can see that A_1 is preferable over A_2 only if

$$240 \cdot n < 4 \cdot n \cdot \log_2(n).$$

This is true precisely for $60 < \log_2(n)$, or

$$n > 2^{60} \approx 10^{18}.$$

In other words, unless we must deal with a data set of size of at least one quintillion, the pedestrian approach of sorting (with an $O(n \cdot \log_2(n))$ time complexity) and then retrieving the kth element (in time $O(1)$) is superior. This holds true even on the basis of algorithms. Since HeapSort is a fairly simple algorithm, without recursion, while the modified Select algorithm is much more complicated, the situation for the programs P_1 and P_2 and their complexities g_1 and g_2 is even worse. In no conceivable practical situation is

---

[7] Recall that in Chapter 1 we defined $k_1(n) = O(k_2(n))$ if and only if there exists an integer $n_0 \geq 1$ and a constant $c > 0$ such that $k_1(n) \leq c \cdot k_2(n)$ for all $n \geq n_0$. Thus, in this comparison of g_1 and g_2, we not only require that $g_1 = O(g_2)$, but also that $c = 1$ in the definition of the order of notation.

[8] While we formulated HeapSort there to yield an array sorted in ascending order, the reverse order is easily obtained by creating the heap with $<$ and $>$ exchanged; this will result in a heap where the first element is the smallest. Since a heap is created by repeated heap insertions, the modification of the heap insertion function ensures the correct functioning of the overall algorithm (in particular, the reinsertion of the element displaced from the last location of the current heap).

[9] In Section 3.2.9 we derived that the time complexity of A_1 is $f_1(n) = 20 \cdot C \cdot n$ where $C \cdot n$ reflects the work to be done in steps 1.1, 1.2, and 2. One can verify that step 2 requires about three instructions, and steps 1.1 and 1.2 about nine; therefore $C = 12$ and $f_1(n) = 240 \cdot n$.

P_1 better than P_2. In other words, the modified Select algorithm is theoretically interesting, but practically totally useless. It will never be faster than sorting.

This situation is not at all uncommon. Numerous algorithms have only theoretical significance. Another example is provided by matrix multiplication. The algorithm we explained in Section 3.2.2 is eminently practical; it runs in time $O(n^{2.81})$. However, this is by no means the asymptotically best algorithm for matrix multiplication: There exist several algorithms that manage to beat the time complexity $n^{2.81}$, the best of which achieves (as of 2005) a time complexity of $O(n^{2.496})$. The crossover point at which this $n^{2.496}$ method beats the $n^{2.81}$ method is so large that it is not (and will never be) of any practical interest. However, the $n^{2.496}$ method illustrates very clearly that there is no nontrivial lower bound for matrix multiplication (see the discussion of lower bounds in Section 1.9).

In practical terms, crossover points are markers that indicate which algorithm should be applied for a particular range. A simple, somewhat contrived example will illustrate this. Suppose we have three algorithms: A_1 has a time complexity of $f_1(n)$, A_2 has a time complexity of $f_2(n)$, and A_3, one of $f_3(n)$. The three complexity functions are defined as follows:

$$f_1(n) = (5n^3 - 10n^2)/(n+50) \quad \text{for all } n \geq 1;$$

$$f_2(n) = 150n\sqrt{n} + 200n + 1000 \quad \text{for all even } n \geq 2;$$

$$f_2(n) = 300n\sqrt{n} + 400n + 1000 \quad \text{for all odd } n \geq 1;$$

$$f_3(n) = 200n\sqrt{n} + 300n + 100 \quad \text{for all } n \geq 1.$$

We can now carry out several calculations, comparing the four functions with each other. Let us denote by $f_{2,even}(n)$ and $f_{2,odd}(n)$ the two parts of $f_2(n)$. It follows that

$$f_1(n) < f_{2,even}(n) \text{ for all } n \leq 1001;$$

$$f_{2,even}(n) < f_{2,odd}(n) \text{ for all } n;^{[10]}$$

$$f_1(n) < f_3(n) \text{ for all } n \leq 1740.$$

Furthermore, $f_3(n)$ is never smaller than $f_{2,even}(n)$ for values of n where $f_1(n)$ does not beat $f_{2,even}(n)$, that is, $n \geq 1002$. We conclude from these calculations that the best algorithm is a hybrid algorithm that must utilize all three algorithms in the following way:

---

[10] Note that we can compare $f_{2,even}(n)$ and $f_{2,odd}(n)$ as functions for all values of n, even though the complexity of the algorithm A_2 uses $f_{2,even}(n)$ only for even n and $f_{2,odd}(n)$ only for odd n.

```
if n ≤ 1001 then call A1
   else if n is even   then call A2
      else if n ≤ 1740   then call A1
         else call A3.
```

Graphically, we can visualize this as follows:

$$1 \text{———} A1 \text{———} 1001 \Big\langle \begin{matrix} 1002 \text{——} \text{even} \text{——} A2 \text{————————} \infty \\ 1003 - \text{odd} - A1 - 1739 - \text{odd} - A3 - \infty \end{matrix}$$

It follows that for practical purposes it may be necessary to consider several algorithms and combine them, for different ranges, into a hybrid algorithm that will have a better performance than any of the original algorithms individually.

9.4   Practical Considerations for Efficient Software: What Matters and What Does Not

We summarize how computational complexity should be employed in the selection of algorithms for implementation as software. While the target platform may play a minor role in this process, for the most part, the determination can be based on a more careful application of computational complexity techniques. We are not interested in squeezing out the last cycle; our focus is on producing reasonably efficient software, starting from good algorithm. If it is the elimination of the last redundant cycle that is of concern, it may be necessary to implement several algorithms and do test runs. We aim to avoid this fairly significant expense, at the risk of ending up with software that is just very good, but not necessarily optimal.[11]

When determining complexity, the programmer should concentrate exclusively on word complexity. Bit complexity is not particularly practical. This holds true for average and worst-case complexity and for time and space complexity.

---

[11] Even if one were willing to go to this extreme, it would result in the best of the candidate programs only for this specific platform. Migrating to another platform might change this outcome considerably. In view of the importance of portability of software (largely motivated by the fact that software greatly outlives hardware), it is probably a bad idea to get fixated on squeezing out the last cycle. We should rather accept that software will be ported to various platforms over its life cycle and consequently concentrate on making a selection that may not be optimal but will not have to be revisited each time the software is ported. Thus, somewhat lower expectations may be a saner approach than chasing optimality.

When determining space complexity, programmers should only consider the worst-case space complexity, not the average complexity. Failure of the program to conform to the average case that the analysis determined will typically have far more dire consequences than missing the mark on time (unless one deals with a hard real-time application, such as air traffic control or nuclear power plant operations, which must be treated much more carefully, typically involving algorithms that are extremely predictable and extensive test runs with various implementations).

Constants are typically hidden in the asymptotical analysis of algorithms. This approach is unacceptable for programs. Instead, great care must be taken to obtain as accurately as possible the actual constants that arise in the analysis. While this will complicate the derivation of the functions, it is nevertheless vital to do so for an accurate assessment of the performance of the software. Occasionally, terms that make a negligible contribution can be suppressed, but the programmer must be very clear about how negligible these terms really are.

Finally, in practical situations it is crucial to consider hybrid algorithms. For different portions of the range of interest, different algorithms may be superior. It cannot be overemphasized that the quality of an algorithm is measured asymptotically, while the quality of a program must be apparent for every input of the practical range. This implies that a programmer should consider several algorithms, determine for which range a particular algorithm is better than the rest, and apply the algorithm for the range to which it is best suited.

Bibliographical Notes

The material in this chapter is directly related to complexity analysis, which can be found in standard textbooks on algorithm design and analysis. We refer to Purdom and Brown: *The Analysis of Algorithms*, which also discusses the unrealistic, but asymptotically very efficient, algorithm for matrix multiplication (which originally appeared in Coppersmith and Winograd: "On the Asymptotic Complexity of Matrix Multiplication"). The actual determination for what range of values which candidate method is most efficient must usually be carried out separately for each set of candidates.

Exercises

Exercise 1

For each of the sets of algorithms, together with their worst-case time complexity functions, determine the ranges for a hybrid algorithm:

a. Algorithms A1 with $f_1(n)$ and A2 with $f_2(n)$, where

$$f_1(n) = 5 \cdot n^2 - 3 \cdot n \cdot \log_2(n) - 2 \cdot n + 10$$

$$f_2(n) = 2 \cdot n^2 + 5 \cdot n \cdot \log_2(n) - 5 \cdot n + 100.$$

b. Algorithms A3 with $f_3(n)$, A4 with $f_4(n)$, and A5 with $f_5(n)$, where

$$f_3(n) = (5 \cdot n^2 + 8n) \cdot \log_2(n) / (n + 4 \cdot \sqrt{n}) - 2 \cdot n + 10$$

$$f_4(n) = 2 \cdot n^2 + n \cdot \log_2(n) - 5 \cdot n + 100$$

$$f_5(n) = (4 \cdot n^2 + 6 \cdot n) \cdot \sqrt{n} / (n + 8 \cdot \log_2(n)) - 3 \cdot n + 50.$$

c. Algorithms A1 with $f_1(n)$, A5 with $f_5(n)$, and A6 with $f_6(n)$, given by

$$f_6(n) = (n^3 - 2 \cdot n^2) / 8 \cdot n \cdot \log_2(n) - 3 \cdot n + 20.$$

Exercise 2

Now assume that the constants c_i and d_i for the relationship between algorithms and programs are given. Under these conditions, determine where the crossover points occur for the resulting hybrid program:

a. $c_1 = 2.5$, $d_1 = 1{,}000{,}000$; $c_2 = 3.2$, $d_2 = 1{,}100{,}000$.
b. $c_3 = 3.5$, $d_3 = 1{,}000{,}000$; $c_4 = 3.2$, $d_4 = 800{,}000$; $c_5 = 6.5$, $d_5 = 2{,}000{,}000$.
c. $c_6 = 1.5$, $d_6 = 500{,}000$.

10

Infeasibility and Undecidability: Implications for Software Development

About This Chapter

There are two aspects of impossibility in computing, absolute and relative. Absolute impossibility is undecidability: it is known that no algorithm exists to solve a given problem. Thus, it denotes algorithmic impossibility. Relative impossibility arises when the complexity of an algorithm is prohibitively large. Both types of impossibility have significant importance for software development. On the one hand, it makes no sense attempting to produce code designed to solve an undecidable problem. On the other hand, if the complexity of an algorithm is excessively large, the user may not be willing or able to wait until a solution is produced. Notwithstanding these different aspects of impossibility, it is imperative to explore what they mean and how one may obtain acceptable answers to legitimate questions, at least in some instances. Of particular interest are approximation algorithms which apply heuristics to obtain solutions that may not be optimal but provably close to optimal.

10.1 Introduction

Occasionally, the theory of algorithm complexity indicates that a problem is impossible to solve. Such an indication is almost always unwelcome. In order to get a clearer picture of what this means in practice, we will explore various aspects of impossibility.

Our first caveat has to do with the question of what exactly is impossible. When we talk about a problem, we tend to commingle the problem in general and a specific instance of that problem. When discussing impossibility, it is important to differentiate these two for two reasons. First, it should be clear that a specific instance of a problem will always have a definite answer. For example, recall the question (posed in Chapter 4) of whether two context-free grammars generate the same language. While the general problem is undecidable, meaning there is not an algorithm that answers for any two grammars, yes or no, it should be perfectly obvious that given any two specific grammars, either they do generate the same language or they do not — there is no third alternative. In other words, for any specific instance of a problem, there is a specific answer. The question that decidability addresses is how we can obtain this answer, in all possible instances.

Second, given a specific instance, even if we have an algorithmic solution approach, it makes no sense to talk about the complexity of solving this instance because of the overall approach of computational complexity. The complexity of a problem is a function of some measure of the input. If one selects a specific instance of the problem, if one can solve it, the measure of that instance is a constant; it may be large, but a constant it is. As a result, the computational complexity of solving this instance is also a constant.[1] Consequently, it makes little sense to talk about the computational complexity of solving an instance; computational complexity can only be used to reflect the effort required to solve all instances of a problem, as a function of the chosen measure of the size of the instances.

The second issue we must address pertains to two types of impossibility. A problem may be such that no algorithm solving it is known. If we can tighten this up and manage to show that no such algorithm can exist, then we say this problem is undecidable. This is, in a way, a positive result. We can actually show that something is impossible. Ordinarily, not being able to do something reflects a lack of effort or success; in other words, we just have not worked hard enough. Were we to spend more time and effort, or were we just smarter, we could find a solution. Undecidability is fundamentally different. We can show that no algorithm exists — not now and not ever in the future.

A very different type of impossibility occurs if the complexity of the problem is prohibitively large. This means larger instances of the problem most likely require more time than we have available. It does not mean we will never be able to obtain a solution. For example, if the measure of the input is very small, even a prohibitively large function may yield a relatively small value for that instance. In addition, if the complexity is worst case, it is possible that instances that are not worst case take significantly less time and effort to solve.

---

[1] For example, assume that the time complexity $f(n)$ of a given algorithm is 2^{5n}, with n the measure of the input (e.g., size). If our instance has a value of n equal to 1000, then the amount of time required to solve this instance of the problem is 2^{5000}, or approximately 10^{1500}. While it is true that (using the current model of the universe) the world has not existed that long, even if time were measured in femtoseconds, it is nevertheless also true that 2^{5000} is a constant, that is $2^{5000} = O(1)$.

Finally, it turns out that in some cases it is very difficult to find an optimal solution, but frequently optimality is not mandatory. A good solution may be entirely acceptable, especially if we can obtain it dramatically faster than an optimal one. This leads to heuristics and approximation algorithms for problems that are considered very hard.

10.2 Undecidability

A problem consisting of infinitely many instances is said to be undecidable if one can prove mathematically that no algorithm exists that solves each instance of the problem.[2] Traditionally, a problem is shown to be undecidable by reducing it to one of two problems that are well known to be undecidable, namely the halting problem for Turing machines and Post's correspondence problem (PCP). A problem P is undecidable if we can show that assuming P were decidable would yield the decidability of a problem known to be undecidable. For example, the question of whether two context-free grammars generate the same language is usually reduced to PCP. One assumes that there exists an algorithm that answers yes or no for any two given context free grammars; then one shows that this algorithm would allow one to solve PCP. However, since this problem is known to be undecidable, a contradiction to the original assumption is obtained. Since the only assumption one made was the existence of the algorithm determining whether two context-free grammars generate the same language, this algorithm cannot exist. The problem is undecidable.

One should be clear that things can be quite tricky. For example, one might approach the problem of the equivalence of two grammars as follows. Take a word and determine if each of the two languages contains that word (whether it is generated by the context-free grammar corresponding to that language).[3] If the word is in one language but not the other, we have proven that the two languages are different; the two grammars do not generate the same language. If the word is in both languages or not in either language, then we choose another word and repeat this process. If at any point we encounter a witness to the differentness of the two languages (that is, the word is in one language but not the other), we know that the two grammars generate different languages. If we never encounter such a witness, the two languages are identical. This is true since we can effectively enumerate all

---

[2] It makes little sense to consider finite classes of problems since it is usually possible to answer each instance, albeit with ad hoc methods. If there are only finitely many such instances, the finite union of these ad hoc methods would constitute an algorithm for the entire class of problems.

[3] This can be done quite efficiently; even in the worst case, the time complexity of parsing a word of length n using an arbitrary context-free grammar is less than n^3.

words,[4] and if the two languages are different, we must eventually encounter a witness to that effect.

There is a fly in the ointment in this argumentation. True, if the two languages are different, we will eventually encounter a witness, but if they are not, if the two grammars generate the same language, then this process never terminates because there are infinitely many words to be checked.

Many undecidable problems are of this type. One of the two outcomes of the question can always be answered, but the other cannot be determined in a finite number of steps. (In the literature this is also referred to as a procedure — a computational recipe that will give the correct answer if it stops but may continue indefinitely without giving an answer. In contrast, an algorithm must always stop and give the correct answer.)[5]

What is a programmer to do when she encounters a problem that turns out to be undecidable?[6] It is important to understand that it is almost always a relatively small portion of the problem that gives rise to its undecidability. In other words, only a rather small[7] subclass of the problem may display characteristics that render the general problem undecidable. While it is impractical to consider the class of all instances that do not give rise to the undecidability,[8] it is usually possible to define subclasses that do not contain any troublesome instances. As we pointed out, often a problem becomes undecidable because we generalized it more than necessary. For example, instead of testing in general whether two grammars generate the same language, it would be better to verify that each transformation rule that changes one grammar into another one does not change the language generated. Thus, in effect, we have a limited version of the test, one that only

---

[4] The enumeration of all words over an alphabet A refers to the task of assigning a positive integer value to each word such that each word is uniquely identified by that value. That this can be done is seen as follows. We first fix an order among the letters of the alphabet A; this induces a lexicographical ordering on words over A. Then we construct first all words of length 0 (there is one, the empty word), then all words of length 1 (in this order; there are exactly card(A) such words), then all words of length 2 (there are [card(A)]^2 of them), and so on. Since any word must have a finite length, say m, we are guaranteed to encounter it eventually during this process. Consequently, all words over the alphabet A are enumerable. The advantage of enumeration is that we can systematically go through all integer values and be sure that we do not miss a word.

[5] A problem for which a procedure exists is called recursively enumerable (r.e.); a problem for which an algorithm exists is called recursive. Any recursive problem is also r.e., but the converse does not hold (see, for example, the equivalence problem for context-free grammars). Any problem that is not recursive is undecidable. There do exist problems that are not even r.e., but such problems tend to be only of theoretical interest. Problems ordinarily encountered in the real world are usually at least r.e., if not recursive.

[6] How the programmer finds out that the problem is undecidable is another issue. This may be known from the literature. Alternatively, having fruitlessly attempted to design a solution method, the programmer in desperation may try to reduce the problem to one known to be undecidable.

[7] The word *small* is to be viewed with caution in this context. Clearly, this subclass must contain infinitely many instances, but relative to the entire class, it may still be vanishingly small.

[8] Let C be the class of all instances of the problem and let C_0 be the subclass of all instances for which no algorithm exists. C_0 is normally not well defined. Even if it were, it would be undecidable to determine which instances belong to C_0.

addresses a specific transformation rule, instead of a general test that pays no attention to the question of how the two grammars were obtained. Such a limited test is almost always quite easy to carry out. It certainly is not an undecidable problem.

From a practical point of view, it may be prudent to take the following approach. Assume one is confronted with a problem that appears to be very difficult. In this case, it behooves the programmer to determine whether the general problem might be undecidable. Few endeavors are as embarrassing as spending much time and effort on obtaining a solution for a problem that does not have one, that is, a problem that is undecidable.

Once one has verified that the problem is undecidable, one should determine whether the problem is needed in its full generality. As pointed out, an individual instance virtually always has a solution. Moreover, if limited classes of instances must be answered, one should determine whether these restricted subclasses are also undecidable. As a general rule, it is quite rare to encounter problems in real life that are fundamentally undecidable. In most cases, closer examination reveals that only certain subclasses are really of interest, not the fully general problem.

If the programmer ultimately determines that the problem is inherently undecidable, the client should be informed that the problem has no solution. Frequently, in such a case the client will use domain-specific knowledge (not easily available to the programmer) to impose restrictions that permit solutions. To help the client understand why the original problem is not solvable may require a good deal of insight into what aspects of the problem render it undecidable.

10.3 Infeasibility

A fundamentally different situation occurs when the algorithmic complexity renders the task of obtaining solutions extremely time-consuming. While the end result for the programmer may be the same (it is impossible to get a general solution), several substantively different aspects may mitigate this conclusion.

Consider the following problem. Modern compilers for programming languages consist of several phases, one of which is the syntactic analysis that employs a parser. This is where we may be interested in determining whether two grammars generate the same (programming) language. Before we get to parsing, a compiler must group together syntactic atoms or tokens, such as keywords, identifiers, operators, and numbers.[9] This is done in the lexical analysis, where regular expressions are used to describe all possible lexical

---

[9] Note that a program starts out as a sequence of characters. These characters must then be grouped together into the program's tokens. While this grouping together may be obvious to a human, a compiler has to use a systematic approach to carry out this task.

tokens of the programming language. While regular expressions are a convenient way of describing all possible tokens, they are not as convenient for processing the program.[10] Instead, the regular expressions are converted to deterministic finite automata (dfa), which are employed in the lexical analysis. For us the important aspect is the conversion from regular expressions to dfa. It should be clear that this is something that occurs frequently, whenever a compiler for a programming language is written. It should also be obvious that because of this ubiquity, the transition from regular expressions to dfa cannot be hopelessly inefficient. Yet algorithmic complexity very clearly states that the size of a dfa (its number of states) can be exponential in the length of the regular expression. This is not just some upper bound. One can construct regular expressions of length n so that the smallest dfa for this regular expression has $2^{O(n)}$ states.[11] This suggests that going from regular expressions to dfa is a hopelessly inefficient step, one that should be avoided at all cost, yet every compiler does it.

To understand this apparent paradox, several remarks are in order. First, the exponential behavior is the worst-case complexity. While there are regular expressions whose dfa have a size exponential in the length of the expression, these are typically pathological examples. Regular expressions representing actual tokens in existing programming languages result in much smaller dfa. Thus, even though the worst-case complexity is indeed exponential, on average this does not happen.[12]

Second, even if the complexity were exponential, note that the construction of dfa occurs once. That is, we convert regular expressions to dfa once for each compiler, and when this operation has been carried out, no more work has to be done on this task. In particular, there is no connection between the number of times the compiler is used to translate programs and the complexity of constructing the dfa. Effectively, we have here a paradigm shift. For the user of the compiler, the complexity of the compiling process is of interest; the user of the compiler has absolutely no interest in the difficulty of creating the compiler. Measured in terms of the effort to compile a program, the transition from regular expressions to dfa is a constant. This effort was expended once and need no longer concern the user of the compiler. Thus, even if the construction of a dfa from a regular expression required time exponential in the expression's length, in terms of compiling programs whose lengths give us the measure n that is the argument of our complexity function, this effort is $O(1)$.

---

[10] Regular expressions are reasonably descriptive for a human; dfa are not. However, dfa are operationally very useful in determining whether something is, or is not, a specific token.

[11] It is not really important to discuss what is meant by the length of a regular expression. We can, for example, count the number of characters and operators in the regular expression, essentially treating it as a word in which we count the number of characters.

[12] Recall that *average* is a loaded term. Here it obviously means average within the context of real tokens in real programming languages. This notion of average would not necessarily be applicable in other contexts.

It follows that the step from regular expression to deterministic finite automaton can be ignored by the user of the compiler, simply because the investment has already been made and does not affect the complexity of using the compiler. As a result, even if this investment was high, it occurred only once. It is not recurring from the point of view of the user of the compiler. In such a situation, one can safely ignore the alarms that computational complexity triggers.

Another situation is the following. Suppose we have an algorithm, say D, for a very important problem. This algorithm has been used for decades very effectively. For most practical problems, the algorithm D produces solutions in linear time, yet it is known that its worst-case time complexity is exponential. There exist problems for which D has exponential run time. Because of the economic significance of the problem and because nobody has been able to show that the problem necessarily is of exponential complexity,[13] extensive additional research provides a radically new algorithm, say K, for the same problem with dramatically different time complexities. K has a polynomial worst-case time complexity, but its average time complexity appears to be significantly slower than that of D. The fact that K has a polynomial worst-case time complexity establishes that the problem has a polynomial worst-case time complexity. In particular, D is clearly not optimal in its worst-case behavior.

This is not a hypothetical example. The problem is linear programming (LP) (for a quick review of this optimization problem, see Section 4.4). Algorithm D is Dantzig's simplex approach to solving LP problems (which predates the widespread use of computers), Algorithm K is Karmarkar's approach (which dates to the mid-1980s). In spite of K's superior worst-case behavior, many of today's LP problems are solved using methods based on Dantzig's simplex method and not on Karmarkar's algorithm. This is primarily due to the faster average case complexity, with *average* of course being in the eye of the beholder. Essentially this means whatever problem I am currently interested in.

Note the fundamental difference between the dfa construction and the LP problem. While the dfa construction is clearly exponential in the worst case, the LP problem is equally obviously not. Yet even though the simplex method does run in exponential time in the worst case, it is still the method of choice. In the first case, there is no other, better alternative; in the second case, there exists one, but because its average time complexity is not as attractive, it tends not to be used.

This raises the practical problem how to guard against encountering an LP problem where the simplex method misbehaves. If this is a significant concern, the programmer should run both algorithms in parallel (on different computer systems). The advantage of this approach is that at the price of

---

[13] Recall the difference between the complexity of an algorithm solving a problem and the complexity of that problem. The algorithm's complexity is an upper bound on that of the problem, but there is no guarantee that it is a good upper bound.

doubling the computational effort (and using twice the hardware), one is guaranteed to get the result as fast as possible.[14]

There is a third, yet again fundamentally different, situation where infeasibility must be sidestepped. This is the case where finding an optimal solution is infeasible but determining an approximation is not. It should be clear that there are instances where optimality it not the driving force; often, people are content if they can obtain a solution that is close to optimal. Such an approach is applicable only in some instances. If one were to decide that converting regular expressions to dfa is just too hard, it would not do to provide an approximation to the correct solution. Furthermore, not every problem where it makes sense to talk about an approximate solution admits approximations that are acceptably good. An example should clarify this.

The bin packing problem can be stated as follows. We are given a set of n rational numbers $w_1, \ldots, w_n$ such that for all $i = 1, \ldots, n$, $0 < w_i < 1$; the problem consists of packing the numbers into the minimum number of bins such that the sum of all numbers in each bin does not exceed 1.[15] The problem of determining the minimum number of bins required is known to be infeasible to solve optimally.[16] While it may be interesting to determine the minimal number of bins, a sufficiently good approximation is probably acceptable in most practical situations. This gives rise to the question of what is *sufficiently good*? It turns out that in the problem at hand, bin packing, we have an excellent answer: We can guarantee that the approximate solution is within a certain fixed percentage of the optimal one.

The first, very simple, heuristic for obtaining an approximation is First Fit. This is an on-line algorithm whereby a number B of bins is maintained (initially $B = 0$), and each rational number w_i is placed into the first bin that can accommodate it. Only if none of the bins in play can store w_i, is a new bin placed in service ($B := B + 1$). It is not difficult to establish an upper bound on the number FF(I) of bins needed by First Fit for the instance I. The number of bins required by First Fit is smaller than twice the optimal number OPT(I) of bins for the instance I:

$$FF(I) < 2 \cdot OPT(I).\text{[17]}$$

---

[14] Objectively, the cost is less than double. We terminate both programs as soon as one provides the result. Thus, if the times for a specific instance are t_D and t_K, we would spend $\min(t_D, t_K)$ on two platforms, for an aggregate time of $2 \cdot \min(t_D, t_K)$.

[15] This is the simplest, one-dimensional (1D) formulation. Bin packing has many generalizations, for example, to more than one dimension. Obviously, the resulting problems are not easier to solve than the original, 1D problem.

[16] Specifically, it is NP-complete (see the following section), meaning that for practical purposes, any algorithm solving it optimally has a time complexity that is exponential in n.

[17] We first verify that $FF(I) < \lceil 2 \cdot (w_1 + \ldots + w_n) \rceil$. This follows if one sets $w_i = 1/2 + \varepsilon$, for all $i = 1, \ldots, n$, with $\varepsilon < 1/(2n)$. Furthermore, it is clear that $\lceil w_1 + \ldots + w_n \rceil \leq OPT(I)$. These two inequalities imply the claim.

In other words, First Fit uses fewer than twice the optimal number of bins.[18] At the same time, First Fit is is an extremely efficient algorithm.[19]

While the first fit heuristic is efficient, it is not particular effective; doubling the number of bins is not very attractive. It turns out that a slight modification of the first fit heuristic has a much better performance. This comes at the price of sacrificing the on-line attribute of the algorithm. We first sort the rational numbers $w_1, ..., w_n$ in decreasing order, yielding $v_1, ..., v_n$. Then we apply First Fit. This is called decreasing First Fit (DFF). One can show that DFF(I) for any instance I of the bin packing problem requires no more than about 22% over OPT(I):

$$DFF(I) \leq 11/9 \cdot OPT(I) + 4.$$

It is instructive to recall that the original optimal bin packing problem has only infeasible algorithms. Yet using a fairly simple heuristic allows one to produce a very practical algorithm, with a time complexity of no more than $O(n^2)$, whose result is guaranteed to be within about 22% of optimal.

In general, some classes of algorithms permit approximate solutions. In all such cases, heuristics play an important role. Some of these algorithms provide provably good solutions, meaning their solutions are within a constant factor of optimal. Other problems may have approximation algorithms, but they do not have provably good solutions; their solutions can differ from the optimal solution by an arbitrarily large constant factor. In most cases, such algorithms are less useful. However, their deficiencies should always be viewed in light of the infeasibility of the algorithms providing exact solutions.

10.4 NP-Completeness

Programmers may occasionally be confronted with the observation that a given problem is NP-complete. While it makes little sense here to go into

---

[18] It turns out that this upper bound can be improved. First Fit requires only about 70% more than optimal, not 100%.

[19] For each of the n rational numbers w_i, a bin must be identified; this can be done in time $O(n)$. Thus, First Fit can easily be carried out in time $O(n^2)$. (This can be improved.) Contrast this with the exponential algorithm to obtain the optimal solution.

the formal definition,[20] it is appropriate to say a few words about the relevance of this to program performance. P and NP are both classes of problems with algorithms of polynomial time complexity, the only difference being that the algorithm must be deterministic for the problem to belong to P, while it can be nondeterministic for NP. Of all the problems in NP, the NP-complete problems are the most difficult to solve.[21] For all practical purposes, the NP-completeness of a problem indicates that the best algorithms solving that problem have exponential worst-case time complexity.[22] Thus, if reference is made to the NP-completeness of a problem in the literature, it means in practice that the problem is as hard as if it had an exponential time complexity. How to deal with such problems was discussed in the previous section.

10.5 Practical Considerations

Programmers should be aware of undecidability and infeasibility, not necessarily as an absolute deterrent, but as an incentive to work around. Both types of impossibility suggest difficulties. However, almost always additional analysis is required to determine whether the problem is inherently without feasible solution or whether techniques can be applied that allow one to sidestep the difficulties in some way. For undecidability, it is imperative to understand whether the class of problems is inherently unsolvable

---

[20] Roughly speaking, the class P consists of all problems for which there exist algorithms whose worst-case time complexity is polynomial. An important aspect of an algorithm is that we know exactly what the next instruction to be executed is. That is, the algorithm is deterministic; it does not require any guessing. One can conceive of a different type of algorithm, namely nondeterministic algorithms, for which guessing, and in particular lucky guessing, is an integral part. To illustrate, consider the problem of finding a path from a node to another node in a graph (discussed in Section 3.2.13). We derived that for a graph with n nodes, represented by its incidence matrix, this problem is of worst-case time complexity $O(n^2)$. However, if we were to use a nondeterministic algorithm, we would stipulate that this algorithm guess correctly whenever there is more than one outgoing edge at a node. In this way, the complexity of this nondeterministic algorithm is $O(n)$. The class NP is then defined as consisting of all problems for which there exist nondeterministic algorithms whose worst-case time complexity is polynomial. Clearly, P is contained in NP, but it is unknown whether P and NP differ (this is one of the most celebrated open problems in theoretical computer science).

[21] More precisely, a problem in NP is NP-complete if the existence of a polynomial time-deterministic algorithm for that problem implies the existence of polynomial time-deterministic algorithms for all problems in NP. In other words, if one NP-complete problem can be shown to belong to P, then all problems in NP belong to P, which means that P = NP. In this sense, an NP-complete problem is as hard as any problem in NP. Note that not all problems in NP are NP-complete. This should be obvious since P is contained in NP. However, not even every problem in NP-P is NP-complete (assuming of course that the two classes are not identical).

[22] Since it is not known whether P ≠ NP, we also cannot say whether using nondeterminism increases the complexity at all. However, no deterministic algorithm of polynomial worst-case time complexity is known that solves an NP-complete problem.

or whether subclasses of interest can be isolated that do have feasible solution techniques. In the case of prohibitively large time[23] complexities, we should first ascertain whether this is worst-case or average complexity. In most such cases, the worst-case complexity is significantly larger than the average complexity. Then we must determine whether the average complexity is tolerable for practical applications. This may require us to examine the basis of our complexity consideration. For example, the lexical analysis requiring the translation of regular expressions into deterministic finite automata may be of little concern to the user of a compiler, even though this step does have an exponential worst-case time complexity.

The most important aspect of this chapter is to alert the programmer that occasionally, for a variety of reasons, a problem may not have a feasible solution. While this may be an unpleasant surprise, it is nevertheless better to recognize this problem than wasting significant amounts of time and effort on obtaining a solution that cannot exist in the first place. In some cases, the size of the problem may be small enough that even a very large complexity, say exponential, may still be acceptable; in such a case, knowing the computational complexity is not particularly useful. In other cases, it may not be necessary that the solution is optimal — a good approximation may be entirely satisfactory. Thus, efficient approximation algorithms should be explored, especially those whose solutions are guaranteed to be within a fixed percentage of the optimal solution. In other cases, the problem may be badly formulated. Investigating more pointedly the actual requirements may reveal that the problem became artificially more complicated than the original question required. In such a case, reverting to the simpler question may resolve the dilemma of needing a solution for a problem that does not seem to have one. Finally, one should always be aware that undecidability is inherently a question of infinitely many instances of a problem. A single instance of a problem will always have a solution, even if it may not be easy to find.

Bibliographical Notes

Undecidability is squarely in the realm of algorithms. Many textbooks covering design and analysis of algorithms devote time to this topic, which clearly imposes a limit on what can be achieved; see, for example, Lewis and Papadimitriou: *Elements of the Theory of Computation*. Nevertheless, given undecidability's pedigree in formal language theory, in particular, Turing machines, some coverage of its fundamentals (most importantly the halting problem for Turing machines) can be found in formal language texts, for

---

[23] As noted before, space complexity should never exceed time complexity. Therefore, we usually concentrate on time complexity.

example, Hopcroft and Ullman: *Introduction to Automata Theory.* Approximation algorithms, for the most part, are a consequence of the realization that
exact solutions may be prohibitively expensive. Only more recent algorithms
texts cover approximation algorithms adequately, for example, Kleinberg
and Tardos: *Algorithm Design.* Infeasibility, owing to prohibitively large complexities, is also covered in algorithm texts, as is NP-completeness, although
the importance of this topic for theoretical computer science has resulted in
texts devoted exclusively to NP-completeness, for example, Garey and
Johnson: *Computers and Intractability.*

Exercises

Exercise 1

Most modern compilers use a variant of LR(k) parsing for their lexical analysis. General parsing of a string of length n based on context-free grammars
requires well in excess of $O(n^2)$ (Earley's algorithm, the standard parsing
algorithm for general context free grammars, is $O(n^3)$, which can be reduced
somewhat, but general context-free parsing is another instance where a
nontrivial lower bound is extremely elusive). However, LR(k) parsing works
in linear time. The nonnegative parameter k indicates the length of the look-
ahead string — essentially how far beyond the end of the already processed
portion of the string one may look ahead to help in processing the remainder.
The boundaries between what can and what cannot be done are exceedingly
sharp here. It is possible to test effectively whether a given context-free
grammar is LR(k) for a specific value of k, but to test whether there exists a
k_0 such that a given context-free grammar is LR(k_0) is undecidable.

Show that testing whether there exists a k_0 such that a given context-free
grammar is LR(k_0) is recursively enumerable, that is, there exists a procedure
that halts if such a k_0 exists but may go on indefinitely otherwise.

Exercise 2

Given any problem P, we may consider its complement P'. For example, the
complement of the equivalence problem of two context-free grammars is the
problem of determining whether two context-free grammars generate different languages.

Show that there are only three possibilities for P and P':

a. P and P' are both recursive (there exist algorithms for both problems).

  b. P is recursively enumerable but not recursive, and P' is not recursively enumerable.
  c. Neither P nor P' are recursively enumerable.

Exercise 3

Instead of formulating problems, one frequently formulates languages when discussing decidability. This is quite natural since its basis is in Turing machines, which can be viewed as devices for accepting languages. The definitions are analogous. A language is recursive if its Turing machine always halts; it is recursively enumerable if its Turing machine halts for every word that is in the language but may go on indefinitely if the word is not in the language. Consequently, if a language is recursively enumerable but not recursive, then all the Turing machines accepting the language have the property that they do not halt for some input (which is of course not in the language).

Let L_1 and L_2 be arbitrary languages, subject to the specification in either (a) or (b). Consider the following four questions:

Q1. Does L_1-L_2 contain a given fixed word w?
Q2. Is L_1-L_2 empty?
Q3. Does $L_1 \cap L_2$ contain a given fixed word w?
Q4. Is $L_1 \cap L_2$ empty?

For each of these four questions determine whether the problem is recursive, not recursive but recursively enumerable, or not recursively enumerable, provided:

  a. Both L_1 and L_2 are recursive.
  b. Both L_1 and L_2 are recursively enumerable but not recursive.

Part 3

Conclusion

We have made the case, convincingly we hope, that many things can go wrong when transitioning from an algorithm to software. We have given concrete examples how this can occur and have described how to avoid some of the disappointments that these difficulties cause. We expect that programmers will come away with a better appreciation of what analysis of algorithms provides, but also what it does not address.

The most important message of this book is that complexity analysis of algorithms has much to offer programmers interested in producing efficient software. It is the only methodology that permits one to predict, with reasonable certainty, how much time a given program will take for a given set of input data, without requiring the execution of the program. Carefully and judiciously applied, complexity analysis is an extremely useful tool that should be viewed as fundamental in any programmer's toolkit.

However, it is crucial to be aware of numerous problems that can cloud the picture. These problems stem from the fundamental differences of the computing paradigms assumed for algorithms and for software. We have carefully outlined these differences and demonstrated how they can influence the conclusions one may draw about the efficiency of software from the complexity analysis of the underlying algorithm.

The most important difference, and definitely the one with the greatest consequences for the efficiency of programs, relates to memory. Algorithm analysis assumes that memory is unlimited and that access to memory is uniform. In contrast, real computing systems have memory hierarchies, consisting in most cases of registers, caches (of various types), main memory, and external memory (magnetic disks), all of them obviously finite. Access characteristics for different types of memory differ greatly, both in access time and in the method of access (lines, blocks/pages, etc.). For example, the time it takes to retrieve an item from external memory typically is between six and seven orders of magnitude (1 to 10 million times) slower than retrieving that item from cache. Furthermore, for most types of memory, it is necessary to retrieve far more than just the desired item; for caches, an entire cache line must be loaded; for main memory, an entire page (for virtual memory management) or block (for out-of-core programming) must be retrieved and installed before an individual item can be accessed. This is complicated by the necessity of managing memory, since the scarcity of memory in cache and main memory implies that installing new lines or pages or blocks ordinarily means displacing older lines or pages or blocks. If these are dirty (have been written to), they must be stored back as well. The upshot of this vastly more complicated process of accessing data is that the location of an item has enormous consequences for the performance of the code. We have demonstrated with concrete (and realistic) code examples that a difference of three orders of magnitude in performance is not at all unheard of. Such a performance difference can make or break a program.

Another important difference between algorithms and software is indirectly related to the management of memory, namely the allocation of dynamic data structures in ordinary programs. Dynamic data structures are ubiquitous in modern programming environments, ranging from explicitly allocated structures such as trees, stacks, and queues (which are obviously dynamic in nature) to recursive functions that may not be quite as obviously dynamic but nevertheless require virtually all the facilities general dynamic memory needs. This means, in particular, the ability to allocate and, perhaps even more importantly, to free memory.

Memory that has been freed, either explicitly by the programmer via an instruction or implicitly (as would be the case for recursion), can then be reused for other purposes. While this is evident, how this reuse can be achieved is not nearly as evident. It requires a good deal of work to attain this goal. In other words, just because memory has been recognized as no longer needed does not mean it is easily put to further use. This is particularly complicated if the sizes of memory units allocated during execution of a program differ. (As we indicated, if all allocations occur in exactly one size, the management of memory is greatly simplified.) This is because components of dynamic data structures must be allocated in contiguous memory space, and here the interplay between allocation and deallocation can result in extensive fragmentation of memory, with the result that the total amount of memory available may significantly exceed the size of an allocation request, but no contiguous chunk of memory of the needed size exists.

This situation calls for the invocation of a process called garbage collection — the gathering of all unused chunks of memory into one contiguous block. Garbage collection can be an extremely costly process. It requires the relocation of large amounts of memory in use. Moreover, it is usually quite unpredictable when it is invoked, resulting in a degree of uncertainty in performance that can be highly disturbing to programmers. Most importantly, it is an aspect of program execution that will never be captured by the complexity analysis of an algorithm.

While the memory model of algorithms is responsible for much of the discrepancies between complexity analysis and program performance, other aspects of the analysis of algorithms may give a distorted picture of the expected behavior of software. These are related to the asymptotic nature of complexity functions and to the finiteness of the representation of numbers in programs.

Complexity analysis emphasizes the eventual behavior of the functions derived as a representation of the time and space complexity of an algorithm. This emphasis justifies the jettisoning of constant factors and lower-order terms. It also focuses predominantly on the behavior in the limit. In contrast, software performance is of interest mainly for a specific range of values, and this range tends to be not just finite but quite limited. Therefore, constant factors and lower-order terms in the functions representing the time (or space) complexity of the algorithm (which are usually ignored when dealing with complexities) may play an important role in determining the performance of a program, especially when we have to decide which of two candidates to choose. In this context crossover points are very important (values where one complexity function becomes larger than another function). Consequently, in practical applications it is quite common to consider hybrid algorithms; these are composite algorithms where for each of a finite set of ranges, a different algorithm is employed.

The finiteness of the number representation has several implications that are not just numerical in nature. In particular, it is important for a programmer to understand the nature of floating point numbers: They do not faithfully represent all numbers a programmer may expect to be represented, and they display unexpected quirks when they are used. Specifically, testing for equality turns out to be quite complicated for floating point numbers. Related to this is the failure of common mathematical properties and identities such as associativity and distributivity to hold.

Finally, we discussed aspects of impossibility, where the situation is somewhat reversed. Algorithm analysis tells us a particular task is impossible to solve, either absolutely (because the problem is undecidable) or relatively (because the complexity of solving the problem is prohibitively large). At the same time, the programmer may have a legitimate interest in obtaining a solution. We outlined possible reasons for the impossibility and suggested ways of avoiding it, including the use of approximation algorithms that may be highly effective whenever solutions are needed, but whose optimality is not crucial.

Appendix I:

Algorithms Every Programmer Should Know

For the most part, this book argues that the disconnect between algorithm analysis and program performance can be bridged. As such, we effectively took the position that the ultimate arbiter of software behavior is the programmer or software engineer. Thus, it appears that we subtly shifted the blame for problems arising from the failure of complexity analysis to predict accurate program performance to the designer of algorithms and away from the software engineer. This is not entirely accurate; we do believe that software engineers, in maintaining that very little useful can be learned from the analysis of algorithms, are seriously shortchanging themselves, primarily because they do not know enough about algorithms in the first place. In this appendix we will briefly enumerate the basics of algorithms — basics in the sense that people who are not fully conversant with them do not have the right to call themselves software engineers. We do not intend to teach these methods, but we do want to list them and stress some aspects that are important for the purpose of this book.

There are generic building blocks for algorithms and there are basic algorithms. Both are equally important. For the most part, the generic building blocks relate to fundamental data structures and their manipulation (often also referred to as abstract data types). These data structures are typically dynamic; while they can be implemented using static data structures (which invariably means fixed-size arrays), such implementations have deficiencies that negate some of the advantages of these data structures.

Minimally, every competent programmer must know stacks,[1] queues[2] (including priority queues), linked lists (of various types: singly, circular, doubly linked, etc.), and trees (of various types: binary, balanced, search, as well as external trees such as B-trees and similar trees). While these are typically viewed as data structures, it should be clearly understood that a data structure is completely useless for the representation of information unless it is coupled with operations. It is these operations that give a data structure its specific quality. For example, a linked list can be used to repre-

---

[1] A stack is also known as a last in first out (LIFO) structure.
[2] A queue is also known as a first in first out (FIFO) structure.

sent both a stack and a queue, but it is the operations that are associated with a stack or a queue that differentiate these data structures. Thus, a stack must support the following operations, and no other operations (such as accessing an element other than that at the top of the stack) are permitted for a pure stack:

1. Test for emptiness
2. Adding an element (adding can only be done at the top of the stack)
3. Removing an element from a nonempty stack (removing can only be done at the top of the stack)
4. Reading an element if the stack is not empty (reading can only be done at the top)

Similarly, a queue must support the following operations, and no other operations are permitted for a pure queue:

1. Test for emptiness
2. Adding an element (adding can only be done at the end of the queue)
3. Removing an element from a nonempty queue (removing can only be done at the front of the queue)
4. Reading an element if the queue is not empty (reading can only be done at the front)

Linear lists and trees have similar types of operations.

It is important that the programmer understand that the operations define the data type, not some internal representation of data items. Only once the operations of a specific data structure are defined does it make sense to address a concrete implementation. This is where questions such as "Is the data structure full?" may be posed. Note that this is not a recognized test for any of these data structures (stack, queue, list, tree). In its pure definition, a stack can never be full. It is a dynamic data structure, and as such there is no upper limit on its size. Such limits only occur when data structures are implemented using structures that impose these limits. Stacks (as well as lists, queues, and trees) can be implemented using fixed-size arrays (not a good idea, but occasionally unavoidable, for example, if the programming language does not support the explicit allocation of dynamic memory) whereby the size of the array imposes an obvious upper bound on the size of the stack. Note that even in the case of dynamic memory, there is an upper bound, namely, the amount of memory in the pool allocated by the run-time support system for the use of dynamic memory (which could be further increased through the use of virtual memory management). This size is typically not known when the program is written; as such, it is not a program constraint, but the programmer should be fully aware that there is an upper

bound of some sort and that exceeding it will result in unpleasant consequences.

In contrast to arrays (at least if they are correctly allocated in main memory), the four data structures stack, queue, linked list, and tree do not preserve the random access property of main memory. To wit, if a stack contains
n elements, accessing the bottom element (the element that was first placed
on the stack) requires removing the $n - 1$ stack elements that are on top of
it. Thus, the complexity of (that is, the amount of work required for) accessing
this element depends on the value of n. If n is small, little work is needed,
but if n is large, a great deal more must be expended. Similarly, accessing
an element just appended to a queue with n elements requires removing
these n elements that precede it. Linked lists and trees have similar examples.

Arrays are data structures of great practical importance, from a theoretical
point of view (consider the mapping functions that we discussed and their
implications), as a structure *sui generis* (representing multidimensional
homogeneous collections of data), and as a representational tool for other
data structures. Most programmers are familiar with the concept of arrays,
although the random access property and the mapping functions that enable
the representation of multidimensional arrays in the one-dimensional main
memory space may be less familiar.

The transition from operations to algorithms is quite fluid. Accessing the
top element of a stack would be considered an operation by most programmers, but what about accessing a leaf in a binary tree? Is it an operation or
an algorithm? This points clearly to an important aspect of operations and
algorithms. They tend to appear as building blocks in more complicated
processes. Another important issue is encapsulation. It is highly desirable to
be able to enclose certain well-defined processes as operations that can be
viewed as abstractions performing certain manipulations. It is then no longer
necessary to be concerned with the implementation of these processes. They
are basic operations that could be replaced by some other implementation
as long as the same effect is achieved on the underlying data structures.[3]
Thus, whether we talk about operations or about algorithms is really just a
question of viewpoint, not an issue of complexity.

In Chapter 3 we formulated a number of algorithms. Most of these should
be considered fundamental. Specifically, the sorting and searching methods
are absolutely basic and indispensable. Beyond the techniques discussed
there, external sorting and searching methods are important,[4] as is interpo-

---

[3] Here is where the importance of the operations and tests associated with a structure becomes
apparent. Any implementation must support them without restriction or exception, and when
replacing one implementation with another, the programmer signally makes use of the availability of this uniform interface to the structure.

[4] External methods refer to data sets stored on disk. In view of the access characteristics of disks,
it is imperative to minimize the number of disk accesses. This has important implications for the
structuring of sorting methods. It also means that searching has to be carried out using different
data structures, for example, fat trees (trees where each node has not just two children as for
binary trees, but many more, allowing one to limit the height of the tree, which corresponds to
the number of disk accesses, if everything is stored on disk).

lation search.[5] Hashing is a related technique that all software engineers must know about, together with its limitations. Balanced search trees are useful for sorting and searching and form an integral part of the instrumentarium all software engineers must know. Finally, there are numerous graph algorithms that we did not touch upon but that are important; the ones we mentioned in Section 3.2 are only the three best known.

Other algorithms we did not mention but that should form part of any competent programmer's arsenal of tools are the following:

Spanning trees: A tree is a minimally connected graph (removing any edge will disconnect the tree into two sets of nodes such that there is no path from any node in one set to any node in the other set). In many applications it is useful to have such a minimally connected skeleton in a general graph. If this skeleton contains all nodes of the original graph, it is called a spanning tree. Numerous algorithms exist for the construction of spanning trees, usually spanning trees that minimize some aspect (cost, for instance, defined as the sum of all edge costs taken over all edges in the spanning tree).

Disjoint path problems: In many applications (network flow, transportation problems) it is desirable to have disjoint paths, which do not have any nodes in common.

Pattern matching and string algorithms: The question of whether a given string occurs within another string is fundamental. Advances in bioinformatics (for example, those related to the human genome project) have assigned increased importance to this class of problems. Numerous, very efficient, algorithms exist that solve this problem and its various generalizations.

Network flow algorithms: A network is a graph in which each edge has a weight (reflecting the capacity of that link). The basis for many network flow algorithms is the min cut max flow theorem, which states that the maximal flow in any network is determined by a minimum cut. A cut is the removal of a set of edges in the network such that the resulting network is no longer connected. A minimum cut is a cut where the sum of the weights of the edges is minimal. Numerous algorithms deal with this and related problems.

Approximation algorithms: In Chapter 10 we showed an approximation algorithm for bin packing. In general, approximation algorithms are employed if the problem at hand is infeasible to solve but is

---

[5] Binary search has a time complexity of $\log_2(n)$ when searching an ordered array of n elements. Most people assume that this cannot be improved upon. This is only true if no additional information is available. However, if a distribution function of the information stored in the sorted array is known, it is possible to do much better. In essence, the distribution function allows one to pinpoint much better the approximate location of an item. Indeed, if the distribution function were infallible, we would have direct access to the item in one probe (assuming it is there, and otherwise detect that the item is not in the location where it would have to be).

amenable to approximation. Not all hard problems are of this type. Of those that are, another important question is whether the approximation is guaranteed to be close to optimal. The bin packing approximation algorithms of Section 10.2 have the property that the number of bins resulting from them is within a constant factor of the optimal number of bins. Not all approximation algorithms give approximate solutions that are within a constant factor of their optimal solution. In general, programmers should research approximation algorithms whenever the optimal solution is infeasible.

Monte Carlo methods and other randomized algorithms: These algorithms are used to solve problems whose properties make them difficult to solve. These are not necessarily problems with infeasible solutions; it may simply be that a randomized algorithm is more efficient for the given objectives. We briefly outline two examples, integration of a function and determination of the probability of getting from point A to point B in a congested environment.

Suppose we are given a function $f(x)$ and two real values a and b ($a < b$). We want to compute the definite integral of f within the interval $[a,b]$. We can use standard integration techniques, such as applying the trapezoid rule, but if the evaluation of $f(x_0)$ at a point x_0 is very hard, the following approach may provide an acceptable answer. One randomly chooses a pair $[x_0,y_0]$ with $a \leq x_0 \leq b$ and tests whether $y_0 < f(x_0)$ (y_0 is below the function f) or $y_0 > f(x_0)$ (y_0 is above the function f).[6] It should be clear that care must taken with the choice of y_0; each randomly chosen y_0 must satisfy $K < y_0 < L$, where K is a fixed value smaller than the minimum of $f(x)$ in the interval $[a,b]$ and L is a fixed value larger than the maximum of $f(x)$ over $[a,b]$. There are functions for which is it much easier to test (for most values y) whether y is above or below $f(x)$; in other words, while ordinary integration approaches require the evaluation of f at certain points, this approach only asks whether the value is above or below the function.

Then we repeat this process, keeping count of all randomly chosen pairs above (C_+) and below (C_-) the function f in the interval $[a,b]$. The area of the rectangle from which all of our randomly chosen points are selected is given by $(b - a)*(L - K)$. Assuming we have $K = 0$, the ratio of $C_-/(C_+ + C_-)$ yields the value of the integral, with $(b - a)*(L - K)$ normalized to 1 (if $K \neq 0$, an appropriate modification provides the desired value of the integral). It is important to see that the number of randomly chosen pairs defines the precision of the result — the larger the number of values, the greater the precision. As a result, it makes little sense to talk about the complexity of this approach, since the primary factor in determining the amount of work to be carried out is the number of pairs of values.

---

[6] Given the general premise of this scenario, the case $y_0 = f(x_0)$ is unlikely to occur. If it does, the overall counts must be adjusted, most likely proportionally to the ratio between values above the function f and values below the faction f in the interval $[a,b]$.

The second type of problem where a Monte Carlo method is very useful is traffic problems. Suppose we are given a map of a city (a directed graph), with two designated points A and B (nodes A and B). Each node in the graph is blocked with a certain probability. The question to solve is, What is the probability for an ambulance to get from A to B? The basic approach is quite similar to the previous one. We fix probabilities for each of the nodes to be blocked and then determine whether a path exists from A to B under these probabilities. If so, we increment the counter $C_{success}$ or otherwise the counter $C_{failure}$. After an appropriately large number of repetitions, each time randomly choosing probabilities for each node to be blocked, we derive a simple formula for the overall probability of the ambulance getting from A to B.

It should be evident that the quality of such randomized approaches depends fundamentally on the quality of the random number generator employed in the process. There is a good deal of fundamental research on generating random numbers (which really can only be pseudo-random, since they are computed by a [nonrandom] program). Most programmers are likely to use system-provided random number generators; however, they should be aware that several such generators have been found to be deficient. One should therefore have at least a glancing knowledge of what constitutes an acceptable random number generator and what tests (e.g., chi-square) such a generator must be able to pass to be considered acceptable.

Numerous other algorithms are of significance in certain areas. We mentioned compiling, where algorithms to construct deterministic finite automata for the lexical analysis and parsing methods for the syntactic analysis are central techniques. We also mentioned linear programming, and, in particular, the Simplex method, which has many applications in minimizing (or maximizing) certain linear functions (for example, operations research). Each discipline has some niche algorithms that tend to be very important within that environment but not so much outside of it. It is not realistic to expect every programmer to know about them.

However, it is realistic to expect programmers to understand that it makes no sense at all to reinvent the wheel. Many algorithms have been implemented, at least as algorithms, very competently and effectively. These algorithms can be found in textbooks and published papers and typically have been reviewed and verified by numerous people in addition to the original author or designer. Thus, one has reasonable assurances that these algorithms are correct. While the programmer still has the ultimate responsibility of verifying the correctness of any chosen computational method, selecting a published algorithm is likely to result in reliable software. This holds in particular for publications that specialize in software. It is therefore the task of the software engineer to make intelligent use of the resources available in the literature. In particular, this means employing canned algorithms as much as possible as the basis for the development of the envisioned software. Deciding which algorithms to use in a particular instance is a separate issue, on which this book should provide some guidance.

Bibliographical Notes

Most standard algorithms are covered in modern comprehensive textbooks on algorithm design and analysis. However, more specialized techniques require that the reader consult texts dedicated to the special areas to which the algorithms are related. The same holds more or less for randomized algorithms and approximation algorithms — not all standard texts cover these. A comprehensive textbook is Kleinberg and Tardos: *Algorithm Design.* An excellent comprehensive discussion of computed randomness is in Knuth: *The Art of Computer Programming,* Vol. 2: *Seminumerical Algorithms.* Moreover, the wealth of network-related algorithms has resulted in texts exclusively covering this discipline, for example, Ahuja, Magnanti, and Orlin: *Network Flows: Theory, Algorithms, and Applications.* The same holds for pattern matching techniques, which are a central part of bioinformatics. The starting point for much of this work is covered in Chapter 9 of Aho, Hopcroft, and Ullman: *The Design and Analysis of Computer Algorithms.*

Appendix II:

Overview of Systems Implicated in Program Analysis

II.1 Introduction

This appendix is a grab bag of concepts that can, and frequently do, have significant effects on program performance. Two of the sections are related to the use of memory (including virtual memory management), one is about a run-time support function (garbage collection), and one is about a translator of source code into optimized object code (optimizing compilers). All of these play important roles whenever software is executed. A good deal of the information contained in this appendix can be found sprinkled among the discussions in the text and in the footnotes. While this appendix is by no means intended to provide a comprehensive treatment of these concepts, our aim is to give a coherent overview in one place that can be consulted instead of having to chase down comments and observations in the text or in footnotes.

II.2 The Memory Hierarchy

Most modern computing systems[1] have a memory hierarchy that consists of registers, caches, main memory, and external memory. Registers are where the action is — literally, because only registers can carry out operations. Since operations need operands, they must be retrieved from storage. Because

---

[1] The only computing systems that neither had caches nor supported virtual memory management (VMM) were Cray systems. Seymour Cray firmly believed that his main memory was as fast as any cache available at the time (thus, there was no need for caches), and he was convinced that VMM was a bad idea since it can lead to enormous inefficiencies. His supercomputer systems offered external memories that were solid state. Essentially, they used the technology that lesser mortals used for main memory. Magnetic disks and tapes were then considered tertiary storage devices.

every application program starts out on disk, as do its data, the usual external memory, both code and data associated with and manipulated by the code, must be first installed in main memory and then in cache before they can be used. It is important to understand how this is carried out. Access to magnetic disks is in terms of blocks; a block is on the order of 10^3 bytes or words. Since magnetic disk drives are mechanical devices,[2] access times have not increased significantly over the past two decades. Retrieving a block from disk takes on the order of tens of milliseconds. This is a lifetime for modern computing systems, equivalent to several million instructions or even more.[3] Note that this only supplies a few thousand words.

Once data are in main memory, they must be transferred into the cache; only from there are registers provisioned with data. Data are transferred to caches in terms of cache lines. Thus, again, it is not the individual data item that is transferred but a collective entity. Cache lines are on the order of hundreds of bytes of words. Access times have decreased in concert with the access times to main memory. Both main memory and caches are solid state, not mechanical devices, so the miniaturization of components that increases processing speed also benefits memories. Caches are typically between three and ten times faster than main memory. Note that the absolute speeds are a moving target, but the ratio between cache and main memory has remained fairly constant over the decades.

A great deal of literature and research has covered using cache memory efficiently. Interestingly, there is far less work on using disks more efficiently, even though the potential savings for caches are no more than the factor by which they are faster than main memory (that is, 3 to 5), while the potential savings for disks are one the order of the size of the block (that is, 10^3). Moreover, owing to the nature of magnetic disk drives (no improvement in access speeds over the past two decades), more and more programs that at some point were compute-bound (when processors were slower) are becoming increasingly I/O-bound. A program is said to be compute-bound if most of its time is spent executing instructions; it is considered I/O-bound if most of its time is used to retrieve data.

For our purposes, caches play a relatively minor role. While cache misses can have some deleterious effect on the efficiency of a program, this is always bounded by the factor by which caches are faster than main memory. In other words, there is a very real danger that we may spend a large amount

---

[2] There is a rotating platter and a read/write head. Increasing the access speed would either increase the rotation speed or reduce the granularity of the magnetic fields used to record and read data. Increasing the rotation rate eventually tears the platter apart; reducing the granularity implies that the read/write head must get closer to the platter, which is not feasible. Finally, moving the head to the correct track cannot be speeded up either, since excessive acceleration and deceleration result in unacceptable vibrations.

[3] Twenty-five years ago, in the early 1980s when Cray supercomputers ruled supreme, 100 million floating point instructions per second of sustained execution was considered very good. Today, even pedestrian desktop computers exceed this, yet magnetic disk drives have not significantly increased their access speed.

of time making cache accesses more efficient when we should instead be spending some time (probably a good deal more) on improving accesses to disks.

II.3 Virtual Memory Management

Virtual memory management (VMM) is ubiquitous in modern computing systems. Its attraction lies in the effortlessness with which memory can be virtually arbitrarily enlarged. What often is forgotten in this calculus is the price that must be paid for the use of VMM. While this price is negligible for small programs (toy programs that would really not need VMM in the first place), many realistic software packages incur a substantial cost through VMM. The main problem is that programmers are for the most part entirely unaware of this cost.[4]

Briefly, VMM functions as follows: Whenever a data item is needed by an instruction, the item's location is determined. If the item is in a register, no data movement is required (in most cases). If the data item is in cache, it is moved from there to a suitable register. If the data item is in main memory, it is moved first, as part of a cache line, into the cache, and from there to a suitable register. Finally, if the data item is only in external memory (that is, on magnetic disk), VMM determines its address and the block in which it resides and retrieves this block (called a page) from disk to main memory. For the purpose of transferring pages, VMM has a portion of the main memory, the active memory set, set aside to accommodate pages that must be installed in main memory. As long as the active memory set is not full, pages can be freely transferred. Once the active memory set is full, bringing in a new page necessitates expelling an old page first. Thus, an integral part of any VMM is the replacement strategy. Most VMMs use some variant of least recently used (LRU), meaning the page that has not been used for the longest time is expelled. Expelling may require writing back to disk if the page is "dirty" — if it has been written to while it was in the active memory set. If a page is not dirty, there is no need to write it back to disk since it has not been changed and therefore still exists in that form on disk.

Because VMM relies on magnetic disk drives, it is subject to the access times of disks. Thus, retrieving a page will take on the order of tens of milliseconds. Reading a block from a track on disk involves two steps. First the beginning address of the required block is determined; this requires up to one entire rotation. Then, in another rotation, that block is read. More time-consuming is finding the track containing the block; this essentially requires moving the read/write head. Since too abrupt a movement will

---

[4] Another aspect contributes to this ignorance. Most students today have only minimal exposure to large programs. Thus, they never experience firsthand the problems that occur when large data spaces are manipulated.

generate deleterious vibrations (recall the mechanical nature of disks), moving the head cannot be speeded up arbitrarily.

In the examples in the text (mainly in Chapter 5), we have pointed out that the use of VMM can have an enormous cost, and the programmer tends not to be aware of that cost. Using simple code fragments, it is not at all difficult to produce two equivalent instruction sequences where one version takes more than one thousand times longer than the other, even though both provide identical results and are completely equivalent in their performance if they are executed in-core. The key issue is the interplay of the VMM with compiler issues, in particular memory-mapping functions. Both of these aspects are generally ignored by programmers. As a result, it comes as a nasty surprise to many programmers when certain code fragments seem to execute at an inexplicably glacial pace.

The culprit is invariable thrashing — excessive paging in and out, usually of pages that have been used only minimally. The obvious objective in the efficient use of paging is that as many elements as possible in a page be used when the page is retrieved (read or written). This is particularly important when every element of the page is used in a computation (but possibly at different times during the program execution).

The most insidious aspect of thrashing is that the programmer is ordinarily not aware of any I/O operations. This is because these I/O operations are implicit. They are not initiated by the programmer, but occur as a consequence of developments outside of the programmer's influence (mainly size of active memory set and replacement policy). It is difficult for a programmer to be concerned about actions that she did not initiate. While VMM is likely to be employed for the foreseeable future in computing systems, a much more efficient way of managing I/O problems is using optimizing compilers to deal with implicit I/O.

II.4 Optimizing Compilers

One of the first software systems any programmer uses is a compiler. Nevertheless, many programmers are only marginally aware of the tasks a compiler carries out. In particular, optimizing compilers do many analyses whose findings could be very useful in reducing the problems caused by the memory hierarchies encountered in modern computing platforms.

Optimizing compilers are designed to modify, automatically and at compile time, the code of a program in such a way that the semantics of the program are maintained (i.e., the results of the original program and the modified one are identical) and the new program is improved with respect to some predefined goal. This goal is usually a reduction in execution time. Optimization is achieved by analyzing an input program and applying a variety of code transformations to it. Which optimizing steps and code transformations can be applied depends on the semantics of the source programming language and the results of the analyses. Modern compilers typically perform optimizations in multiple phases, each with a distinct purpose. Usually, certain sequences of analyses and transformations are combined into an optimization strategy that is accessible via a compiler switch. Thus, the user may choose between several predefined collections of optimizations when the compiler is invoked.

II.4.1   Basic Optimizations

Several optimizations are useful for improving code written in many different programming languages and for execution on most modern architectures. They include optimizations to eliminate statements that will never be executed (useless code), to replace certain operations by faster, equivalent ones (e.g., strength reduction), and to eliminate redundant computations, possibly by moving statements in the code to a new location that permits the results to be used subsequently in multiple locations. Examples of this last optimization include hoisting code from loops, so that it is executed just once rather than during each loop iteration, and partial redundancy elimination, variants of which attempt to move statements so that an expression is computed only once in a given execution path. Another popular optimization, constant propagation, attempts to determine all variable references that have a constant value no matter what execution path is taken and to replace those references with that value. This, in turn, may enable the application of further optimizations. These optimizations are generally known as scalar optimizations, since they are applied to scalar variables without regard to the internal structuring of a program's complex data objects.

II.4.2   Data Flow Analysis

Data flow analysis studies the flow of values of data objects throughout a program. Many data flow optimizations are closely related to the so-called use-definition (UD) and definition-use (DU) chains. A UD chain links a use of a variable to the set of all definitions of that variable that may reach it, that is, all possible sources of the value that will be used in the program. A DU chain links a definition of a variable to all of its possible uses. The task of determining all the points in the program where a specific optimization is applicable, or where a specific property holds, is known as a data flow problem. For example, the live variables problem may be solved by traversing a single-exit flow graph, starting with its unique exit node, and propagating information on outward-exposed uses to nodes that precede them on paths from the start node. (Any variable definition for which there is a subsequent outward-exposed use is live.)

In copy propagation a variable is replaced with one that is equivalent to it. Constant folding evaluates expressions at compile time when their operands are known to be constant, especially when they are integers. Common sub-expression elimination and value numbering are techniques supporting the identification and removal of computations that are unnecessary because the values have already been determined. Partial redundancy elimination is a more powerful approach to handling this problem and is increasingly preferred over these alternatives. Bounds checking elimination is applicable to programming languages that require tests to determine whether array references are within the defined range of index values. Loop invariant code motion finds computations that produce the same result each time a loop is executed and moves them out of the loop. The compiler must also be able to simplify algebraic and logical expressions to reduce the work of computing them, but also to facilitate the implementation of those optimizations that require them to be compared or evaluated.

II.4.3 Interprocedural Optimizations

The strategies discussed so far are typically applied to individual procedures of a program. However, it is also possible to optimize code across procedure boundaries. The growing utilization of structured programming techniques has led to the increased modularization of programs, which consequently consist of a large number of relatively small procedures. Thus, it has become important to consider how to improve code in a way that takes procedure and function invocations into account. Interprocedural analysis (IPA) gathers information about the calling relationships between different program units; optimizations based upon them are called interprocedural optimizations. A compiler generally translates input code one procedure at a time. Strategies for applying optimizations interprocedurally must take this into account. Interprocedural analysis may produce superior results, since without it, worst-case assumptions must be made with respect to the impact of procedure calls during (intraprocedural) data flow analysis. It must be assumed that the call modifies every variable that is visible to both it and the calling procedure, including every global variable. Thus, IPA can be used to improve the results. It may also be used explicitly to improve code that spans multiple procedures.

II.4.4 Data Dependence Analysis

The optimizations discussed above are applied to individual scalar variables; they are not explicitly applicable to structured data objects such as arrays. In particular, they cannot deal with subscripted variables or analyze the data access patterns in loops, where a statement may be executed many times, each time reading and writing a different set of subscripted variables. As a result, important optimizations may be missed. The ability of the compiler to analyze accesses to structured data objects, especially arrays, in the presence of nonconstant subscript expressions is crucial for a number of advanced optimization techniques. The foundation of this is (data) dependence analysis, a collection of techniques that allow the automatic determination, at compile time, of whether two references to an array both refer to the same element of that array, that is, whether the regions of the array accessed by them will overlap. If they do not overlap, the compiler is free to reorganize the code in these statements as desired to optimize it. If they do overlap, and (at least) one of them writes the variable, then it is essential that the relative order of those accesses be maintained. The results of this analysis will enable the compiler to determine whether certain code transformations are semantically valid (produce the same results) in a specific context.

Numerous dependence tests have been developed and published; they are either exact or approximate. Exact tests determine precisely whether or not there is a dependence. Approximate tests use conditions whose validity implies that there is no dependence. If the condition is not satisfied, one assumes that a dependence is present. (This is what is known as a nonfatal assumption: It may be that no dependence is present even though the condition is not satisfied, but since the presence of a dependence merely impedes the application of a code transformation, not being able to transform the code will leave the semantics unchanged. We may simply miss out on some possible optimization, which an exact test would have allowed us to carry out.) Exact tests tend to be computationally intensive, if not infeasible, so approximate tests are commonly used in compilers dedicated to this type of optimization (typically vectorizing and parallelizing compilers).

II.4.5 Code Transformations

Once dependence analysis for a code has been carried out, code transformations can be applied. It is of paramount importance that the semantics of the code not be affected by these transformations. Since loops tend to account for a significant portion of the computation time of many programs, most code transformations focus on loops and arrays. Very common are loop distribution (replacing one big loop by several smaller ones; see, for example, the code fragment in Section 5.4) and loop interchange (where the inner and outer loops of nested loops are interchanged). Other code transformations are the wavefront method, replication and alignment, loop fusion and fission, and strip mining. These techniques were designed with specific objectives in mind, typically automatic vectorization or parallelization; in other words, the objective is the parallel execution of instructions.

II.4.6 I/O Issues

In conventional programming, source code is compiled by a compiler, and then the resulting object code is turned over to a run-time support system operating under the operating system, which knows very little about the program. In contrast, a compiler, especially an optimizing compiler, knows a good deal about the program. The information we are interested in is routinely collected by the compiler and consists mainly of dependence information, which in turn determines what code transformations are semantically valid for a given program fragment. We are particularly interested in two problems related to input and output, namely reducing memory bank conflicts and minimizing implicit block transfers.

Memory is frequently organized in banks, each with its own controller. This allows a degree of parallelism when accessing memory because I/O requests involving different memory banks can be carried out simultaneously. This allows the pipelining of memory accesses. Given a program, together with information about memory mapping, the number of cycles required to access main memory, and the number of memory banks, a compiler can carry out an analysis (at compile time) of the number and type of bank conflicts that the program causes. This is based on the assumption that the dimensions of the arrays are known at compile time. There are two ways in which a compiler can attempt to reduce bank conflicts: by changing the shape of arrays and by inserting a filler of an appropriate length.

Automatic minimization of implicit block transfers uses the standard code transformation techniques, but with the goal of reducing block transfers. Based on the results of dependence analysis, the compiler can carry out semantically valid code transformations. Since the compiler knows about the program, the code transformations can be very specific and informed by the program behavior. Since a reduction in the number of block transfers implies a disproportionate reduction in the execution time, the potential savings involved in this approach can be substantial.

In general, optimizing compilers are an important tool in improving the performance of programs. While the ostensible goal of an optimizing compiler is of course reducing the overall execution time, using compiling techniques — especially dependence analysis and code transformations based on it — to ameliorate problems caused by the memory hierarchy is relatively novel. The ultimate goal is the complete elimination of VMM.

II.5 Garbage Collection

Garbage collection is the process of determining which memory locations are no longer accessible in a program and making them available for further use. Usually, when using dynamic data structures, we should not only allocate them when needed but also deallocate, or free, them when they are no longer of use. How this can be done is dependent on the programming language. At any rate, one must be aware that recursion necessarily employs dynamic data structures. The recursion stack consists of the activation records, which must be maintained for every invocation of a recursive function.

If the programming language provides explicit instructions for the deal-location of dynamically allocated space, this space can be marked for reuse. Note that in this case it is the responsibility of the programmer to make sure the program does not use this space at some later time.[5] The administration of the recursion stack can also be done in this way. If there is no way for the programmer to indicate directly that space is no longer needed, this infor-mation may be imparted indirectly, for example, by reassigning (or setting to null) a pointer to the node of a structure. If no other pointers to that node exist, the node becomes inaccessible, and the space associated with that node can then be reused. Determining whether space can be reused is part of what garbage collection is concerned with.

A secondary objective of garbage collection is frequently the consolidation of reusable memory. Because of allocation and deallocation requests, mem-ory fragmentation may occur. As a result, it is possible (in fact, quite likely) that a request for memory (which must be contiguous memory) cannot be satisfied since no chunk of the required size is available, even though the sum of all available memory chunks exceeds the size of the request. In such a case, the extant small chunks of free memory must be compacted into a large, contiguous chunk of reusable memory. After some more allocation and deallocation requests, this process has to start again.

Depending on the type of chunks of memory that a programming language allocates, different approaches are required. By far the simplest is the situation where all requests are of the same (unit) size. The programming language Lisp is the primary representative of this situation. The available dynamic memory is initially divided into chunks of unit size and placed in a queue. Any allo-cation request is satisfied by removing the chunk at the front of the queue. Any deallocation request consists of placing (an address to) the freed chunk at the end of the queue. In this way, each request takes time $O(1)$ — clearly optimal. Moreover, there is never any need for compaction.

Most programming languages supporting dynamic data structures (or recursion) employ more complicated schemes, because the sizes of the chunks of requests are not uniform. In this case, a number of strategies can be applied, with varying complexities. The fundamental goal is to reduce the number of compaction operations because compaction is an extremely expensive process, since it involves copying large amounts of data from one location to another. In order to satisfy this objective, different ways of allo-cating requests have been studied and implemented. First fit allocates the requested memory from the first chunk of free space (in some linear order) that is sufficiently large. Best fit allocates the requested memory from the chunk whose overage is minimal (that is, one finds the smallest available chunk that is sufficiently large). Worst fit allocates the requested memory

---

[5] Depending on the sophistication of the programming language, explicitly deallocating space that is later accessed may or may not result in a run-time error. One should be aware that it is often quite difficult, if not impossible (that is, undecidable), to determine whether freed space is later referenced in a program. If such a reference were to occur, it would be to information that is entirely unrelated to the operation at hand, so the program is semantically invalid.

from the chunk whose overage is maximal (that is, one allocates from the largest chunk, as long as it is sufficiently large). The size of the overage (the amount of space that is left free once the request is satisfied from a given chunk) is an important consideration. This is why the intuitively obvious best fit is actually anything but best. It tends to leave one with very small overages that most likely are quite unsuitable (too small) for subsequent requests. In contrast, the counterintuitive worst fit approach tends to leave large overages and is usually a better scheme. Other approaches, such as buddy schemes, have also been used and studied. However, ultimately, every one of these schemes must resort to memory compaction (and must therefore provide compaction facilities).

Common to all garbage collection schemes is that they occur at unexpected times. Moreover, they typically also occur at unpredictable times.[6] This is made more serious because garbage collection tends to be an expensive process. In most instances it is driven by allocation requests. Thus, an allocation instruction is executed that triggers a search for available memory. If an appropriate chunk is identified, the request is satisfied (usually fairly rapidly); however, if no such suitable chunk is found, garbage collection together with memory compaction must be initiated. Since a significant percentage of the total memory may be involved in a compaction process, it is easily seen that compaction can take a considerable amount of time. Because the way in which memory is allocated during the execution of a program is usually unknown to the programmer, the execution of substantially similar programs may result in very different execution times — simply because the allocation requests of one run may require fewer garbage collection processes than those of the other. While this explanation may be cold comfort to the programmer, at least it provides some help in understanding why such differences may occur.

In summary, garbage collection and related processes should always be considered when executing code. Any program with dynamic aspects (dynamic memory, recursion) is likely to require this system service. In this sense, it is unavoidable (in contrast to VMM, for example, where one could always write an out-of-core version of the program). Since it is an expensive service, and since it occurs at unpredictable times, programmers should be prepared to tolerate its consequences.

Bibliographical Notes

The memory hierarchy and virtual memory management are generally covered in operating systems textbooks. We refer to Silberschatz, Gavin, and

---

[6] Unexpected and unpredictable are different and generally independent concepts. Something may occur unexpectedly, but once we understand why it occurs, it may be easy to predict it. Garbage collection tends not to conform to this behavior.

Gagne: *Operating Systems Concepts* and other works cited in Chapter 5. Optimizing compilers and the techniques they employ are covered in texts devoted to compilers and their construction and techniques. We refer to Muchnik: *Advanced Compiler Design and Implementation* and Zima and Chapman: *Supercompilers for Parallel and Vector Computers*. Section II.4 is an abridgment of the article "Optimizing Compilers" by B. Chapman and E. L. Leiss. More information about I/O management, especially the use of code transformations to reduce implicit I/O transfers, is also contained in Chapter 7 of Leiss: *Parallel and Vector Computing*. Finally, garbage collection is covered in operating systems textbooks.

Appendix III:

NP-Completeness and Higher Complexity Classes

III.1 Introduction

In Chapter 1 we introduced the complexity classes that are of greatest interest for us. However, there are slightly different ways of defining complexity classes, the most important upshot of which is the notion of NP-completeness. Since programmers may encounter references to NP-completeness and higher-complexity classes in the literature, it is useful to provide a brief sketch of these concepts.

III.2 NP-Completeness

We must first define the complexity classes P and NP; then we explain NP-completeness. Before we outline the formal definition involving Turing machines, it is useful to give an informal characterization. Intuitively, a problem is in P if there exists an (ordinary) algorithm solving it in polynomial time. Thus, all the complexity classes we defined in Chapter 1 except for the exponential class are subsets of P. NP is then the class of all problems where we can check a solution in polynomial time (even though we may not necessarily find it).

Formally, the definition involves Turing machines. These are abstract machines that encapsulate the notion of computation in the most comprehensive way. A Turing machine consists of a finite state control and an unbounded tape consisting of cells, each of which can contain one data item, together with a read/write head that can look at and change the contents of a cell. Thus, a Turing machine M can be written as a sextuple,

$$M = (Q, T, T_0, \delta, q_0, F),$$

where Q is a finite nonempty set of states, the initial state q_0 is an element of Q, and the set of final states F is a subset of Q. The alphabet[1] T contains all the tape symbols, including a distinguished character □ denoting the blank, and the alphabet T_0 is a subset of T consisting of all input symbols (in particular, the blank symbol is not contained in T_0: □ ∈ $T-T_0$). Finally, the move function δ is a (partial) function taking a state p and a tape symbol t and returning a triple, consisting of a state q, a tape symbol s, and a direction instruction dir that is either L or R:

$$\delta(p,t) = (q,s,dir).[2]$$

The interpretation of this is as follows: The finite state control is in state p and the read/write head looks at a certain cell whose content is t; then the control changes to q, the contents of the cell the head inspects is changed from t to s, and the head is moved to the cell either immediately to the left of the inspected cell (dir = L) or to the right (dir = R). The Turing machine is initially presented with its (finite) input (a string over the alphabet T_0) on a portion of its tape, with the head looking at the first input symbol and the finite state control in the initial state q_0. All cells not occupied by the input string are assumed to be blank (that is, contain □). Then M executes one transition move after another in sequence. This process can terminate in two ways. Either M enters a final state (any state in F), in which case the input string is considered accepted and the Turing machine halts, or M reaches a point where δ(p,t) is not defined [δ(p,t) = ∅] for the given actual state p and the contents t of the cell currently inspected, in which case the Turing machine rejects the input string and halts. It is possible that the Turing machine does not reach either of these two configurations; in this case the Turing machine does not halt (consequently, no statement can be made regarding acceptance or rejection of the given input string).

The definition above is for a deterministic Turing machine because there is at most one triple in each of the entries δ(p,t). In other words, given a state and a cell content, we know deterministically (without any guessing or choosing) where the next transition takes us. If we relax this requirement and permit δ(p,t) to contain more than one triple, we have a nondeterministic Turing machine. In this model, when carrying out a transition move, we must first select one of the alternatives.

Using Turing machines, one can define complexity classes as follows. For a given input string of length n, we determine the number of moves the Turing machine makes for this input, assuming the machine halts. If it does not, then the complexity is not defined. Here, the length of the input string n is the measure of the input we assumed in our discussion in Chapter 1.

---

[1] An alphabet is a finite nonempty set of atomic symbols called letters. The alphabet of decimal digits is an example (with 10 elements).
[2] The move function is partial since it is permitted that no result is specified for a given pair (p,t): δ(p,t) = ∅ where ∅ denotes the empty set.

The number of moves is then the complexity $f(n)$. It can be defined for average[3] and for worst case.[4]

Turing machines are useful because anything that can be computed can be computed using a Turing machine.[5] [6] Moreover, all generally used deterministic computational models can be simulated using deterministic Turing machines in such a way that the complexity of the Turing machine model is no more than a polynomial function of the complexity of the other model. This is referred to as polynomial reduction.

Now we can define the two classes P and NP. P is the set of all problems that can be solved in (worst-case) polynomial time using a deterministic Turing machine. NP is the set of all problems that can be solved in (worst-case) polynomial time using a nondeterministic Turing machine.

While algorithms are polynomially reducible to deterministic Turing machines, it is not known whether nondeterministic Turing machines are polynomially reducible to deterministic Turing machines. Thus, it is not known whether P = NP (although P is contained in NP, P ⊆ NP, since any deterministic Turing machine can be viewed as a nondeterministic one). However, in practical terms, if we want to simulate a nondeterministic Turing machine using a deterministic one, the complexity increases exponentially.

Within the set of all problems in NP, there is subset, called NP-complete problems, consisting of all those that are maximally difficult in the following sense. If we find that one NP-complete problem has a polynomial time algorithm (in other words, if it is in P), then all problems in NP have polynomial time complexity algorithms. Thus, the open question P = NP could be solved affirmatively if one were able to devise a polynomial time algorithm for a single NP-complete problem. However, no such NP-complete problem is known, as of this writing (2005). Thus, the best algorithm for any NP-complete problem has exponential time complexity.

From a practical point of view, finding out that a problem is NP-complete is generally undesirable since it means the best algorithm solving it has exponential time complexity. However, one should note that NP-completeness is based on worst-case time complexity; occasionally, the average time complexity is much better. Moreover, using approximation algorithms, one

---

[3] This requires assigning probabilities to each input string of length n, determining the number of moves for each string, and then forming the weighted average (weighted with these probabilities) of these numbers to obtain the average complexity $f(n)$.

[4] This requires determining the number of moves for each string of length n and finding the maximum of all these values to obtain the worst-case complexity $f(n)$.

[5] It is quite difficult to come up with something intuitively understandable that cannot be effectively computed. My best candidate is the following instruction for finding a location. "Take the one-way street and turn left two miles before the rail-road crossing." While it can be described, it cannot be executed, since we would have to backtrack two miles, which is impossible with a one-way street.

[6] Strictly speaking, this is not a fact or an observation, but a thesis, known as Church's thesis. It is essentially not possible to prove it, since defining in its full generality what is "computable" is infeasible.

can frequently obtain a solution that may not be optimal but is nevertheless acceptable.

III.3 Higher Complexity Classes

The hierarchy of complexity classes is infinite, so neither NP nor the exponential time algorithms are the most complicated classes. There are infinitely many more time-consuming classes between NP and the class of undecidable problems. We have, for instance, doubly exponential classes, exemplified by the number 2^{2^n} of boolean functions in n variables. In the higher reaches of this complexity hierarchy are nonelementary problems, (decidable) problems whose time complexity is so large that it cannot be expressed as a bounded stack of exponentials. This means that given an arbitrary integer M, there exists a value n (dependent on M) such that the time complexity of solving this problem requires more time than the function denoted by a stack of M powers of 2 followed by n:

$$2^{2^{\cdot^{\cdot^{2^n}}}}$$

.

   This complexity is exemplified by extended regular expressions, regular expressions in whose formulation we admit not just the three operations involved in ordinary regular expressions, namely union, concatenation, and star,[7] but also the operation complementation.[8] While the smallest deterministic finite automaton for an ordinary regular expression of length n may have up to 2^n states, the smallest deterministic finite automata for an extended regular expression of length n may have a nonelementary number in n states.

   None of these higher complexity classes has great practical significance for programmers. Essentially, finding out that a problem belongs to one of these classes means that for all but the smallest instances, trying to solve this problem is an exercise in futility.

---

[7] Union allows one to provide alternatives (e.g., "a constant is either an integer or a real"). Concatenation allows one to compose one regular expression by appending one to another (e.g., "an assignment statement consists of a variable, concatenated to the assignment operator, concatenated to an expression"). Star captures unbounded iteration (e.g., "an integer consists of a digit, concatenated to zero or more digits").

[8] Complementation captures negation. Instead of describing what we want, we describe what we do not want. For example, we may be interested in all strings that do not contain a certain substring. The extremely surprising aspect of complementation is that is has an incredible effect on the complexity of the resulting expressions, from singly exponential to nonelementary.

Bibliographical Notes

NP-completeness and higher complexity classes, including nonelementary problems, are covered in texts on algorithms and abstract computational complexity, for example in Kleinberg and Tardos: *Algorithm Design*; Garey and Johnson: *Computers and Intractability: A Guide to the Theory of NP-Completeness*; and Aho, Hopcroft, and Ullman: *The Design and Analysis of Computer Algorithms*. Turing machines and regular expressions are covered in texts on formal language and automata theory, for example in Hopcroft and Ullman: *Introduction to Automata Theory*.

Appendix IV:

Review of Undecidability

IV.1 Introduction

Undecidability captures the ultimate in (algorithmic) impossibility. It means that no algorithm can exist to solve the problem at hand. We have argued (in Chapter 10) that in some cases at least, undecidability is the result of overgeneralization and could be remedied by restricting our attention to a subset of specific interest instead of considering the general problem. In this appendix we briefly review the two fundamental undecidable problems that are typically used to demonstrate the undecidability of some other problem by reducing it to one of the two. These two are the halting problem for Turing machines (HTM) and Post's correspondence problem (PCP). The basic approach is the following: We are given a problem P and assume that there exists an algorithm that solves P. Then we show that under this assumption, either HTM or PCP is also solvable. Since this is known to be false, it follows that our original assumption, namely that P is solvable, must also be false; hence, P is undecidable.

IV.2 The Halting Problem for Turing Machines

We first define the notion of a Turing machine;[1] then we explain the halting problems for Turing machines. A Turing machine consists of a finite state control and an unbounded tape consisting of cells, each of which can contain one data item, together with a read/write head that can look at and change the contents of a cell. Thus, a Turing machine M can be written as a sextuple,

$$M = (Q,T,T_0,\delta,q_0,F)$$

---

[1] There is a good deal of overlap here with Appendix III. We tolerate this repetition in the interest of keeping the appendices independent.

where Q is a finite nonempty set of states, the initial state q_0 is an element of Q, and the set of final state F is a subset of Q; the alphabet[2] T contains all the tape symbols, including a distinguished character $\Box$ denoting the blank, and the alphabet T_0 is a subset of T consisting of all input symbols (in particular, the blank symbol is not contained in T_0: $\Box \in T - T_0$). Finally, the move function δ is a (partial) function taking a state p and a tape symbol t and returning a triple, consisting of a state q, a tape symbol s, and a direction instruction dir, which is either L or R,

$$\delta(p,t) = (q,s,\text{dir}).[3]$$

The interpretation of this is as follows. The finite state control is in state p, and the read/write head looks at a certain cell whose content is t. Then the control changes to q, the contents of the cell the head inspects is changed from t to s, and the head is moved to the cell either immediately to the left of the inspected cell (dir = L) or to the right (dir = R). The Turing machine is initially presented with its (finite) input (a string over the alphabet T_0) on a portion of its tape, with the head looking at the first input symbol and the finite state control in the initial state q_0. All cells not occupied by the input string are assumed to be blank (that is, contain $\Box$). Then M executes one transition move after another in sequence. This process can terminate in two ways. Either M enters a final state (any state in F), in which case the input string is considered accepted and the Turing machine halts, or M reaches a point where $\delta(p,t)$ is not defined [$\delta(p,t) = \varnothing$] for the given state p and the contents t of the cell currently inspected, in which case the Turing machine rejects the input string and halts. It is possible that the Turing machine does not reach either of these two configurations; in this case the Turing machine does not halt (consequently, no statement can be made regarding acceptance or rejection of the given input string).

The above definition is that of a deterministic Turing machine, as there is at most one triple in each of the entries $\delta(p,t)$. In other words, given a state and a cell content (tape symbol), we know deterministically (without any guessing or choosing) where the next transition takes us. One can relax this requirement, permitting $\delta(p,t)$ to contain more than one triple. This results in a nondeterministic Turing machine. Since any nondeterministic Turing machine can be simulated by a deterministic one (although it may make many more moves), as far as the halting problem is concerned, it makes no difference whether the Turing machine is deterministic or nondeterministic. If the original nondeterministic one halts, the deterministic simulation halts as well. Similarly, if the nondeterministic Turing machine does not halt, the deterministic one simulating it does not halt either.

---

[2] An alphabet is a finite nonempty set of atomic symbols, called letters. The alphabet of decimal digits is an example (with 10 elements).

[3] The move function is partial since it is permitted that no result is specified for a given pair (p,t): $\delta(p,t) = \varnothing$, where $\varnothing$ denotes the empty set.

The HTM can then be stated as follows. Given an arbitrary Turing machine M (in view of the comment in the last paragraph, we may assume that M is deterministic) and a specific input string α over the alphabet T_0 of input symbols, does M halt when presented with input α? While this appears to be a reasonable question, one can show formally that no algorithm for answering it can exist.[4] Thus, HTM is undecidable.

One should be quite clear that there are Turing machines for which one can definitely determine whether they halt for a given input; this is not in doubt. Instead, the question is whether one can always do this for all Turing machines. The answer to this question is no.

Consequently, any problem whose solvability would imply the solvability of HTM must also be undecidable. HTM is a powerful tool for demonstrating the undecidability of numerous questions of practical interest. One undecidable question of very practical significance to programming is whether an arbitrary program, when started with a certain input, will ever enter into an infinite loop.

IV.3 Post's Correspondence Problem

Turing machines are complicated theoretical systems, and the practically oriented programmer may harbor the suspicion that this complicatedness is responsible for the undecidability of the halting problem. Here then is a far simpler problem, PCP,[5] which is also undecidable.

Let T be a fixed alphabet of symbols and let A and B be two lists of strings or words over the alphabet T such that both lists have the same number of, say k, elements:

$$A = v_1, v_2,..., v_k \quad \text{and} \quad B = w_1, w_2,..., w_k .$$

We say that the instance (A,B) of PCP has a solution if there exists a sequence of integers $i_1, i_2, ..., i_m$ for some $m \geq 1$, with all $1 \leq i_j \leq k$ such that selecting the words with these indices from list A and concatenating them yields a word that is identical to the word obtained by taking the words with these indices from list B and concatenating them:

$$v_{i_1} \cdot v_{i_2} \cdot ... \cdot v_{i_m} = w_{i_1} \cdot w_{i_2} \cdot ... \cdot w_{i_m} .$$

PCP is then the problem of determining for any given instance (A,B) whether a solution $(i_1, i_2, ..., i_m)$ exists. This problem is undecidable; there

---

[4] The proof is automata-centric, fairly lengthy, and of little importance for this book. We therefore suppress it here and refer the interested reader to the literature.
[5] It is named after the Norwegian mathematician Emil Post.

does not exist an algorithm that will determine for arbitrary lists A and B, whether or not such a sequence of integers i_1, i_2, ..., i_m exists solving the given instance.

Again, there is no difficulty in coming up with specific lists where there is a solution,[6] or perhaps more interesting, where there is no solution.[7] The question is whether we can answer this for any two lists A and B in general. The answer is no.

In contrast to HTM, PCP is very easy to formulate. In particular, it does not require an elaborate formalism, but instead uses two simple, finite lists of words. Nevertheless, it is an undecidable problem.

The undecidability of PCP is usually proven by reducing it to the HTM. PCP is often a more convenient mechanism for proving undecidability, partly because it is significantly simpler to formulate and hence to apply. For example, the question of whether two context-free grammars generate the same context-free language is very easily formulated in terms of PCP for grammars based on the two lists, thereby rendering the equivalence problem for context-free grammars undecidable.

Bibliographical Note

Both the HTM and PCP are covered in standard texts of algorithmic complexity, for example in Lewis and Papadimitriou: *Elements of the Theory of Computation*, as well as in formal language texts such as Hopcroft and Ullman: *Introduction to Automata Theory*.

---

[6] Here is a simple example. Assume the binary alphabet {0,1}, $k = 3$, and let $v_1 = 1$, $v_2 = 10111$, $v_3 = 10$, $w_1 = 111$, $w_2 = 10$, $w_3 = 0$. Then a solution is given by the sequence 2,1,1,3, since $v_2 v_1 v_1 v_3 = 10111 \cdot 1 \cdot 1 \cdot 10 = 10 \cdot 111 \cdot 111 \cdot 0 = w_2 w_1 w_1 w_3$.

[7] Here is another simple example. Assume the binary alphabet {0,1}, $k = 3$, and let $v_1 = 10$, $v_2 = 011$, $v_3 = 101$, $w_1 = 101$, $w_2 = 110$, $w_3 = 011$. One can show directly that no solution can exist. First one notes that any possible solution can only start with index 1, since the other two indices correspond to words in the two lists starting with different symbols. Thus, any solution must begin with 10 from the first list and 101 from the second. To achieve equality, we need an index where the word from the first list starts with 1; this is achieved by 1 and 3. If we chose 1, we get a clash on the fourth character, since the first list produces 1010 and the second 101101. Therefore, we must select 3, which yields 10101 and 101011. Continuing in this fashion, there is always exactly one forced choice, but it never yields strings of equal length. Thus, no solution of this instance can exist.

Bibliography

A. V. Aho, J. E. Hopcroft, and J. D. Ullman: *The Design and Analysis of Computer Algorithms*, Addison-Wesley, Reading, MA, 1975.

A. V. Aho, R. Sethi, and J. D. Ullman: *Compilers, Principles, Techniques, and Tools*, Addison-Wesley Publishing Company, Reading, MA, 1987.

A. V. Aho and J. D. Ullman: *The Theory of Parsing, Translation, and Compiling, Vol. I*: Parsing, Prentice-Hall, Englewood Cliffs, NJ, 1972.

A. V. Aho and J. D. Ullman: *The Theory of Parsing, Translation, and Compiling, Vol. II*: Compiling, Prentice-Hall, Englewood Cliffs, NJ, 1973.

R. K. Ahuja, T. L. Magnanti, and J. B. Orlin: *Network Flows: Theory, Algorithms, and Applications*, Prentice Hall, Englewood Cliffs, NJ, 1993.

J. D. Aron: *The Program Development Process*, Addison-Wesley, Reading, MA, 1974.

L. J. Arthur: *Software Evolution*, John Wiley, New York, NY, 1988.

J. Asserrhine, J.-M. Chesneaux, and J.-L. Lamotte: Estimation of Round-Off Errors on Several Computers Architectures, *Journal of Universal Computer Science*, Vol. 1, No. 7, 1995.

M. J. Bach: *The Design of the Unix Operating System*, Prentice Hall, Englewood Cliffs, NJ, 1986.

K. Beck: *Test Driven Development: By Example*, Addison-Wesley Professional, Reading, MA, 2002.

K. Beck and M. Fowler: *Planning Extreme Programming*, Addison-Wesley Professional, Reading, MA, 2000.

J. L. Bentley: *Programming Pearls*, 2nd ed., Addison-Wesley, Reading, MA, 2000.

J. L. Bentley: *More Programming Pearls: Confessions of a Coder*, Addison-Wesley, Reading, MA, 1990.

B. Bezier: *Software Testing Techniques*, 2nd ed., Van Nostrand, New York, NY, 1990.

L. Bic and A. C. Shaw: *Operating Systems*, Prentice-Hall, Englewood Cliffs, NJ, 1990.

G. Booch: *Object-Oriented Analysis and Design with Applications*, Benjamin Cummings, Menlo Park, CA, 1987.

F. P. Brooks: *The Mythical Man Month*, Addison-Wesley, Reading, MA, 1975.

F. P. Brooks: No Silver Bullet: Essence and Accidents of Software Engineering, *IEEE Computer*, April 1987.

B. Chapman and E. L. Leiss: Optimizing Compilers, in *Encyclopedia of Computer Science and Engineering*, Benjamin Wah (ed.), John Wiley, New York, NY, 2006.

E. G. Coffman and P. J. Denning: *Operating Systems Theory*, Prentice-Hall, Englewood Cliffs, NJ, 1973.

D. Coppersmith and S. Winograd: On the Asymptotic Complexity of Matrix Multiplication, *SIAM J. Comput.*, 11, 472–492, 1982.

E. W. Dijkstra, O. J. Dahl, et al.: *Structured Programming*, Academic Press, London, UK, 1972.

E. Gamma, R. Helm, et al.: *Design Patterns: Elements of Reusable Object-Oriented Software*, Addison-Wesley, Reading, MA, 1995.

M. R. Garey and D. S. Johnson: *Computers and Intractability: A Guide to the Theory of NP-Completeness*, Morgan Freeman, San Francisco, CA, 1979.

D. Goldberg: What Every Computer Scientist Should Know about Floating-Point Arithmetic, *ACM Computing Surveys*, Vol. 23, No. 1, 5–48, 1991.

D. Goldberg: Computer Arithmetic, in: *Computer Architecture: A Quantitative Approach*, J. L. Hennessy and D. A. Patterson (editors), Morgan Kaufmann, San Francisco, CA, 1995

G. H. Golub and C. F. Van Loan: *Matrix Computations*, 2nd ed., Johns Hopkins Press, Baltimore, MD, 1989.

G. H. Gonnet: *Handbook of Algorithms and Data Structures*, Addison-Wesley, London, UK, 1984.

N. J. Higham: *Accuracy and Stability of Numerical Algorithms*, SIAM, 2nd ed., 2002.

J. E. Hopcroft and J. D. Ullman: *Introduction to Automata Theory*, Addison-Wesley, Reading, MA, 1969.

A. Hunt and D. Thomas: *The Pragmatic Programmer: From Journeyman to Master*, Addison-Wesley Professional, Reading, MA, 1999.

I. Jacobson, G. Booch, and J. Rumbaugh: *The Unified Software Development Process*, Addison-Wesley Professional, Reading, MA, 1999.

C. Jones: *Software Project Management Practices: Failure Versus Success*, last access Feb. 6, 2006: www.stsc.hill.af.mil/crosstalk/2004/10/0410Jones.html

J. H. Kingston: *Algorithms and Data Structures, Design, Correctness, Analysis*, Addison-Wesley, Reading, MA, 1990.

E. Kit: *Software Testing in the Real World: Improving the Process*, Addison-Wesley, Reading, MA, 1995.

J. Kleinberg and E. Tardos: *Algorithm Design*, Pearson Addison-Wesley, Boston, MA, 2005.

D. E. Knuth: *The Art of Computer Programming, Vol. 1: Fundamental Algorithms*, 2nd ed., Addison-Wesley, Reading, MA, 1973.

D. E. Knuth: *The Art of Computer Programming, Vol. 2: Seminumerical Algorithms*, Addison-Wesley, Reading, MA, 1969.

D. E. Knuth: *The Art of Computer Programming, Vol. 3: Sorting and Searching*, Addison-Wesley, Reading, MA, 1973.

P. Krutchen: *The Rational Unified Process – An Introduction*, Addison-Wesley, Reading, MA, 2000.

C. Larman: *Agile and Iterative Development: A Manager's Guide*, Addison-Wesley Professional, Reading, MA, 2003.

C. Larman and V. R. Basili: Iterative and Incremental Development: A Brief History, *IEEE Computer*, June 2003.

S. J. Leffler, M. K. McKusick, M. J. Karels, and J. S. Quaterman: *The Design and Implementation of the 4.3BSD Unix Operating System*, Addison-Wesley, Reading, MA, 1989

E. L. Leiss: *Parallel and Vector Computing, A Practical Introduction*, McGraw-Hill, New York, NY, 1995.

A. V. Levitin: *Introduction to the Design and Analysis of Algorithms*, 2nd ed., Addison-Wesley, Reading, MA, 2007.

H. R. Lewis and C. H. Papadimitriou: *Elements of the Theory of Computation*, Prentice-Hall, Englewood Cliffs, NJ, 1981.

B. Liskov and J. Guttag: *Abstraction and Specification in Program Development*, MIT Press, Cambridge, MA, 1986.

A. C. McKellar and E. G. Coffman: Organizing Matrices and Matrix Operations for Paged Memory Systems, *Comm. ACM*, Vol. 12, No. 3, 1969.

C. B. Moler: Technical Note: Double-Rounding and Implications for Numeric Computations, *The MathWorks Newsletter*, Vol. 4, No. 1, 6, 1990.

S. S. Muchnik: *Advanced Compiler Design and Implementation*, Morgan Kaufmann, San Francisco, CA, 1997.

J. Neilsen: *Usability Engineering*, Academic Press, New York, NY, 1993.

P. W. Purdom, Jr. and C. A. Brown: *The Analysis of Algorithms*, Holt, Rinehart and Winston, New York, NY, 1985.

S. Rosen (ed.): *Programming Systems and Languages*, McGraw-Hill, New York, NY, 1960.

J. Rumbaugh, M. Blaha, et al.: *Object-Oriented Modeling and Design*, Prentice-Hall, Englewood Cliffs, NJ, 1991.

A. Silberschatz, P. Gavin, and G. Gagne: *Operating Systems Concepts*, 7th ed., John Wiley, New York, NY, 2004.

W. Stallings: *Operating Systems: Design and Principles*, 4th ed., Prentice-Hall, Englewood Cliffs, NJ, 2002.

R. Startz: *8087/80287/80387 for the IBM PC and Compatibles*, 3rd ed., Brady, New York, NY, 1988.

A. S. Tanenbaum: *Operating Systems — Design and Implementation*, Prentice-Hall, Englewood Cliffs, NJ, 1987.

J. H. Wilkinson: *Rounding Errors in Algebraic Processes*, Prentice-Hall, Englewood Cliffs, NJ, 1963.

J. H. Wilkinson: *The Algebraic Eigenvalue Problem*, Clarendon Press, Oxford, UK, 1965.

N. Wirth: Good Ideas, through the Looking Glass, *IEEE Computer*, January 2006.

E. Yourdon: When Good-Enough Software Is Best, *IEEE Software*, 1995.

W. Zhang and E. L. Leiss: Compile Time Data Transfer Analysis, 5th Int'l Conf. on Algorithms and Architectures for Parallel Processing (ICA3PP2002), IEEE Computer Society Press, 2002.

H. Zima and B. M. Chapman: *Supercompilers for Parallel and Vector Computers*, Addison-Wesley, Reading, MA, 1991.

Index